GROWING UP

RUSSELL BAKER began his career in journalism in 1947, when he
was hired by the *Baltimore Sun*. In 1954 he joined *The New
York Times*, for which he covered the White House, Congress,
and national politics. He has written his "Observer" column for
the *Times* since 1962. In 1979 he won the George Polk Award
for Commentary and the Pulitzer Prize for Distinguished Commentary. His columns were most recently collected in *So This
Is Depravity*. He received the 1983 Pulitzer Prize for biography
for *Growing Up*.

Russell and Doris.

RUSSELL BAKER
GROWING UP

A PLUME BOOK

NEW AMERICAN LIBRARY

NEW YORK AND SCARBOROUGH, ONTARIO

NAL BOOKS ARE AVAILABLE AT QUANTITY DISCOUNTS WHEN USED TO PROMOTE
PRODUCTS OR SERVICES. FOR INFORMATION PLEASE WRITE TO PREMIUM MARKETING
DIVISION, NEW AMERICAN LIBRARY, 1633 BROADWAY,
NEW YORK, NEW YORK 10019.

PLUME TRADEMARK REG. U.S. PAT. OFF. AND FOREIGN COUNTRIES
REGISTERED TRADEMARK—MARCA REGISTRADA
HECHO EN HARRISONBURG, VA., U.S.A.

SIGNET, SIGNET CLASSIC, MENTOR, ONYX, PLUME, MERIDIAN
and NAL BOOKS are published in the United States by NAL PENGUIN INC.,
1633 Broadway, New York, New York 10019, in Canada by The New American
Library of Canada Limited, 81 Mack Avenue, Scarborough, Ontario M1L 1M8

Library of Congress Cataloging in Publication Data

Baker, Russell, 1925-
  Growing up.

   Reprint. Originally published: New York : Congdon &
Weed, c1982.
   1. Baker, Russell, 1925-   —Biography—Youth.
2. Authors, American—20th century—Biography.
3. Journalists—United States—Biography. I. Title.
[PS3552.A4343Z466 1983b] 070′.92′4 [B] 83-8213
ISBN 0-452-25550-3

First Plume Printing, October, 1983

11 12 13 14 15 16 17 18

PRINTED IN THE UNITED STATES OF AMERICA

To Doris

GROWING UP

CHAPTER ONE

AT the age of eighty my mother had her last bad fall, and after that her mind wandered free through time. Some days she went to weddings and funerals that had taken place half a century earlier. On others she presided over family dinners cooked on Sunday afternoons for children who were now gray with age. Through all this she lay in bed but moved across time, traveling among the dead decades with a speed and ease beyond the gift of physical science.

"Where's Russell?" she asked one day when I came to visit at the nursing home.

"I'm Russell," I said.

She gazed at this improbably overgrown figure out of an inconceivable future and promptly dismissed it.

"Russell's only this big," she said, holding her hand, palm down, two feet from the floor. That day she was a young country wife with chickens in the backyard and a view of hazy blue Virginia mountains behind the apple orchard, and I was a stranger old enough to be her father.

Early one morning she phoned me in New York. "Are you coming to my funeral today?" she asked.

I

It was an awkward question with which to be awakened. "What are you talking about, for God's sake?" was the best reply I could manage.

"I'm being buried today," she declared briskly, as though announcing an important social event.

"I'll phone you back," I said and hung up, and when I did phone back she was all right, although she wasn't all right, of course, and we all knew she wasn't.

She had always been a small woman—short, light-boned, delicately structured—but now, under the white hospital sheet, she was becoming tiny. I thought of a doll with huge, fierce eyes. There had always been a fierceness in her. It showed in that angry, challenging thrust of the chin when she issued an opinion, and a great one she had always been for issuing opinions.

"I tell people exactly what's on my mind," she had been fond of boasting. "I tell them what I think, whether they like it or not." Often they had not liked it. She could be sarcastic to people in whom she detected evidence of the ignoramus or the fool.

"It's not always good policy to tell people exactly what's on your mind," I used to caution her.

"If they don't like it, that's too bad," was her customary reply, "because that's the way I am."

And so she was. A formidable woman. Determined to speak her mind, determined to have her way, determined to bend those who opposed her. In that time when I had known her best, my mother had hurled herself at life with chin thrust forward, eyes blazing, and an energy that made her seem always on the run.

She ran after squawking chickens, an axe in her hand, determined on a beheading that would put dinner in the pot. She ran when she made the beds, ran when she set the table. One Thanksgiving she burned herself badly when, running up from the cellar oven with the ceremonial turkey, she tripped on the stairs and tumbled back down, ending at the bottom in the debris of giblets, hot gravy, and battered turkey. Life was combat, and victory was not to the lazy, the timid, the slugabed, the drugstore cowboy, the

2

libertine, the mushmouth afraid to tell people exactly what was on his mind whether people liked it or not. She ran.

But now the running was over. For a time I could not accept the inevitable. As I sat by her bed, my impulse was to argue her back to reality. On my first visit to the hospital in Baltimore, she asked who I was.

"Russell," I said.

"Russell's way out west," she advised me.

"No, I'm right here."

"Guess where I came from today?" was her response.

"Where?"

"All the way from New Jersey."

"When?"

"Tonight."

"No. You've been in the hospital for three days," I insisted.

"I suggest the thing to do is calm down a little bit," she replied. "Go over to the house and shut the door."

Now she was years deep into the past, living in the neighborhood where she had settled forty years earlier, and she had just been talking with Mrs. Hoffman, a neighbor across the street.

"It's like Mrs. Hoffman said today: The children always wander back to where they come from," she remarked.

"Mrs. Hoffman has been dead for fifteen years."

"Russ got married today," she replied.

"I got married in 1950," I said, which was the fact.

"The house is unlocked," she said.

So it went until a doctor came by to give one of those oral quizzes that medical men apply in such cases. She failed catastrophically, giving wrong answers or none at all to "What day is this?" "Do you know where you are?" "How old are you?" and so on. Then, a surprise.

"When is your birthday?" he asked.

"November 5, 1897," she said. Correct. Absolutely correct.

"How do you remember that?" the doctor asked.

"Because I was born on Guy Fawkes Day," she said.

3

"Guy Fawkes?" asked the doctor. "Who is Guy Fawkes?"

She replied with a rhyme I had heard her recite time and again over the years when the subject of her birth date arose:

"Please to remember the Fifth of November,
Gunpowder treason and plot.
I see no reason why gunpowder treason
Should ever be forgot."

Then she glared at this young doctor so ill informed about Guy Fawkes' failed scheme to blow King James off his throne with barrels of gunpowder in 1605. She had been a schoolteacher, after all, and knew how to glare at a dolt. "You may know a lot about medicine, but you obviously don't know any history," she said. Having told him exactly what was on her mind, she left us again.

The doctors diagnosed a hopeless senility. Not unusual, they said. "Hardening of the arteries" was the explanation for laymen. I thought it was more complicated than that. For ten years or more the ferocity with which she had once attacked life had been turning to a rage against the weakness, the boredom, and the absence of love that too much age had brought her. Now, after the last bad fall, she seemed to have broken chains that imprisoned her in a life she had come to hate and to return to a time inhabited by people who loved her, a time in which she was needed. Gradually I understood. It was the first time in years I had seen her happy.

She had written a letter three years earlier which explained more than "hardening of the arteries." I had gone down from New York to Baltimore, where she lived, for one of my infrequent visits and, afterwards, had written her with some banal advice to look for the silver lining, to count her blessings instead of burdening others with her miseries. I suppose what it really amounted to was a threat that if she was not more cheerful during my visits I would not come to see her very often. Sons are capable of such letters. This one was written out of a childish faith in the eternal strength of parents, a naive belief that age and wear could be overcome by an effort of will, that all she needed was a good pep talk to recharge

4

a flagging spirit. It was such a foolish, innocent idea, but one thinks of parents differently from other people. Other people can become frail and break, but not parents.

She wrote back in an unusually cheery vein intended to demonstrate, I suppose, that she was mending her ways. She was never a woman to apologize, but for one moment with the pen in her hand she came very close. Referring to my visit, she wrote: "If I seemed unhappy to you at times—" Here she drew back, reconsidered, and said something quite different:

"If I seemed unhappy to you at times, I am, but there's really nothing anyone can do about it, because I'm just so very tired and lonely that I'll just go to sleep and forget it." She was then seventy-eight.

Now, three years later, after the last bad fall, she had managed to forget the fatigue and loneliness and, in these free-wheeling excursions back through time, to recapture happiness. I soon stopped trying to wrest her back to what I considered the real world and tried to travel along with her on those fantastic swoops into the past. One day when I arrived at her bedside she was radiant.

"Feeling good today," I said.

"Why shouldn't I feel good?" she asked. "Papa's going to take me up to Baltimore on the boat today."

At that moment she was a young girl standing on a wharf at Merry Point, Virginia, waiting for the Chesapeake Bay steamer with her father, who had been dead sixty-one years. William Howard Taft was in the White House, Europe still drowsed in the dusk of the great century of peace, America was a young country, and the future stretched before it in beams of crystal sunlight. "The greatest country on God's green earth," her father might have said, if I had been able to step into my mother's time machine and join him on the wharf with the satchels packed for Baltimore.

I could imagine her there quite clearly. She was wearing a blue dress with big puffy sleeves and long black stockings. There was a ribbon in her hair and a big bow tied on the side of her head. There had been a childhood photograph in her bedroom which

5

showed all this, although the colors of course had been added years later by a restorer who tinted the picture.

About her father, my grandfather, I could only guess, and indeed, about the girl on the wharf with the bow in her hair, I was merely sentimentalizing. Of my mother's childhood and her people, of their time and place, I knew very little. A world had lived and died, and though it was part of my blood and bone I knew little more about it than I knew of the world of the pharaohs. It was useless now to ask for help from my mother. The orbits of her mind rarely touched present interrogators for more than a moment.

Sitting at her bedside, forever out of touch with her, I wondered about my own children, and their children, and children in general, and about the disconnections between children and parents that prevent them from knowing each other. Children rarely want to know who their parents were before they were parents, and when age finally stirs their curiosity there is no parent left to tell them. If a parent does lift the curtain a bit, it is often only to stun the young with some exemplary tale of how much harder life was in the old days.

I had been guilty of this when my children were small in the early 1960s and living the affluent life. It galled me that their childhoods should be, as I thought, so easy when my own had been, as I thought, so hard. I had developed the habit, when they complained about the steak being overcooked or the television being cut off, of lecturing them on the harshness of life in my day.

"In my day all we got for dinner was macaroni and cheese, and we were glad to get it."

"In my day we didn't have any television."

"In my day . . ."

"In my day . . ."

At dinner one evening a son had offended me with an inadequate report card, and as I leaned back and cleared my throat to lecture, he gazed at me with an expression of unutterable resignation and said, "Tell me how it was in your days, Dad."

I was angry with him for that, but angrier with myself for

6

Lucy Elizabeth as a child, at home in Lancaster County, Virginia, 1906.

having become one of those ancient bores whose highly selective memories of the past become transparently dishonest even to small children. I tried to break the habit, but must have failed. A few years later my son was referring to me when I was out of earshot as "the old-timer." Between us there was a dispute about time. He looked upon the time that had been my future in a disturbing way. My future was his past, and being young, he was indifferent to the past.

As I hovered over my mother's bed listening for muffled signals from her childhood, I realized that this same dispute had existed between her and me. When she was young, with life ahead of her, I had been her future and resented it. Instinctively, I wanted to break free, cease being a creature defined by her time, consign her future to the past, and create my own. Well, I had finally done that, and then with my own children I had seen my exciting future become their boring past.

These hopeless end-of-the-line visits with my mother made me wish I had not thrown off my own past so carelessly. We all come from the past, and children ought to know what it was that went into their making, to know that life is a braided cord of humanity stretching up from time long gone, and that it cannot be defined by the span of a single journey from diaper to shroud.

I thought that someday my own children would understand that. I thought that, when I am beyond explaining, they would want to know what the world was like when my mother was young and I was younger, and we two relics passed together through strange times. I thought I should try to tell them how it was to be young in the time before jet planes, superhighways, H-bombs, and the global village of television. I realized I would have to start with my mother and her passion for improving the male of the species, which in my case took the form of forcing me to "make something of myself."

Lord, how I hated those words. . . .

CHAPTER TWO

I began working in journalism when I was eight years old. It was my mother's idea. She wanted me to "make something" of myself and, after a levelheaded appraisal of my strengths, decided I had better start young if I was to have any chance of keeping up with the competition.

The flaw in my character which she had already spotted was lack of "gumption." My idea of a perfect afternoon was lying in front of the radio rereading my favorite Big Little Book, *Dick Tracy Meets Stooge Viller*. My mother despised inactivity. Seeing me having a good time in repose, she was powerless to hide her disgust. "You've got no more gumption than a bump on a log," she said. "Get out in the kitchen and help Doris do those dirty dishes."

My sister Doris, though two years younger than I, had enough gumption for a dozen people. She positively enjoyed washing dishes, making beds, and cleaning the house. When she was only seven she could carry a piece of short-weighted cheese back to the A&P, threaten the manager with legal action, and come back triumphantly with the full quarter-pound we'd paid for and a few ounces extra thrown in for forgiveness. Doris could have made something of herself if she hadn't been a girl. Because of this defect, however, the best she could hope for was a career as a nurse or schoolteacher, the only work that capable females were considered up to in those days.

This must have saddened my mother, this twist of fate that had allocated all the gumption to the daughter and left her with a son who was content with Dick Tracy and Stooge Viller. If disappointed, though, she wasted no energy on self-pity. She would make me make something of myself whether I wanted to or not. "The Lord helps those who help themselves," she said. That was the way her mind worked.

She was realistic about the difficulty. Having sized up the material the Lord had given her to mold, she didn't overestimate what she could do with it. She didn't insist that I grow up to be President of the United States.

Fifty years ago parents still asked boys if they wanted to grow up to be President, and asked it not jokingly but seriously. Many parents who were hardly more than paupers still believed their sons could do it. Abraham Lincoln had done it. We were only sixty-five years from Lincoln. Many a grandfather who walked among us could remember Lincoln's time. Men of grandfatherly age were the worst for asking if you wanted to grow up to be President. A surprising number of little boys said yes and meant it.

I was asked many times myself. No, I would say, I didn't want to grow up to be President. My mother was present during one of these interrogations. An elderly uncle, having posed the usual question and exposed my lack of interest in the Presidency, asked, "Well, what *do* you want to be when you grow up?"

I loved to pick through trash piles and collect empty bottles, tin cans with pretty labels, and discarded magazines. The most desirable job on earth sprang instantly to mind. "I want to be a garbage man," I said.

My uncle smiled, but my mother had seen the first distressing evidence of a bump budding on a log. "Have a little gumption,

Russell," she said. Her calling me Russell was a signal of unhappiness. When she approved of me I was always "Buddy."

When I turned eight years old she decided that the job of starting me on the road toward making something of myself could no longer be safely delayed. "Buddy," she said one day, "I want you to come home right after school this afternoon. Somebody's coming and I want you to meet him."

When I burst in that afternoon she was in conference in the parlor with an executive of the Curtis Publishing Company. She introduced me. He bent low from the waist and shook my hand. Was it true as my mother had told him, he asked, that I longed for the opportunity to conquer the world of business?

My mother replied that I was blessed with a rare determination to make something of myself.

"That's right," I whispered.

"But have you got the grit, the character, the never-say-quit spirit it takes to succeed in business?"

My mother said I certainly did.

"That's right," I said.

He eyed me silently for a long pause, as though weighing whether I could be trusted to keep his confidence, then spoke man-to-man. Before taking a crucial step, he said, he wanted to advise me that working for the Curtis Publishing Company placed enormous responsibility on a young man. It was one of the great companies of America. Perhaps the greatest publishing house in the world. I had heard, no doubt, of the *Saturday Evening Post?*

Heard of it? My mother said that everyone in our house had heard of the *Saturday Post* and that I, in fact, read it with religious devotion.

Then doubtless, he said, we were also familiar with those two monthly pillars of the magazine world, the *Ladies Home Journal* and the *Country Gentleman.*

Indeed we were familiar with them, said my mother.

Representing the *Saturday Evening Post* was one of the weightiest honors that could be bestowed in the world of business, he said. He was personally proud of being a part of that great corporation.

My mother said he had every right to be.

Again he studied me as though debating whether I was worthy of a knighthood. Finally: "Are you trustworthy?"

My mother said I was the soul of honesty.

"That's right," I said.

The caller smiled for the first time. He told me I was a lucky young man. He admired my spunk. Too many young men thought life was all play. Those young men would not go far in this world. Only a young man willing to work and save and keep his face washed and his hair neatly combed could hope to come out on top in a world such as ours. Did I truly and sincerely believe that I was such a young man?

"He certainly does," said my mother.

"That's right," I said.

He said he had been so impressed by what he had seen of me that he was going to make me a representative of the Curtis Publishing Company. On the following Tuesday, he said, thirty freshly printed copies of the *Saturday Evening Post* would be delivered at our door. I would place these magazines, still damp with the ink of the presses, in a handsome canvas bag, sling it over my shoulder, and set forth through the streets to bring the best in journalism, fiction, and cartoons to the American public.

He had brought the canvas bag with him. He presented it with reverence fit for a chasuble. He showed me how to drape the sling over my left shoulder and across the chest so that the pouch lay easily accessible to my right hand, allowing the best in journalism, fiction, and cartoons to be swiftly extracted and sold to a citizenry whose happiness and security depended upon us soldiers of the free press.

The following Tuesday I raced home from school, put the canvas bag over my shoulder, dumped the magazines in, and, tilting to the left to balance their weight on my right hip, embarked on the highway of journalism.

We lived in Belleville, New Jersey, a commuter town at the northern fringe of Newark. It was 1932, the bleakest year of the Depression. My father had died two years before, leaving us with a few pieces of Sears, Roebuck furniture and not much else, and my mother had taken Doris and me to live with one of her younger brothers. This was my Uncle Allen. Uncle Allen had made something of himself by 1932. As salesman for a soft-drink bottler in Newark, he had an income of $30 a week; wore pearl-gray spats, detachable collars, and a three-piece suit; was happily married; and took in threadbare relatives.

With my load of magazines I headed toward Belleville Avenue. That's where the people were. There were two filling stations at the intersection with Union Avenue, as well as an A&P, a fruit stand, a bakery, a barber shop, Zuccarelli's drugstore, and a diner shaped like a railroad car. For several hours I made myself highly visible, shifting position now and then from corner to corner, from shop window to shop window, to make sure everyone could see the heavy black lettering on the canvas bag that said THE SATURDAY EVENING POST. When the angle of the light indicated it was suppertime, I walked back to the house.

"How many did you sell, Buddy?" my mother asked.

"None."

"Where did you go?"

"The corner of Belleville and Union Avenues."

"What did you do?"

"Stood on the corner waiting for somebody to buy a *Saturday Evening Post*."

"You just stood there?"

"Didn't sell a single one."

"For God's sake, Russell!"

Uncle Allen intervened. "I've been thinking about it for some time," he said, "and I've about decided to take the *Post* regularly. Put me down as a regular customer." I handed him a magazine and he paid me a nickel. It was the first nickel I earned.

Afterwards my mother instructed me in salesmanship. I would have to ring doorbells, address adults with charming self-confidence, and break down resistance with a sales talk pointing out that no one, no matter how poor, could afford to be without the *Saturday Evening Post* in the home.

13

I told my mother I'd changed my mind about wanting to succeed in the magazine business.

"If you think I'm going to raise a good-for-nothing," she replied, "you've got another think coming." She told me to hit the streets with the canvas bag and start ringing doorbells the instant school was out next day. When I objected that I didn't feel any aptitude for salesmanship, she asked how I'd like to lend her my leather belt so she could whack some sense into me. I bowed to superior will and entered journalism with a heavy heart.

My mother and I had fought this battle almost as long as I could remember. It probably started even before memory began, when I was a country child in northern Virginia and my mother, dissatisfied with my father's plain workman's life, determined that I would not grow up like him and his people, with calluses on their hands, overalls on their backs, and fourth-grade educations in their heads. She had fancier ideas of life's possibilities. Introducing me to the *Saturday Evening Post*, she was trying to wean me as early as possible from my father's world where men left with their lunch pails at sunup, worked with their hands until the grime ate into the pores, and died with a few sticks of mail-order furniture as their legacy. In my mother's vision of the better life there were desks and white collars, well-pressed suits, evenings of reading and lively talk, and perhaps—if a man were very, very lucky and hit the jackpot, really made something important of himself—perhaps there might be a fantastic salary of $5,000 a year to support a big house and a Buick with a rumble seat and a vacation in Atlantic City.

And so I set forth with my sack of magazines. I was afraid of the dogs that snarled behind the doors of potential buyers. I was timid about ringing the doorbells of strangers, relieved when no one came to the door, and scared when someone did. Despite my mother's instructions, I could not deliver an engaging sales pitch. When a door opened I simply asked, "Want to buy a *Saturday Evening Post*?" In Belleville few persons did. It was a town of 30,000 people, and most weeks I rang a fair majority of its doorbells. But I rarely sold my thirty copies. Some weeks I canvassed the entire town for six days and still had four or five unsold magazines on Monday evening; then I dreaded the coming of Tuesday morning, when a batch of thirty fresh *Saturday Evening Post*s was due at the front door.

"Better get out there and sell the rest of those magazines tonight," my mother would say.

I usually posted myself then at a busy intersection where a traffic light controlled commuter flow from Newark. When the light turned red I stood on the curb and shouted my sales pitch at the motorists.

"Want to buy a *Saturday Evening Post?*"

One rainy night when car windows were sealed against me I came back soaked and with not a single sale to report. My mother beckoned to Doris.

"Go back down there with Buddy and show him how to sell these magazines," she said.

Brimming with zest, Doris, who was then seven years old, returned with me to the corner. She took a magazine from the bag, and when the light turned red she strode to the nearest car and banged her small fist against the closed window. The driver, probably startled at what he took to be a midget assaulting his car, lowered the window to stare, and Doris thrust a *Saturday Evening Post* at him.

"You need this magazine," she piped, "and it only costs a nickel."

Her salesmanship was irresistible. Before the light changed half a dozen times she disposed of the entire batch. I didn't feel humiliated. To the contrary. I was so happy I decided to give her a treat. Leading her to the vegetable store on Belleville Avenue, I bought three apples, which cost a nickel, and gave her one.

"You shouldn't waste money," she said.

"Eat your apple." I bit into mine.

"You shouldn't eat before supper," she said. "It'll spoil your appetite."

Back at the house that evening, she dutifully reported me for wasting a nickel. Instead of a scolding, I was rewarded with a pat

15

on the back for having the good sense to buy fruit instead of candy. My mother reached into her bottomless supply of maxims and told Doris, "An apple a day keeps the doctor away."

By the time I was ten I had learned all my mother's maxims by heart. Asking to stay up past normal bedtime, I knew that a refusal would be explained with, "Early to bed and early to rise, makes a man healthy, wealthy, and wise." If I whimpered about having to get up early in the morning, I could depend on her to say, "The early bird gets the worm."

The one I most despised was, "If at first you don't succeed, try, try again." This was the battle cry with which she constantly sent me back into the hopeless struggle whenever I moaned that I had rung every doorbell in town and knew there wasn't a single potential buyer left in Belleville that week. After listening to my explanation, she handed me the canvas bag and said, "If at first you don't succeed . . ."

Three years in that job, which I would gladly have quit after the first day except for her insistence, produced at least one valuable result. My mother finally concluded that I would never make something of myself by pursuing a life in business and started considering careers that demanded less competitive zeal.

One evening when I was eleven I brought home a short "composition" on my summer vacation which the teacher had graded with an A. Reading it with her own schoolteacher's eye, my mother agreed that it was top-drawer seventh grade prose and complimented me. Nothing more was said about it immediately, but a new idea had taken life in her mind. Halfway through supper she suddenly interrupted the conversation.

"Buddy," she said, "maybe you could be a writer."

I clasped the idea to my heart. I had never met a writer, had shown no previous urge to write, and hadn't a notion how to become a writer, but I loved stories and thought that making up stories must surely be almost as much fun as reading them. Best of all, though, and what really gladdened my heart, was the ease of the writer's life. Writers did not have to trudge through the town peddling from canvas bags, defending themselves against

16

angry dogs, being rejected by surly strangers. Writers did not have to ring doorbells. So far as I could make out, what writers did couldn't even be classified as work.

I was enchanted. Writers didn't have to have any gumption at all. I did not dare tell anybody for fear of being laughed at in the schoolyard, but secretly I decided that what I'd like to be when I grew up was a writer.

Chapter Three

My mother's efforts to turn poor specimens of manhood into glittering prizes began long before she became my mother. As the older daughter in a family of nine children, she had tried it on her younger brothers without much success. When she married she had tried it on my father with no success at all.

Her attitudes toward men were a strange blend of twentieth-century feminism and Victorian romance. The feminism filled her with anger against men and a rage against the unfair advantages that came with the right to wear trousers. "Just because you wear pants doesn't mean you're God's gift to creation, sonny boy," she shouted at me one day when I said something about the helplessness of women. Of a man vain about his charm with women: "Just because he wears pants he thinks he can get through life with half a brain."

The unfair advantage bestowed by pants was a lifelong grievance. As a girl of sixteen she denounced it while arguing the case for women's suffrage in her 1913 high school debate. "Women do not ask to be placed on a throne as goddess or queen," she said. "They are content to be equal. At present they are only half-citizens. Is the right to vote to be not a matter of right or justice, but a mere matter of pantaloons?"

She was so pleased with the phrase that she underlined "pantaloons" twice on her script before concluding: "A noted man once said to a young man starting out to practice law, 'Young man, espouse some righteous unpopular cause.' That is just what I have been called upon to do, and whether I win or lose, 'I had rather be right than President'—and perhaps, when women shall have won the ballot, some one of the Lancaster High School girls will be both right *and* President."

And yet some part of her did want to be queen. Her modern feminist passion for equality was at war with her nineteenth-century idea of women as the purifying, ennobling element of society, special creatures who ought to be protected and treasured as precious assets of civilization. She wanted the equality, but she also wanted to be a lady. Somewhere she had picked up the tyrannical spirit of the ladies of the Mauve Decade and, like them, looked upon men as naturally brutish creatures whose licentious and lazy instincts could be overcome only by the guidance of a good woman. "Behind every successful man you'll find a good woman" was another favorite in her storehouse of maxims.

Her model of male excellence, the paragon of manhood against whom she measured all other men, was her father. "Papa," she always called him.

Poor mythic Papa. As I was growing up, my mother loved to tell me about the happiness of her childhood days, and I loved to listen, for I knew only the ruined and colorless landscape of the Depression, and her talk evoked beautiful pictures of a world that was bright and sunny. When she spoke of it, I saw her as a little girl in a great Virginia country house. Sleek horses and fancy buggies, roaring fireplaces in the autumn, summer romps through the woods with carefree brothers, her "Mama" playing hymns on the piano in the parlor on Sunday nights. In that world, Tuesday mornings brought no soul-crushing bundle of *Saturday Evening Posts*. Then she inevitably came to the part that always began, 'Now Papa was a real gentleman . . .'' and my interest faded.

Though he was my grandfather, I couldn't abide him being such a splendid man, and knew I could never match him in quality. I took my revenge by shutting him out of mind. It took years for me to care enough to look into the Papa matter. A surprise awaited. The fact was, Papa had not made anything at all of himself. He had tried hard enough, no doubt about that, but he had failed disastrously.

A country lawyer in Tidewater Virginia, he mixed religious piety unhealthily with capitalistic ambition. His urge to make money led him into timber speculation. His religion led him to abhor insurance. When an agent tried to sell him a life-insurance policy, he lectured the fellow on the sinfulness of his trade. "God hates a gambler," Papa said, "and life insurance is gambling with God." Papa was a good Methodist, and a good Methodist he died at the modest age of fifty-three, felled by a heart attack during a business trip to Richmond. Debt-ridden from timber speculation and uninsured out of respect for God, he left his family destitute.

The year was 1917. My mother was in college at Petersburg—Papa had had grand plans for his children—but she had to quit and go to work. Her education qualified her to teach school, but not for the choice assignments. To find jobs she traveled northward, out of the genteel old Tidewater culture, where her family had been "quality folk" for 250 years, and into primitive backwaters where mountain children came barefoot to school and dropped out after fourth grade to take dollar-a-week work in the fields. Her youth became a succession of two-room schoolhouses, boarding with families of preachers and farmers prosperous enough to have a spare couch to rent for a few dollars a month.

In her middle twenties she came at last to the Arlington School in the northernmost reaches of Loudoun County, a two-room schoolhouse at the foot of the Short Hill Mountain. A few miles beyond to westward lay the Blue Ridge, a few miles to the north, the Potomac River.

Four hundred yards to the west, between the schoolhouse and the mountain, lay a festering center of sin, a bootleg whiskey still operated by the celebrated anti-Prohibition guerrilla Sam Reever.

The dirt road running past the school carried a steady traffic of horseback riders, buggies, cars, and strolling pilgrims to and fro in ceaseless quest of moonshine.

My mother hated whiskey and admired men who could leave it alone. In her family the men never used it. "Papa," she told me over and over again, "never touched a drop of whiskey in his life." She believed alcohol brought out men's innate brutishness, made them foolish and quarrelsome, and destroyed their ability to make something of themselves. The traffic outside the schoolhouse saddened and disgusted her. So many of the men looked so young to be traveling that road to perdition.

When she was outside for recess with her students one day, a sputtering old Model T en route from Sam Reever's coughed and died right beside the schoolyard. She watched a lanky, dark-haired young man step out, lift the hood, and peer in at the engine. He wore a shapeless gray cap, coarse work clothes, and heavy clodhopper shoes.

After studying the engine, he opened the tool chest on the fender and took out a wrench and a Mason jar. He had the cap off the jar and was lifting it to drink before he noticed her watching him from the playground. "Like a gentleman," she later recalled, he quickly put the jar out of sight, flashed her a broad smile, and lifted his cap in salute.

He was still tinkering with the engine when recess ended. Back in her schoolroom, her anger about his exposing children to the sight of whiskey was softened by feelings of sadness. What a shame for such a nice-looking young man to be ruining his life with whiskey. He looked like a man who might be able to make something of himself if a good woman took him in hand. Her chance to do so came a few days later.

She was boarding at Ep Ahalt's farm. Ep owned the biggest barn, the mightiest silo, and the fanciest house in the neighborhood. Ep's wife, Bessie, a tiny, sweet-tempered woman with grown sons, was different from most women thereabouts. She too wanted her boys to make something of themselves. She fretted about all the bad influences, all the temptations to idleness which surrounded her sons. One of those tempters dropped in one evening. He wore a shapeless gray cap and arrived in a sputtering old Model T and knocked at the door asking if Walton was there. Walton, one of Bessie's sons, was not there, for which Bessie was probably grateful, but the schoolmarm boarder was, and Bessie, being the soul of politeness, introduced them.

He was tall and lean in the angular, graceless mountaineer style. His hands were rough, callused, competent. Workman's hands. Not at all like Papa's hands. He was not at all like Papa in any respect. With coarse black hair and dark brown skin, he might have been part Indian.

Maybe it was his utter difference from Papa that stirred her. Despite her preference for gentlemen, she was not without a healthy feminine interest in tall, dark, and handsome specimens with the adventurer's gleam in their eyes. Much later, when Robert Taylor was Hollywood's newest sex symbol, I was surprised to overhear her tell a group of women discussing Taylor's charms, "He can park his shoes under my bed anytime." She was joking, of course, being one of the girls. Still, it forced me to concede that she was capable of more varieties of love than her girlish love for Papa and her motherly love for me.

The young man in Bessie Ahalt's parlor was obviously no gentleman. Gentlemen didn't visit Sam Reever. In his favor, though, he was quick to smile, and he was not a complete Hottentot. He had enough manners to say "ma'am" when he talked to Bessie. There was a sense of fun in him too. Unlike most men she met, he was not so blinded by awe of a schoolteacher that he couldn't see a woman. Though he'd left school after fourth grade, her learning didn't scare him. Cheekily he asked if she'd like to go riding in his Model T.

She said she'd like that.

Among other things, she planned to improve him. Her first goal was to stop his drinking, but as months passed and the courtship became complicated her program went awry, and then there was a crisis. She was pregnant.

Out-of-wedlock pregnancies were fairly commonplace in that

22

Benny before his marriage.

part of Virginia. They occasioned mild scandal when the news spread, but there was no taint or disgrace if a man "did the right thing" and a marriage ensued. If he refused, people looked on him as a bad sport for a while, until he found another woman, married, and "settled down." The rejected mother-to-be, on the other hand, faced a lifetime of shame and ostracism.

In either case a schoolteacher's career was ended. In this terrible moment when she faced ruin, my mother was confronted by a redoubtable enemy. This was her prospective mother-in-law, whose plans for her son did not include marriage with an outsider she heartily disliked.

An obedient son, he had taken the schoolteacher home to meet his mother when the courtship began, and the two women promptly developed a lively aversion to each other. When his mother learned of the pregnancy, she declared violently against marriage. She told him he was a young fool who had been tricked by a hussy ready to stoop to any scheme to trap herself a husband.

She was a domineering woman, who had trained her sons to march to her command. Normally, her opposition to a marriage of this sort would have closed the case against the mother-to-be. This case, though, was different. She was pitted against a woman as fierce as she.

In March of 1925 her son and his schoolteacher went discreetly down to Washington to be married. They were both twenty-seven years old. I was born six months later and immediately became the darling of my doting grandmother. With all her love for me, however, she never forgave my mother, and my mother returned the scorn measure for measure.

Ep Ahalt's farm looked down across sloping cornfields toward a small village a quarter mile to the south. The village consisted of seven houses and a general store, a few vegetable gardens, a couple of straw ricks, and a scattering of barns, chicken houses, and pigpens. On a summer afternoon the whole place dozed in the sun, under silences broken only by the occasional cluck of a hen, the solitary clack of a closing screen door.

The wedding picture of Ida Rebecca and George Baker, 1880.

This was the center of the universe in the days of my innocence. Its name, Morrisonville, dated from the early part of the nineteenth century. By the time I came along it could have been appropriately renamed Bakerville, for almost every soul in the community was a member in some degree of the prodigious Baker family, which had settled in the region around 1730.

Why a settlement rose there in the first place is a mystery. The village sat a third of a mile back from the only paved road in the territory, and the sole waterway was a creek so shallow I could wade across it and barely get my feet wet. To get in from the main highway, travelers had to wind through thick stands of brush along a dirt road that could swallow an automobile all the way to the axles in the mud season. When it finally arrived at Morrisonville, this road forked. One branch ambled toward my Uncle Irvey's house, then lurched to avoid hitting the creek and disappeared into a briar patch. The other branch ran smack through the middle of town as though intending to become a real road, but it lost heart after it passed my grandmother's house and meandered off in a lackadaisical path toward the mountain.

This was the same road that ran past the Arlington School to Sam Reever's bootleggery. It came to rest smack against the mountain two miles west of Morrisonville. My great-grandfather Daniel Baker used to live in a log house back there. He was a gunsmith who turned to tailoring after the declining need for full-time gunmakers made the craft unprofitable. Born shortly after the War of 1812, he could still walk five miles carrying a sack of cornmeal when he was eighty years old, and he lived to see the arrival of the twentieth century.

His son George moved down to Morrisonville around 1880 and went into blacksmithing. George was short and on the slender side, not the towering, heavily muscled stereotype of the blacksmith celebrated in Longfellow's poem. His devotion to Christian worship was remarkable. He required a minimum of two church services each Sunday to keep his soul in sound repair, and after partaking of the Gospel at morning and afternoon servings he often set out across the fields for a third helping at dusk if he heard of a church with lamps lit for nocturnal psalming.

Shortly before moving into Morrisonville, he had married Ida Rebecca Brown, the daughter of a local farmer. Ida Rebecca was only nineteen at her marriage, but she took to power as naturally as George took to toil. George built his blacksmith shop hard by the stone-and-log house in which Ida Rebecca ruled, and there he pursued a life of piety, toil, and procreation.

He was as vigorous at procreation as he was at churchgoing. In the first year of their marriage, Ida Rebecca produced a son. In the next ten years she produced nine more, including twin boys. In 1897, after an uncommonly long pause of more than four years, an eleventh son was born. He was to become my father. They named him Benjamin.

The line didn't stop there, though. Two years later there was, at last, a daughter; and five years after her, a twelfth son. Thirteen children was not a record for the neighborhood, nor even very remarkable. One family close by produced children in such volume that the parents ran out of names and began giving them numbers. One of their sons, whom I particularly envied for his heroic biceps, was named Eleven.

How big my father's family might have become eventually is hard to say, for Grandfather George suffered a stroke in 1907 and died at home, at the still fruitful age of fifty-two. There was a family mystery about his dying words. These, according to Ida Rebecca, were "into midget and out of midget." At least they sounded like "into midget and out of midget," though Ida Rebecca never knew if this was exactly what he was trying to say or, if it was, what he meant by it. Nor did she ask him. He belonged to the Order of Red Men, one of those lodge brotherhoods common at the turn of the century which cherished secret handshakes and mumbo-jumbo passwords. Ida Rebecca hesitated to ask him what he meant by "into midget and out of midget" for fear she might be delving improperly into the sacred mysteries of the lodge.

In the eighteen years between Grandfather George's death and my arrival in Morrisonville, Ida Rebecca established herself as the iron ruler of a sprawling family empire. Her multitude of sons, some of them graying and middle-aged, were celebrated for miles around as good boys who listened to their mother. If one of them kicked over the traces, there was hell to pay until he fell obediently back into line. In Morrisonville everybody said, "It's her way or *no* way."

Her sons' wives accepted the supremacy of mother-in-law rule as the price of peace and kept their resentments to themselves. When her boys married the women she approved, their wives were expected to surrender their swords in return for being allowed to keep their husbands for the spring planting. Among them, only my mother refused to bend the knee. It's easy to understand why the two disliked each other instinctively from the first meeting, long before the awkward question of marriage arose. One can readily imagine the scene at that first confrontation:

Ida Rebecca would have been sitting in state in the front porch rocker that served as her throne, waiting for Benny to arrive from Ep Ahalt's with his new girl. Her porch commanded a view fit for an empress. It sat high above the road overlooking Morrisonville's rooftops and behind them the distant rampart of the Blue Ridge Mountains. Arriving visitors had to look up to her, for the road lay three steps below the level of her lawn, and after climbing those steps and passing through the whitewashed picket gate, they had to mount another set of broad stone steps before reaching the presence.

My mother could only have been impressed when she finally attained the topmost level and Ida Rebecca rose to meet her. Seated, Ida Rebecca looked much like any other country woman whose style had been formed in the 1870s. She wore home-sewn gray that enclosed her from neck to wrists to ankles and, if there was the smallest glint of sunshine, a gray bonnet with a wide bill that kept her face buried in shadow. When she stood, though, she projected physical power and moral authority. Fully erect, she was six feet tall and seemed to look down on the world. She certainly looked down on my mother, who was almost a foot shorter.

Under the enveloping gray dress were shoulders square and broad. The hands were big and gnarled. They were hands that could prepare a feast for thirty people, deliver a baby, grow a year's supply of canning vegetables in a summer of garden toil, or butcher a hog, and they had done all these things many times long before my mother was born and many times after. The long jaw under her bonnet was combatively prominent. Her hair was a glistening silvery white. Peering through steel-rimmed spectacles were chilly gray eyes that found little to be amused by. What my mother saw was an overpowering figure accustomed to command.

What Ida Rebecca saw was a frail little creature with her hair cut in the sassy new pageboy bob. A suspicious touch of the city flapper, that haircut. Decent women let their hair grow and tied it in a knot on the back of the head. And skinny little ankles and wrists like twigs that looked as if they'd snap if they had to do any real work. What in the world did Benny see in her? She certainly wasn't pretty. Didn't have enough weight on her to be pretty. Hardly an ounce of flesh anywhere.

Conversation couldn't have improved matters. Ida Rebecca's respect for schoolteachers was slight. Her sons left school when they were big enough to work. By then they could read, write, and do sums and knew who George Washington and Abraham Lincoln were and had learned a little geography. How to find Europe on a map, and Virginia, and China. That was enough. Man was born to work, not to sit around with his nose in a book. She was totally uninterested in the proposition that a man ought to make something of himself. A man's duty was to provide. Provide for his wife, provide for his children. And pay his duty to his mother. Beyond that . . . It's doubtful she ever thought much beyond that.

My mother, always education-proud, wouldn't have hesitated to talk too much and show off her learning. Maybe just to prove her spunk, she mentioned how backward the children around Morrisonville seemed, compared to the youngsters where she came from, for she was appalled by the unworldliness of her students. One day she asked one of them if she had ever been to Frederick over in Maryland. "No indeed, ma'am, and I don't ever

29

expect to," the girl replied. "I once went all the way to Brunswick and just about knocked my brains out *there* looking at all the buildings."

Ida Rebecca had small book learning but highly developed sensitivity, particularly when it came to judging outsiders. In Morrisonville outsiders were under suspicion until they proved they could fit comfortably into Morrisonville society. Ida Rebecca must have sensed immediately what her eleventh son failed to: that this book-proud schoolteacher who gave herself airs about her fancy family would never accommodate to Morrisonville.

My father's decision to defy Ida Rebecca with a marriage she hated may have been the bravest act of his life. With enough money he would probably have moved away, out toward Lovettsville or down toward Waterford, to put distance between bride and mother and to avoid being pulled and torn in their war for his loyalties. Well, there wasn't enough money. There was almost no money at all. He was a stonemason by trade, but in a region where stone was plentiful and stonework common, stonemasons were also plentiful and earnings were small. And he was a man who liked a good time. What little he earned went into repairs for the failing Model T, flings in the urban sinks of Lovettsville, Brunswick, and Purcellville, and the moonshine Sam Reever ladled into Mason jars.

Without money he had no choice. He brought my mother to Morrisonville. Not to live with Ida Rebecca; that promised only nightmare. Temporary shelter was offered by his oldest brother, who was well-to-do by Morrisonville standards and owned his own house, which was situated a comfortable hundred yards from Ida Rebecca's. The brother offered to keep the newlyweds until they could save enough to "go to housekeeping."

This brother, who was my first great benefactor, was my Uncle Irvey. I was born in his second-floor bedroom just before midnight on Friday, August 14, 1925. Ida Rebecca was there, prepared to deliver me into the world when it seemed that the doctor from Lovettsville would never arrive. He did, however, in the nick of time, and I was issued uneventfully into the governance of

Ida Rebecca as a girl of sixteen
and with a grandchild in 1925.

Calvin Coolidge. World War I was seven years past, the Russian Revolution was eight years old, and the music on my grandmother's wind-up Victrola was "Yes, We Have No Bananas." Unaware of history's higher significance, I slumbered through the bliss of infancy, feeling no impulse whatever to make something of myself.

When I woke from that slumber—this is my earliest memory —I was staring into two huge eyes glaring at me from a monstrous skull. I screamed, and the monster emitted a terrifying rumble. My mother came running and scooped me out of the crib.

"Get away from there!" she shouted.

The horror vanished.

"It's just a cow," she said.

Grazing against the house, the cow had raised its head to look through the open window at the crib, she explained. Cows were nice. They didn't hurt people. Would I like her to carry me outside to look at it?

I understood her perfectly. Sometime during my slumber, when I seemed to be aware of nothing at all, I had learned to understand English.

We'd moved from Uncle Irvey's by then, and were living in a tenant farmhouse near Ep Ahalt's farm. When I next noticed the world, we were living in a yellow frame house in Morrisonville directly across the road from Ida Rebecca's high front porch. Looking up, I saw my grandmother across the road looking down upon me. I liked that because I loved my grandmother dearly and knew she loved me just as much. She was not comfortable on my mother's side of the road, and my mother was uneasy when she crossed to Ida Rebecca's, but I happily occupied both worlds. Walking through Morrisonville to survey her kingdom, my grandmother took my hand and led me beside her. In her vegetable garden she taught me how to pick potato bugs. In her dark cellar kitchen she showed me how to lay the kindling and pour kerosene to fire her wood-burning stove. When a summer thunderstorm roared off the mountain, she scurried into the road, dragging me

32

behind her, to scoop up newborn chicks soft as cotton wool in the hand and so fragile they could be pelted to death by the rain. When we hurried back to her house and the storm struck with a blast of hail on the tin roof, we sat behind sealed windows in her stone-walled sitting room and watched the lightning dance in the fields and shuddered when the thunder boomed like heavy artillery. We were two people alone in a fortress under siege, but she sat calmly in a rocker by her cast-iron stove teaching me about the perils of storms.

"Don't sit there," she cautioned. "You're right between the door and the fireplace."

And that was a dangerous place to be?

"Lawsa mercy, child, it's the worst place in the room during a thunderstorm. I've seen lightning bolts come right down the chimney and roll across the floor in a ball of fire and go right on through the door."

My mother, frantic about my safety, was impatient when I came in after the storm and told her I'd been at grandmother's. "Why don't you stay on this side of the road where you belong? I was scared half to death about you."

My grandmother thought my mother kept me under too much discipline and delighted in taking me to her cellar pantry and stuffing me with forbidden treats. One afternoon she took me down there in the darkness to feed me on her homemade bread. Slicing a thick piece for each of us, she laid on a coat of butter, then said, "You want jelly on top of it?"

"Yes ma'am, please."

She took a jar from the shelf and removed the wax and had the knife poised to plunge in when we were caught.

"Russell, what're you doing back in there?" My mother was silhouetted in the doorway.

"Grandma's fixing me a piece of jelly bread."

My mother spoke to Ida Rebecca. "You know I don't want him eating between meals." Her voice was terrible with anger.

So was Ida Rebecca's. "Are you going to tell *me* how to raise a boy?"

"I'm telling you I don't want him eating jelly bread between meals. He's my child, and he'll do as I tell him."

"Don't you come in here telling me how to raise children. I raised a dozen children, and not one of them ever dared raise their voice to me like you do."

I cowered between them while the shouting rose, but they had forgotten me now as the accumulated bitterness spewed out of them. Finally my mother noticed I was still standing there with the buttered bread in my hand.

"I want you to stay on the other side of the road where you belong," she said to me.

"He belongs over here just as much as he belongs over there," my grandmother exclaimed.

The anger seemed to drain suddenly out of my mother. She started to leave but turned at the door and said, very much in control of her temper, "You can eat the butter bread, but I don't want any jelly put on it."

At this Ida Rebecca jabbed her knife into the jar and smeared the bread with a thick coat of jelly, all the time glaring at my mother.

"Eat it," she commanded.

I waited until my mother marched out, very near tears, I judged, and then I ate it while Ida Rebecca watched. I didn't dare not to.

Not going to my grandmother's side of the road was an impossibility, and my mother acknowledged it, and went frequently herself in calmer moments, for Ida Rebecca's house was the capitol of Morrisonville. Once in the middle of a winter night my parents shook me awake to announce that we were going across to grandmother's. My father carried me, still in bedclothes, up the broad stone steps, across the porch, and through cold black rooms until we came to the parlor, the grim, forbidding parlor that was never used except for funerals and which I believed to be haunted with the ghosts of the dead who had lain there. There my father opened the door on a baffling scene. In one corner I saw his sister, several of his brothers, and my grandmother standing in a group, most of

34

them in nightclothes. Somebody held a kerosene lamp. They were staring at a tree.

I had never seen my grandmother looking so strange. She wore a nightgown, and her silvery hair streamed free over her shoulders. She was smiling at me. I had never seen her smile before. Smiling like that, she looked more like a girl than a grandmother.

"Look who's been here," she said to me.

They were all smiling, and at me. This was very, very strange. They were not people who smiled much, least of all at children.

By the dim kerosene lamp I saw that the tree's branches were filled with objects of many colors and odd shapes. Someone held the lamp close against the branches so I could see its light reflecting from these glistening objects.

"Merry Christmas!" my grandmother said, taking me from my father and thrusting my nose against the pine needles. "Kris Kringle's been here. Look what he brought for you."

On the floor I saw a toy steam shovel with black sides and a red roof. The shovel itself had metal teeth so it could bite into a pile of dirt. With a string mechanism, the shovel could be lifted into the air and its bottom released to dump the dirt back onto the ground.

To my grandmother and father and uncles it must have seemed like an educational toy. Metalworkers, stonemasons, carpenters, people with a tradition of craftsmanship and building, they naturally assumed that giving me a toy steam shovel was giving me something more lasting than a toy. They were also giving me a way to start thinking about my life.

Left to her own devices, my mother, I suspect, would not have thought of such a beautiful, ingenious machine but would have given me a book.

CHAPTER FOUR

DURING all these years my father was under a sentence of death. In 1918 he had been drafted by the Army and discharged after five days with papers stating he had "a physical disability." From his childhood it had been Morrisonville's common knowledge that Benny had "trouble with his kidneys." What the Army doctors found is not clear from the records. Maybe they told him the truth—that he had diabetes—but if so he kept their terrible diagnosis a secret. In 1918 insulin was still unknown. As a twenty-year-old diabetic, whether he knew it or not, he was doomed to early death.

The discovery of insulin in 1921 would have lifted that sentence and offered him a long and reasonably healthy life. If he ever learned about insulin, though, he certainly never used it, for the needle required for daily injections was not part of our household goods. Perhaps he didn't know how seriously ill he was, but the state of medicine in Morrisonville must also be allowed for. New medical wonders were slow to reach up the dirt roads of backcountry America. Around Morrisonville grave illness was treated mostly with prayer, and early death was commonplace. Children were carried off by diphtheria, scarlet fever, and measles. I heard constantly of people laid low by typhoid or mortally ill with "blood poisoning." Remote from hospitals, people with ruptured appendixes died at home waiting for the doctor to make a house call.

Since antibiotics lay far in the future, tuberculosis, which we called "T.B." or "consumption," was almost always fatal. Pneumonia, only slightly less dreaded, took its steady crop for the cemetery each winter. Like croup and whooping cough, it was treated with remedies Ida Rebecca compounded from ancient folk-medicine recipes: reeking mustard plasters, herbal broths, dosings of onion syrup mixed with sugar. Boils and carbuncles were covered with the membrane of a boiled egg to "draw the core" before being lanced with a needle sterilized in a match flame.

When my cousin Lillian stepped barefoot on a rusty nail, my grandmother insisted on treating the puncture by applying a slab of raw bacon. When my cousin Catherine's hand touched a red-hot wood stove, my grandmother seized her arm and with fingertips light as feathers stroked the blistering skin while murmuring an incoherent incantation in a trancelike monotone. Catherine's screaming stopped. "My hand doesn't hurt anymore, Grandma," she said.

This was called "powwowing," a form of witch-doctoring still believed in then by the old people around Morrisonville and prescribed on at least one occasion by a local medical man. This doctor, after failing to rid Lillian of a severe facial rash with the tools of science, prescribed a visit to an old woman on the mountain whose powwowing, he said, sometimes cured such rashes. "But don't you ever dare tell anybody I sent you to her," he cautioned. Lillian did not go for the powwow treatment; her rash subsided without help from either science or witchcraft.

Very few people ever saw the inside of a hospital. When my grandfather George had a stroke he was led into the house and put to bed, and the Red Men sent lodge brothers to sit with him to exercise the curative power of brotherhood. Red Men who failed to report for bedside duty with their stricken brother were fined a dollar for dereliction. Ida Rebecca called upon modern technology to help George. From a mail-order house she ordered a battery-operated galvanic device which applied the stimulation of low-voltage electrical current to his paralyzed limbs.

Morrisonville had not developed the modern disgust with death. It was not treated as an obscenity to be confined in hospitals and "funeral homes." In Morrisonville death was a common part of life. It came for the young as relentlessly as it came for the old. To die antiseptically in a hospital was almost unknown. In Morrisonville death still made house calls. It stopped by the bedside, sat down on the couch right by the parlor window, walked up to people in the fields in broad daylight, surprised them at a bend in the stairway when they were on their way to bed.

Whatever he knew about his ailment, my father made no concessions to it. If anything he lived a little too intensely, as though determined to make the most of whatever time he was to be allowed. By 1927 he had saved enough money to rent and furnish a small house of his own—the tenant house where grazing cows peered through windows—and there, that August, my sister Doris was born. In 1928 we were back in Morrisonville in a larger house, looking up at Ida Rebecca's porch, and there my second sister was born in January of 1930. They named her Audrey.

Benny's development into "a good family man" was evidence of my mother's success at improving his character. His refusal to forswear moonshine, however, mocked her with the most painful failure of all. After pleasing her with long bouts of sobriety, he often came home from work with the sour smell of whiskey on him and turned violently ill. With diabetes, his drinking was lethal. He paid terribly for whatever pleasure he took from Sam Reever's Mason jars. My mother didn't know about the diabetes; all she knew was that drinking acted like poison on him. When he came home smelling of whiskey, she abused him fiercely in cries loud enough to be heard across the road at Ida Rebecca's. He never shouted back, nor argued, nor attempted to defend himself, but always sat motionless as her anger poured down on his bowed head —sick, contrite, and beaten.

One evening when we waited supper long past his usual arrival time and finally ate without him, he came in while the dishes were being washed. He was smiling and holding something behind his back.

"Where have you been?" my mother asked.

"I bought a present for Doris."

"Do you know what time it is? Supper's been over for hours." All this in a shout.

Holding his smile in place, trying to ignore her anger, he spoke to Doris. "You want to see what Daddy brought you?"

Doris started toward him. My mother pulled her back.

"Leave that child alone. You're drunk."

Well—and he kept smiling—actually he had taken a drink along the way, but just one—

"Don't lie about it. You're stinking drunk. I can smell it on you."

—had been in town looking for a present for Doris, and run into a man he knew—

"Aren't you ashamed of yourself? Letting your children see you like this? What kind of father are you?"

His smile went now, and he didn't try to answer her. Instead he looked at Doris and held the present in front of him for her to take. It was a box with top folded back to display a set of miniature toy dishes made of tin, little tin plates, little tin saucers, little tin teacups.

"Daddy brought you a set of dishes."

Delighted, Doris reached for the box, but my mother was quicker. Seizing his peace offering, she spoke to him in words awful to me. It wasn't bad enough that he wasted what little money he had on the poison he drank, not bad enough that he was killing himself with liquor, not bad enough that he let his children see him so drunk he could hardly stand up. He had to squander our precious money on a box of tin junk.

In a rage she ran to the kitchen screen door, opened it wide, and flung Doris's present into the darkening twilight. My father dropped onto a chair while I watched this unbelievable waste of

39

brand-new toys. When I turned back to see if he intended to rescue the dishes, I saw that he was just sitting there helplessly.

Doris and I ran out into the gloaming to recover the scattered dishes. While we scrambled on hands and knees groping for tiny cups and saucers, the sounds of my mother's anger poured from the kitchen. When the shouting subsided, I crept back to the door. My father was slumped on the chair, shoulders sagging, head bowed, his forearms resting lifelessly on his thighs in a posture of abject surrender. My mother was still talking, though quietly now.

"For two cents," I heard her say, "I'd take my children out of here tomorrow and go back to my own people."

I sneaked back into the darkness and found Doris and tried to interest myself in the dishes for a while. The screen door banged. My father was silhouetted against the light for an instant, then he came down the steps, walked toward the pear tree, and started vomiting.

There were also sweet times in that house. On breathless summer nights my parents brought blankets down from the steamy upstairs bedroom to make a bed on the living room floor. The summer I was four years old my mother bought me my first book and started teaching me to read. One night at bedtime she and my father stretched out on the blankets for sleep, but before dousing the lamp my father wanted to see how I was progressing with the written word.

They placed me between them with the opened book. I knew a few words, but under pressure to perform forgot everything. It was beginner material: "cat," "rat," "boy," "girl," "the." I didn't recognize a word.

My mother was disappointed that I could do nothing but stare stupidly at the printed page. My father saved my pride. "Have a little patience with him," he said. Taking the book in hand, he moved me close against him and rubbed his cheek against mine. "Now," he said, pointing to a word, "you know that word, don't you?"

I did indeed. " 'The,' " I said.

40

Russell at four, Morrisonville, 1929.

"You're a smart boy. I bet you know this one too."

" 'Boy,' " I said.

When I read most of the sentence without too much help, he said to my mother, "You're doing good with him. Maybe we ought to send him to college." Pleased, my mother reached across me and kissed him on the cheek. Smiling down at me, he said, "You want to go to college?" They both laughed a little at this. Maybe he liked the extravagance of the idea as much as she did. Then he turned off the kerosene lamp. That night they let me sleep between them.

The occasional outbursts of passion that flickered across my childhood were like summer storms. The sky clouded suddenly, thunder rumbled, lightning flashed, and I trembled a few moments, then just as swiftly the sky turned blue again and I was basking contentedly in the peace of innocence.

Morrisonville was a poor place to prepare for a struggle with the twentieth century, but a delightful place to spend a childhood. It was summer days drenched with sunlight, fields yellow with buttercups, and barn lofts sweet with hay. Clusters of purple grapes dangled from backyard arbors, lavender wisteria blossoms perfumed the air from the great vine enclosing the end of my grandmother's porch, and wild roses covered the fences.

On a broiling afternoon when the men were away at work and all the women napped, I moved through majestic depths of silences, silences so immense I could hear the corn growing. Under these silences there was an orchestra of natural music playing notes no city child would ever hear. A certain cackle from the henhouse meant we had gained an egg. The creak of a porch swing told of a momentary breeze blowing across my grandmother's yard. Moving past Liz Virts's barn as quietly as an Indian, I could hear the swish of a horse's tail and knew the horseflies were out in strength. As I tiptoed along a mossy bank to surprise a frog, a faint splash told me the quarry had spotted me and slipped into the stream. Wandering among the sleeping houses, I learned that tin roofs crackle under the power of the sun, and when I tired and came back to my grandmother's house, I padded into her dark cool living room, lay flat on the floor, and listened to the hypnotic beat of her pendulum clock on the wall ticking the meaningless hours away.

I was enjoying the luxuries of a rustic nineteenth-century boyhood, but for the women Morrisonville life had few rewards. Both my mother and grandmother kept house very much as women did before the Civil War. It was astonishing that they had any energy left, after a day's work, to nourish their mutual disdain. Their lives were hard, endless, dirty labor. They had no electricity, gas, plumbing, or central heating. No refrigerator, no radio, no telephone, no automatic laundry, no vacuum cleaner. Lacking indoor toilets, they had to empty, scour, and fumigate each morning the noisome slop jars which sat in bedrooms during the night.

For baths, laundry, and dishwashing, they hauled buckets of water from a spring at the foot of a hill. To heat it, they chopped kindling to fire their wood stoves. They boiled laundry in tubs, scrubbed it on washboards until knuckles were raw, and wrung it out by hand. Ironing was a business of lifting heavy metal weights heated on the stove top.

They scrubbed floors on hands and knees, thrashed rugs with carpet beaters, killed and plucked their own chickens, baked bread and pastries, grew and canned their own vegetables, patched the family's clothing on treadle-operated sewing machines, deloused the chicken coops, preserved fruits, picked potato bugs and tomato worms to protect their garden crop, darned stockings, made jelly and relishes, rose before the men to start the stove for breakfast and pack lunch pails, polished the chimneys of kerosene lamps, and even found time to tend the geraniums, hollyhocks, nasturtiums, dahlias, and peonies that grew around every house. By the end of a summer day a Morrisonville woman had toiled like a serf.

At sundown the men drifted back from the fields exhausted and steaming. They scrubbed themselves in enamel basins and, when supper was eaten, climbed up onto Ida Rebecca's porch to watch the night arrive. Presently the women joined them, and the twilight music of Morrisonville began:

The swing creaking, rocking chairs whispering on the porch planks, voices murmuring approval of the sagacity of Uncle Irvey as he quietly observed for probably the ten-thousandth time in his life, "A man works from sun to sun, but woman's work is never done."

Ida Rebecca, presiding over the nightfall from the cane rocker, announcing, upon hearing of some woman "up there along the mountain" who had dropped dead hauling milk to the creamery, that "man is born to toil, and woman is born to suffer."

The timelessness of it: Nothing new had been said on that porch for a hundred years. If one of the children threw a rock close to someone's window, Uncle Harry removed his farmer's straw hat, swabbed the liner with his blue bandanna, and spoke the wisdom of the ages to everyone's complete satisfaction by declaring, "Satan finds work for idle hands to do."

If I interrupted the conversation with a question, four or five adults competed to be the first to say, "Children are meant to be seen and not heard."

If one of my aunts mentioned the gossip about some woman "over there around Bollington" or "out there towards Hillsboro," she was certain to be silenced by a scowl from Ida Rebecca or Uncle Irvey and a reminder that "little pitchers have big ears."

I was listening to a conversation that had been going on for generations.

Someone had a sick cow.

The corn was "burning up" for lack of rain.

If the sheriff had arrested a local boy for shooting somebody's bull: "That boy never brought a thing but trouble to his mother, poor old soul."

Old Mr. Cooper from out there around Wheatland had got his arm caught in the threshing machine and it had to be taken off, "poor old soul."

Ancient Aunt Zell, who lived "down there around Lucketts," had to be buried on a day "so hot the flowers all wilted before they could get her in the ground, poor old soul."

When the lamps were lit inside, someone was certain to say to the children, "Early to bed and early to rise makes a man healthy, wealthy, and wise."

Uncle Harry usually led the departures, for he lived outside Morrisonville proper and had to walk a half mile to get home. Only a year younger than Uncle Irvey, Harry was Ida Rebecca's quiet son. A dour man in sweat-stained work shirts, baggy trousers held up by yellow galluses, he worked in the fields, did some carpentry, turned up on a building job occasionally. He was gray, solemn, and frosty. A lonely man. His wife had died in childbirth twenty years earlier.

I knew he was slightly scandalous. Lately he had taken an interest in a younger woman who had borne an illegitimate child and been abandoned by her lover. Everybody knew Uncle Harry had "gone to housekeeping" with her and was devoted to her child, but he did not bring either mother or daughter to sit on Ida Rebecca's porch. Morrisonville's social code was rigid about such things.

Another person who did not join our evening assemblies was Annie Grigsby, Ida Rebecca's next-door neighbor. Annie had been born in slavery, and this made her a notable citizen. Her log house was pointed out to travelers as one of the Morrisonville sights not to be ignored. "Annie was born in slavery," the visitor was always advised.

"Born in slavery." That phrase was uttered as though it were an incredible accomplishment on Annie's part. Elsewhere, people boasted of neighbors who had tamed lightning, invented the wind-up Victrola, and gone aloft in flying machines, but we in Morrisonville didn't have to hang our heads. We had Annie. "Born in slavery." My mother told me about Abraham Lincoln, a great man who freed the slaves, and living so close to Annie, who had been freed by Lincoln himself, made me feel in touch with the historic past.

Annie was not much older than Ida Rebecca, who was born in 1861. She was a short, gray-haired, rotund woman of weary carriage and a dignity appropriate to her remarkable birth. Now and then she unbent enough to invite Doris or my cousin Kenneth or me into her dark kitchen for a piece of butter bread, Morrisonville's universal treat. One afternoon I wandered into

45

her backyard to find her hacking the meat out of a huge, freshly killed terrapin.

"What's that, Annie?"

"It's a tarpon."

"What's a tarpon?"

"Tarpon's big turtle, child."

"Why're you cutting it up like that?"

"To make soup. You come back over here when I get it done, and I'll give you some."

White Morrisonville's hog-meat diet hadn't prepared me for terrapin soup. I hurried back across the road giggling to my mother that colored people ate turtles.

"Colored people are just like everybody else," she said.

Despite the respect accorded Annie, no one else in Morrisonville held my mother's radical view. Nor did Annie. Only when there was death or sickness did Annie presume the social freedom of white households. Then she came to help in the sickroom or sit in a rocker on Ida Rebecca's porch comforting a sobbing child in her lap. In time of crisis her presence was expected, for she was a citizen of stature. An historical monument. A symbol of our nation's roots. "Born in slavery."

For occasional treats I was taken on the three-mile trip to Lovettsville and there had my first glimpse of urban splendors. The commercial center was Bernard Spring's general store, a dark cavernous treasure house packed with the riches of the earth. Staring up at the shelves, I marveled at the bulging wealth of brand-new overalls, work shirts, gingham fabrics, shoe boxes, straw hats, belts, galluses, and neckties and intoxicated myself inhaling the smell of plug tobacco, chewing gum, gingersnaps, cheese, leather, and kerosene, all of which Bernard Spring sold across the same polished counter on which he cut bolts of cloth for the women to sew into new dresses.

Nearby stood the Spring family's mansion, the most astonishing architectural monument I had ever seen, a huge white wedding cake of a building filled with stained glass and crowned with turrets and lightning rods. The whole business had been ordered from the Sears, Roebuck catalog and erected according to mail-order instructions. Since Mr. Spring insisted on top-of-the-line in all his dealings, Lovettsville could boast that it contained the finest house in the Sears, Roebuck warehouse.

Just as wonderful to me was a contrivance my Uncle Etch kept behind his Lovettsville house. Uncle Etch, Ida Rebecca's fourth son, was married to the town undertaker's daughter and had inherited custody of a hearse, which he kept in his backyard shed. It was not one of your modern internal-combustion hearses, but a beautiful black antique horse-drawn hearse with glass windows on all four sides and elegant wood carvings jutting out hither and yon. It was a hearse fit for a royal corpse, but I never saw anything in it but a few of Uncle Etch's chickens who enjoyed nesting down inside during the heat of the afternoon.

My cousin Leslie, Uncle Etch's oldest son, much older than I, assisted in the family undertaking business and took part in one of the most appropriate buryings ever held in our part of the country. The customer was Sam Reever, the famous bootlegger.

For several months before their triumph Leslie and his grandfather had been unnaturally depressed. The cause of their sorrow was a unique coffin foisted upon them by their chief supplier of funeral goods. The thing was made entirely of glass. They hadn't ordered it; the supplier had just had it delivered out of the blue one day. His covering letter explained that glass coffins were the wave of the future. To help popularize them, he was sending specimens to a few lucky customers for showroom display. Leslie's grandfather had been selected to be among the few let in on the ground floor of the glass-coffin boom.

The price was staggering, and so was the weight. Leslie and his grandfather tried to move it but couldn't.

"Lord, it's heavy," the old man groaned.

"Must weigh a ton," Leslie grunted.

They had to step outside and corral six other men to help before they could position it tastefully in the showroom. Weeks passed, then months, and though death took its steady toll, there

47

were no customers rich enough to afford glass interment. Leslie's grandfather sank into despair.

"We're never going to be able to sell it," he told Leslie.

Then, hope: news that Sam Reever had died. Everybody knew bootlegging was one of the richest businesses in the county. Leslie and his grandfather collected Sam and carried him to Lovettsville. Close behind came his widow, Liz, determined to put Sam away in dandy style.

"Now here's a really wonderful coffin," Leslie's grandfather said, after showing her the pauper's pine model to rouse her appetite for higher quality. "Look how heavy this glass top is."

He and Leslie demonstrated that two men could scarcely budge it.

"And look all around the edge of the lid here," Leslie said. "That's a rubber gasket, just like you use to seal the cap on a Mason jar."

"When you seal it up with that gasket in there," said his grandfather, "it's completely airtight. With a coffin like this, Sam'll look as good a hundred years from now as he does the day you bury him."

The widow would have nothing else. Maybe it was the gasket sealing the glass that sold her on it. Maybe she saw the esthetic beauty of burying Sam in the symbol of his profession. Like most country bootleggers, Sam bottled his moonshine in canning jars. When they took him to the graveyard the mourners approved of the fitting way in which Liz, as a grace note to his life, had him buried in the fanciest Mason jar ever sold in Loudoun County.

Beyond Lovettsville, on the outer edge of my universe, lay Brunswick. I first walked in that vision of paradise hand-in-hand with my father, and those visits opened my eyes to the vastness and wonders of life's possibilities. Two miles north of Lovettsville, across the Potomac on the Maryland shore, Brunswick was as distant and romantic a place as I ever expected to see. To live there in that great smoking conurbation, rumbling with the constant thunder of locomotives, filled with the moaning of train whistles

48

Russell and Doris with Aunt Pat, Morrisonville, 1929.

coming down the Potomac Valley, was beyond my most fevered hopes.

Brunswick was a huge railway center on the B&O Main Line, which linked the Atlantic coast to Chicago and midwestern steel centers. Approaching it was almost unbearably thrilling. You crossed an endless, rickety cantilever bridge after pausing on the Virginia bank to pay a one-dollar toll. This was a powerful sum of money, but Brunswick was not for the pinchpennies of the earth. As you neared the far end of the bridge, its loose board floor rattling under the car wheels, the spectacle unfolding before you made the dollar seem well spent.

In the foreground lay a marvelous confusion of steel rails, and in the midst of them, on a vast cinder-covered plain, the great brick roundhouse with its doors agape, revealing the snouts of locomotives undergoing surgery within. Smaller yard locomotives chugged backward and forward, clacking boxcar couplings together and sending up infernos of black gritty smoke which settled over the valley in layers.

If the crossing gate was down, you might be treated to the incredible spectacle of a passenger express highballing toward glory, the engineer waving down at you from the cab window, sparks flying, cinders scattering, the glistening pistons pumping with terrifying power. And behind this hellish monstrosity throbbing with fire and steam, a glimpse of the passengers' faces stately and remote as kings as they roared by in a gale of wind powerful enough to knock you almost off your feet.

Between the mountains that cradled the yard there seemed to be thousands of freight cars stretching back so far toward Harpers Ferry that you could never see the end of them. And flanking the tracks on the far side, a metropolis: Brunswick had electric light bulbs, telephones, radios. Rich people lived there. Masons, for heaven's sake. Not just Red Men and Odd Fellows and Moose such as we had around Morrisonville, but Masons. And not just Masons, but Baptists, too—genuine dress-to-the-teeth-and-give-yourself-fancy-airs Baptists.

Three of my uncles lived there: Uncle Tom, Uncle Harvey,

50

and Uncle Lewis. They were expected to come back to Morrison-ville and sit on Ida Rebecca's porch too, but only on Sundays. As citizens of Brunswick, they had crossed over into a world of Byzantine splendor.

Brunswick had a department store and a movie house. There was a street stretching for two or three blocks lined with stores, including a drugstore where you could sit down at a round marble-top table and have somebody bring you an ice-cream soda. There were whole blocks of houses jammed one right up against another, the blocks laid out in a grid pattern on hills steep enough to tire a mountain goat.

Uncle Harvey lived with his wife and daughter at the crest of one such hill. He was one of God's favored people, a locomotive engineer. I was in terror that he might try to engage me in conversation. When he heard a train whistle echoing off the valley below, I goggled in admiration as he produced his big railroad watch, studied it coolly, and announced, "The three-fifty-four's running five minutes late today."

My Uncle Tom worked as a blacksmith in the B&O yards near Harpers Ferry. That was a good job too. Though he walked the four-mile round trip to and from the shop daily in sooty rail-roader's clothes, Uncle Tom was well off. His house contained a marvel I had never seen before: an indoor bathroom. This was enough to mark Uncle Tom a rich man, but in addition he had a car. And such a car. It was an Essex, with windows that rolled up and down with interior hand cranks, not like my father's Model T with the isinglass windows in side curtains that had to be buttoned onto the frame in bad weather. Uncle Tom's Essex even had cut-glass flower vases in sconces in the backseat. He was a man of substance. When he rolled up in his Essex for Ida Rebecca's command appearances on Sunday afternoons in Morrisonville, wearing a white shirt and black suit, smoking his pipe, his pretty red-haired wife Goldie on the seat beside him, I felt pride in kinship to so much grandeur.

Lewis, Ida Rebecca's youngest son, also thrived in Brunswick, at the barbering trade. Though scarcely twenty-five years old, he had his own shop and called by appointment on the Brunswick ladies to cut their hair at home in the new boyish bobs and sometimes, according to people envious of Uncle Lewis's reputation for gallantry, to render more knightly service. Uncle Lewis was my first vision of what male elegance could be. He had glistening black hair always parted so meticulously that you might have thought he needed surveyor's instruments to comb a line so straight. Thin black sideburns extended down to his earlobes in the style cartoonists adopted as the distinguishing mark of high-toned cads. With a high gloss on his city shoes, in his crisp white barber's smock, he wisecracked with the railroad men as he presided in front of a long wall of mirrors lined with pomades, tonics, and scents. I admired him as the ultimate in dandyism.

On those magic occasions when my father took me to Brunswick, the supreme delight was to have Uncle Lewis seat me on a board placed across the arms of his barber chair, crank me into the sky, and subject me to the pampered luxury of being clippered, snipped, and doused with heavy applications of Lucky Tiger or Jeris hair tonic, which left my hair plastered gorgeously to the sides of my head and sent me into the street reeking of aromatic delight.

After one such clipping I climbed a hill in Brunswick with my father to call at Uncle Tom's house. Though Uncle Tom was fourteen years older, my father loved and respected him above all his brothers. Maybe it was because he saw in Tom the blacksmith some shadow of the blacksmith father who died when my father was only ten. Maybe it was because Tom, living in such splendor with his indoor bathroom and his Essex, had escaped Morrisonville and prospered. Maybe it was for Tom's sweetness of character, which was unusual among Ida Rebecca's boys.

Uncle Tom was at work that day, but Aunt Goldie gave us a warm welcome. She was a delicate woman, not much bigger than my mother, with hair of ginger red, blue eyes, and a way of looking at you and turning her head suddenly this way and that which reminded me of an alert bird. She was also a notoriously fussy housekeeper, constantly battling railroad grime to preserve her house's reputation for not containing "a speck of dust anywhere in it." Before admitting us to her spotless kitchen, she had my father and me wipe our shoes on the doormat, then made a fuss about how sweet I smelled and how handsome I looked, then cut me a huge slab of pie.

My great joy in calling on Aunt Goldie was the opportunity afforded to visit the indoor bathroom, so naturally after polishing off the pie I pretended an urgent need to use the toilet. This was on the second floor and required a journey through the famously dust-free dining room and parlor, but Aunt Goldie understood. "Take your shoes off first so you don't track up the floor," she said. Which I did. "And don't touch anything in the parlor."

With this caution she admitted me to the sanctum of spotlessness. I trod across immaculate rugs and past dining room furniture, armchairs, side tables, a settee, like a soldier walking in a mine field. There would be no dust left behind if I could help it.

At the top of the stairs lay the miracle of plumbing. Shutting the door to be absolutely alone with it, I ran my fingers along the smooth enamel of the bathtub and glistening faucet handles of the sink. The white majesty of the toilet bowl, through which gallons of water could be sent rushing by the slightest touch of a silvery lever, filled me with envy. A roll of delicate paper was placed beside it. Here was luxury almost too rich to be borne by anyone whose idea of fancy toiletry was Uncle Irvey's two-hole privy and a Montgomery Ward catalog.

After gazing upon it as long as I dared without risking interruption by a search party, I pushed the lever and savored the supreme moment when thundering waters emptied into the bowl and vanished with a mighty gurgle. It was the perfect conclusion to a trip to Brunswick.

CHAPTER FIVE

WHEN my father came home from work that evening he ate hurriedly, bathed in the tin basin, and changed into his blue serge suit, white shirt, necktie, and low shoes. It was a Wednesday in November. We were all going on a trip.

Doris, Audrey, my mother, and I were already dressed in our best clothes and the suitcase was packed when my father arrived. It was the first time the family had ever made a trip together. I had been itching to get away all afternoon, annoying my mother with the same question repeated a hundred times—"Is it almost time to go? Is it almost time to go?"—and she had gone about the preparations singing happily to herself.

When the supper dishes were cleared it was dark and chilly. My father buttoned up the isinglass windows of the Model T and hoisted Doris and me onto the high backseat. My mother climbed into the front with Audrey in her arms, my father spun the crank, the motor caught, he jumped in behind the wheel, and we rolled merrily out of Morrisonville.

We were headed for Taylorstown, five miles away, to spend the night with Uncle Miller. It was the hog-butchering season, a time of communal festivals which ended the long harvest season. Uncle Miller, Ida Rebecca's fifth son, had invited my father to bring us all for the festivities at his house. These would start with the predawn slaughter of Miller's hogs and turn into a sixteen-hour bout of boiling, scraping, grinding, chopping, slicing, stuffing, feasting, gossip, and high-spirited jocularity.

For my mother there were risks in a visit with Miller, for he was fond of drink. A tall cadaverous man with a nose like a hatchet blade, he was, of all Ida Rebecca's boys, the closest to being a blithe spirit. His passions were antique furniture and shrewd bargaining. When his eyes sparkled with the stimulus of a few drinks, his furniture standards fell and he began bargaining for anything for the sheer love of bargaining. In this mood he even tried to draw my father into barter deals for our mail-order furniture. "I'll tell you what I'm going to do, Ben. I'm going to make you a proposition. . . ." Uncle Miller was constantly making propositions, and to develop a mood more congenial to bargaining he passed the whiskey freely.

Since we would all be together at Uncle Miller's house, though, the risks were not high. Aunt Edmonia would be there to keep things in hand. Aunt Edmonia, Miller's wife, fit my mother's idea of a good woman. She exercised woman's power for decency. Uncle Miller minded his ways when Aunt Edmonia was in the house.

The car trip through the cold and darkness felt like an immense journey to me. I had exhausted myself with the excitement of anticipating it and drowsed off in fatigue, and then woke, and it seemed we had been driving for hours, and then dozed again, and then woke, and dozed again. . . .

For my mother, a trip outside Ida Rebecca's territory was worth a little risk. I had just turned five, and my mother was more and more unhappy about Ida Rebecca's growing influence on me. The latest tension involved ghosts.

My grandmother believed firmly in the existence of ghosts and the importance of heeding omens. I was with her one day when a bird flew into her house. When we had shooed it out she told me, "Somebody's going to die."

I didn't understand.

"A bird coming into the house is an omen," she said. "It means somebody in that house is going to die."

Since I was in that house when the bird came in, I went to my mother in alarm and told her the awful news.

"Don't pay any attention to stuff like that. It's just ignorant superstition."

Ida Rebecca had evidence, though. She had told me of a woman not far from Morrisonville who died after a bird got into her house. I told this too to my mother.

"Naturally she died," my mother said. "People die every day. Birds don't have anything to do with it. If there hadn't been a bird for miles around she'd have died just the same."

I wasn't too reassured.

"Listen here, Buddy, when the Lord's ready to take you away from here you're going to go, and not before, and the Lord's not going to send a bird to tell you to get ready. Don't believe things like that. It's heathenish."

The night a ghost appeared in my grandmother's parlor door made my mother even angrier. It was in the dark of the evening with kerosene lamps casting gigantic shadows on the stone walls of my grandmother's sitting room, and I was there with her and three of my uncles when she started up to her bedroom. The trip took her into a narrow adjoining room and past the closed parlor door, through which I'd seen my first Christmas tree.

I heard her cry out, then she was back among us in a frightful state.

"Raymond's in there," she said.

Raymond, one of her twins, had died in 1917, eight years before I was born, at the age of twenty-three.

"He's standing there in the doorway right at the foot of the stairs."

As oldest son, Uncle Irvey sought to reassure her.

"He's there. Standing in the doorway," she insisted.

56

Uncle Irvey.

While I huddled on a chair in a fever of terror, Uncle Irvey took a lamp and led his brothers into the next room to search for dead Raymond. There was silence. Soon I heard doors being opened and closed, then heavy shoes stamping overhead.

Returning, Uncle Irvey said, "We've been over the whole house, Mother, and there's nothing here."

"I saw him just as plain as I see you now," she said.

Naturally I reported Raymond's appearance to my mother the instant I crossed the road. Normally my mother did not speak disrespectfully to me of Ida Rebecca, but this time impatience overcame restraint.

"That old woman's going soft in the head."

"But she saw him, Mama, just as plain as I see you."

"There's no such thing as ghosts. People just make them up and think they see them."

I still wasn't persuaded. I had been there and seen the ghost's dreadful effect on my grandmother.

"Listen here, Buddy, the dead don't come back. You never have to worry about the dead hurting you. It's the living you've got to worry about in this world."

Supper was almost ready when we arrived that night at Uncle Miller's. In the few minutes before we sat down Uncle Miller asked my father to come out to the pigpen for a look at the porkers to be slaughtered in the morning. I heard them outside talking and laughing and knew they were having a drink in the darkness. In Morrisonville you learned the symptoms young. There was a certain change in the level of the voice, a laughter slightly more enthusiastic than laughter usually sounded. But they were only outside a few minutes, not long enough to overdo it, and when they returned and we all sat at the table, they looked fine.

We started with fried oysters. Presently my father put his fork down, rose from the table, and went into the yard; we all sat there not saying a word, listening to him outside vomiting. Uncle Miller

58

and my mother went outside then, and after a while my mother returned and took Doris and me off to the bedroom where Audrey was already asleep.

The house was unnaturally quiet next morning. The butchering festival I'd expected was not in progress, and my father was not in the bedroom with us. My mother said he was in Uncle Miller's bedroom because a doctor was coming to see him.

I wandered around the backyard until the sun burned off the frost. After a while my mother came out.

"The doctor's here," she said. "He's going to take Daddy to the hospital in Frederick so he can get better. Come and kiss him good-bye."

To my surprise my father was fully dressed and seated in the doctor's small roadster at the front of the house. He was wearing his blue serge suit, white shirt, and necktie, and looked all right to me. I walked across the lawn to the car, and he leaned out the window on the passenger's side and smiled, but he didn't have much to say to me. Just, "Daddy'll be home in a day or two. Be a good boy till I get back."

My mother held me up, and he gave me a kiss.

"We'd better get going," the doctor said.

My mother set me down and leaned into the car and kissed him. She and I watched the roadster together until it passed over the brow of the hill headed for the Maryland side of the Potomac.

By afternoon we were back in Morrisonville. Next day before sunup she rose to visit the hospital. Uncle Irvey would drive her.

"Is Daddy coming home today?"

"Maybe we'll bring him back with us," she said.

It was a gentle Indian summer morning, and my grandmother told me to go out and play while she minded Doris and Audrey. I set off on one of my daily wandering expeditions, taking the road down toward the creek.

I was down there by myself. You could always find something entertaining to do around Morrisonville. Climb a fence. Take a stick and scratch pictures in the dirt. There were always cows

59

around, or a horse. Throw pebbles at a locust tree. I was busy at this sort of thing when I saw my cousins, Kenneth and Ruth Lee, coming down the road.

Besides Doris, Audrey, and me, they were the only other children living in Morrisonville. Kenneth, two years older than I, was our leader. He was coming down the road with Ruth Lee following as usual. I was happy to see them. We usually played in the fields and around the barns and straw ricks together. Sometimes we ripped open a burlap grain sack to build a tepee in the apple orchard, or picked through the junk pile behind Liz Virts's house to collect enough tin cans and broken dishes to play store. I was glad now to have company.

When Kenneth walked right up to me, though, he stared at me with such a stare as I'd never seen.

"Your father's dead," he said.

It was like an accusation that my father had done something criminal, and I came to my father's defense.

"He is not," I said.

But of course they didn't know the situation. I started to explain. He was sick. In the hospital. My mother was bringing him home right now. . . .

"He's dead," Kenneth said.

His assurance slid an icicle into my heart.

"He is not either!" I shouted.

"He is too," Ruth Lee said. "They want you to come home right away."

I started running up the road screaming, "He is not!"

It was a weak argument. They had the evidence and gave it to me as I hurried home crying, "He is not. . . . He is not. . . . He is not. . . ."

I was almost certain before I got there that he was.

And I was right. Arriving at the hospital that morning, my mother was told he had died at four A.M. in "acute diabetic coma." He was thirty-three years old.

When I came running home, my mother was still not back from Frederick, but the women had descended on our house, as women there did in such times, and were already busy with the housecleaning and cooking that were Morrisonville's ritual response to death. With a thousand tasks to do, they had no time to handle a howling five-year-old. I was sent to the opposite end of town, to Bessie Scott's house.

Poor Bessie Scott. All afternoon she listened patiently as a saint while I sat in her kitchen and cried myself out. For the first time I thought seriously about God. Between sobs I told Bessie that if God could do things like this to people, then God was hateful and I had no more use for Him.

Bessie told me about the peace of Heaven and the joy of being among the angels and the happiness of my father who was already there. This argument failed to quiet my rage.

"God loves us all just like His own children," Bessie said.

"If God loves me, why did He make my father die?"

Bessie said I would understand someday, but she was only partly right. That afternoon, though I couldn't have phrased it this way then, I decided that God was a lot less interested in people than anybody in Morrisonville was willing to admit. That day I decided that God was not entirely to be trusted.

After that I never cried again with any real conviction, nor expected much of anyone's God except indifference, nor loved deeply without fear that it would cost me dearly in pain. At the age of five I had become a skeptic and began to sense that any happiness that came my way might be the prelude to some grim cosmic joke.

While I came to grips with death in Bessie's kitchen, its rites were being performed by other Morrisonville women in my father's house. Our floors were being scrubbed, windows washed, furniture dusted, beds made. Visitors would be arriving by the dozen. It was a violation of the code to show them anything but a spotless house.

Prodigies of cooking were already under way in surrounding houses. Precious hams were being removed from smokehouses, eggs and butter were being beaten in cake bowls, pie crusts were being rolled, canning jars of pickles and preserved fruits were being lifted from pantry shelves. Death was also a time for feasting.

It was growing dark when, pretty well cried out and beginning to respond to the holiday excitement in the air, I left Bessie Scott's and walked back down the road to home. The place sparkled with cleanliness, and the women sat clustered in the kitchen, exhausted, I suppose. The men had just begun to arrive, looking uncomfortable in their good dark suits, their shirts and neckties and low shoes. I went outside and stood around with the men in the road. So late in November, the dusk came early. The men seemed unusually quiet. I did not know many of them. They stood in little groups talking quietly, almost in whispers, probably not saying anything very interesting, just feeling self-conscious in their Sunday suits with nothing to do but stand. The men standing and waiting and talking quietly with nothing to do in their good dark suits was part of the ritual too. It was important to have a powerful turnout of humanity. That showed the dead man had been well liked in the community, and it was therefore considered an important source of comfort to the widow.

It was fully dark when someone told me to move around and wait in the backyard, which I did. After a while Annie Grigsby came out and hugged me and said it was all right to come into the kitchen. "They've brought your daddy home," she said.

My mother was in the kitchen, but most of the other women had left now. It was the first time I had seen her since she left for the hospital that morning. She was sitting on a chair looking very tired. Annie took a chair beside her. It was terribly quiet. I wondered where my father was. Annie finally broke the silence.

"Maybe he'd like to see his father."

"Do you want to see your father?" my mother asked.

"I guess so," I said.

The undertaker had come and gone while I was in the backyard, and now that most of the bustle was over and most of the people had gone home for supper, the house felt empty and still. My mother did not seem up to showing me the undertaker's handiwork.

"I'll take him in," Annie said, rising in her weary fashion, taking my hand.

She led me into the adjoining living room. The blinds were drawn. A couple of kerosene lamps were burning. Annie lifted me in her arms so I could look down. For some reason there was an American flag.

"There's your daddy, child," Annie said. "Doesn't he look nice?"

He was wearing his blue serge suit and a white shirt and necktie.

"Yes. He looks nice," I told Annie, knowing that was what I was supposed to say. But it wasn't the niceness of the way he was dressed and the way his hair was so carefully combed that impressed me. It was his stillness. I gazed at the motionless hand laid across his chest, thinking no one can lie so still for so long without moving a finger. I waited for the closed eyelids to flutter, for his chest to move in a slight sigh to capture a fresh breath of air. Nothing. His motionlessness was majestic and terrifying. I wanted to be away from that room and never see him like that again.

"Do you want to kiss your daddy?" Annie asked.

"Not now," I said.

Then I went back to the warmth of the kitchen with Annie, born in slavery, and sat there until bedtime with my mother and Doris while the neighbors came back and stood whispering in the living room.

Everything happened quickly after that.

First the funeral and the New Jerusalem Lutheran Church outside Lovettsville packed with mourners, the congregation snuffling as the preacher led us in singing "In the sweet bye and bye, we shall meet in that sweet bye and bye." My mother had vetoed "We are going down the valley one by one."

Then her decision to leave Morrisonville. That was reached on Sunday evening immediately after the funeral. For the first time in her life she needed charity. It was extended by one of her younger brothers, Allen, who had settled in the North, in New

Jersey. He offered to take us in. She accepted without hesitation. Her alternative, remaining in Morrisonville dependent on the kindness of Ida Rebecca and her sons, she never considered.

Her decision to give up Audrey took a little longer. That was how she always thought of it afterwards: as "giving up" Audrey. It was the only deed of her entire life for which I ever heard her express guilt. Years later in her old age, she was still saying, "Maybe I made a terrible mistake when I gave up Audrey."

The giving up of Audrey was done in a time of shock and depression for her. When the undertaker was paid she was left with a few dollars of insurance money, a worthless Model T, several chairs, a table to eat from, a couple of mail-order beds, a crib, three small children, no way to earn a living, and no prospects for the future. The grimness of her situation touched Ida Rebecca's sense of family duty, and she sent Uncle Irvey to intercede and try to arrange for our security. By then my mother had announced her intention to move away and live with her brother, which was fine with Ida Rebecca, who must have been tempted to say "Good riddance." Ida Rebecca's grandchildren were another matter. Uncle Irvey sat in our kitchen and talked about children's need for a home and about possibilities of placing the three of us here or there among members of the family who could give us one.

My mother rejected the idea immediately. She intended us now to grow up among her people. No matter how dark things looked, she would not break up her family.

Uncle Irvey focused the talk on Audrey, a dimpled blond infant ten months old with a perpetual smile. My Uncle Tom and Aunt Goldie, childless after a long marriage, wanted a baby desperately, and loved Audrey, and would happily give her a comfortable home and a good life, which was more than my mother could promise her.

My mother had to concede the point.

Tom and Goldie came to argue their own case. They were persuasive. Like my father, my mother admired Uncle Tom above all Ida Rebecca's other sons. He was the only one the least bit like Papa, with his Essex automobile, his sparkling white Sunday

64

shirts, his good cigars, his fine house spotlessly clean. He didn't drink, either. "Your Uncle Tom is a good man," was my mother's judgment.

She admired Aunt Goldie with reservations, possibly because Goldie had succeeded at a task that had defeated my mother. In his youth Tom had been a heavy drinker. After the marriage, Aunt Goldie turned him into a model of sobriety. This was admirable proof of Aunt Goldie's womanly strengths, but it also mocked my mother's failure to reform my father. Sensitive to the comparison, my mother preferred to look for shortcomings in Aunt Goldie. She laughed about Aunt Goldie's passion for spotlessness and sometimes criticized her for playing the duchess among her poor relations in Morrisonville. "Goldie gives herself airs," she said.

On balance, though, Aunt Goldie had to be recognized as a woman with iron in her, and my mother respected her for that. When she and Uncle Tom arrived in Morrisonville to plead for Audrey, my mother saw the handsome car and the expensive clothes. Could she deny her child a life that offered every comfort with decent, loving "parents"?

A lonely winter was coming, and she looked toward the future from a deepening melancholy. There were too many big decisions to be made. Moving numbly through the ruins of her life, she found it harder and harder to sort out anymore what was worth saving and how best to save it. Goldie helped her reach the decision, saying: "Benny sat in my kitchen just last summer and told us if anything ever happened to him he wanted Tom and me to take care of Audrey." If God granted them the chance to raise Audrey, she promised, Audrey would always know who her real mother was, and that I was her brother and Doris her sister, and all of us would always be welcome as such in Uncle Tom's house.

A few days later Uncle Tom and Aunt Goldie arrived in Morrisonville again. My mother helped them carry out the crib and the boxes packed with baby clothes. When the car was loaded, my mother bundled Audrey into blankets, carried her outside, handed her to Aunt Goldie, and kissed her good-bye.

When their car was out of sight I went back into the house.

My mother was sitting in the straight-backed oak rocker, the fanciest piece of furniture we owned, staring at the stove.

"When's Audrey coming back, Mama?"

She didn't answer. Just sat staring at the stove and rocking for the longest while. I went back out into the road, but she came out right behind me and touched my shoulder.

"Do you want me to fix you a piece of jelly bread?" she asked.

Chapter Six

M Y mother brought us to Newark in January 1931. The stock market had collapsed fifteen months earlier, but though business was bad, Washington people who understood these things did not seem alarmed. President Hoover refused to use the scare word "recession" when speaking about the slump. It was merely "a depression," he said. Nothing to panic about. Good times were just around the corner.

My mother intended to live with her brother Allen a few months until she could find work and rent a place of her own. Allen was twenty-eight, five years younger than she, and blessed with the optimism of youth. He was shocked when she arrived in Newark without Audrey and scolded her gently for breaking up her family.

"Three can starve as cheap as two," he told her.

Uncle Allen had no intention of starving. He had left school in tenth grade after "Papa" died and had worked since he was fourteen years old, moving from job to job and always improving his income, and he was now confident he could cope with whatever lay ahead.

The daily news stories of deepening hard times did not unnerve him. For Uncle Allen the truly hard times seemed all behind him. He had been a day laborer in a Virginia sawmill crew, fished in New England waters aboard a commercial trawler, jerked sodas in a cigar store, and sold groceries over the counter in Washington. In his early twenties he had moved up to a suit-and-necktie job as a salesman in New York.

He was short—scarcely five feet six inches tall—and spoke in a quiet southern drawl. After the men of Morrisonville, who were cut to the long-shanked mountaineer pattern and sat down to supper in overalls, he seemed to me the complete city slicker with his dapper manners and his white shirts with sleeve garters and detachable collars starched stiff as iron. I studied him in fascination as he polished his shoes each night after supper and inspected his suits for wrinkles and stains. He owned two suits, which was a sign of great wealth in my eyes, and pressed them on an ironing board in the basement every Sunday, with a gallon jug of benzine and a white cloth at hand to remove spots encountered along the way.

Like my mother, Uncle Allen believed that with hard work, good character, and an honest nature a man could make something of himself in spite of bad times, and he worked at the salesman's trade with total dedication. He had sold wholesale groceries in Brooklyn and cheap tobacco in Yonkers and Staten Island. An oleomargarine distributor gave him a chance to improve himself with a $25-a-week route in north Jersey and he moved to Newark, but after giving haven to my mother, Doris, and me, he went looking for something that would pay him even more.

The daily firings produced by the withering economy offered loopholes of opportunity for a young man who kept his eyes open. One night just before we arrived from Virginia, Uncle Allen called at the Newark plant of the Kruger Beverage Company to ask if they needed a salesman.

"I don't need anybody right now, but there may be an opening in the morning," the sales-crew chief told him. This was Depression code talk. Uncle Allen had heard it before. Translated, it

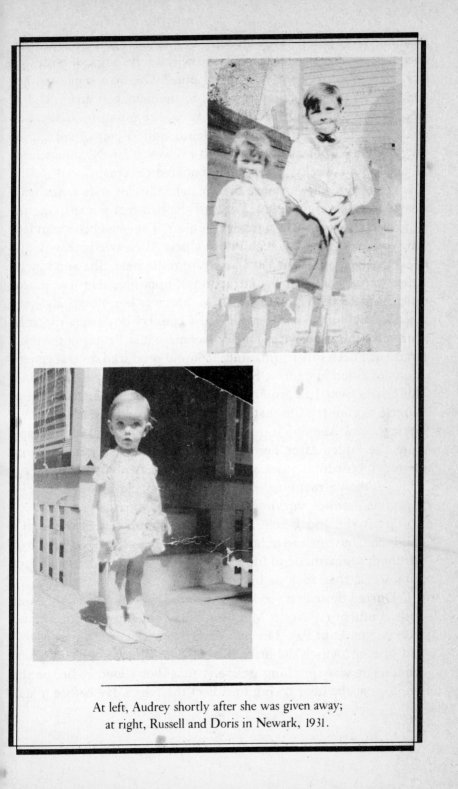

At left, Audrey shortly after she was given away;
at right, Russell and Doris in Newark, 1931.

meant: "We're going to fire a couple of men later tonight and will need a new salesman tomorrow who will do the work of both for less salary than we're paying either one." The man suggested he come back in the morning to speak to the manager, and added a piece of advice: "And be dressed like you're going to your own wedding." That evening Uncle Allen bought a pair of spats and put $5 down on a black overcoat with a velvet collar. Next morning he had a $30-a-week job selling carbonated beverages.

His optimism was more than matched by his wife's. She was a sassy, rambunctious New York girl he had met while living in Brooklyn. Aunt Pat was now twenty-four. They had been married four years and were as yet childless. Uncle Allen awed me with his cool elegance, but Aunt Pat I loved from the start. She and Uncle Allen were a study in the attraction of opposites. He was short, quiet, neat to the point of fussiness. She was big, noisy, and relished messy human combat. He was a country boy from Virginia with a southern drawl and a dry laconic wit, a Protestant whose family had been in Virginia since 1666 and produced several generations of colonial gentry. She was a New Yorker, half Irish and half Cuban, who had grown up in a Catholic orphanage and knew so little of country life that she proposed cutting the milk bill by buying a cow, keeping it in the backyard, and feeding it on scraps from the table. After her orphanage childhood she roomed in Brooklyn boardinghouses, working at a variety of jobs: waiting on tables in Wall Street lunchrooms, running an elevator at Gimbel's department store, working telephone switchboards.

What she and Uncle Allen had in common was the waif's childhood, but, instead of hardening them against the world, it had left them sympathetic to life's other losers. And so, cheerfully, on $30 a week, they took us in.

During those first weeks in Newark I was enchanted by Aunt Pat's ebullient city style. Morrisonville women were reticent and weary. Not Aunt Pat. The house rang to her cry of "Jesus, Mary, and Joseph!" which she uttered whenever something startled her, whether it was splashing grease, a neighbor's loud radio, or the landlord at the door trying to collect the rent a day before it was due She was a full-time combatant in the battle of life and flung herself into it with zest, and when she encountered an enemy or a challenger she gave him "a piece of her mind."

"They'd better not tangle with your Aunt Pat," my mother would say, "because she'll give them a piece of her mind."

Childless, she doted on children and rarely left the house without dragging Doris or me behind her to introduce us to the marvels of urban living. She hauled me with her to the corner delicatessen one day to buy three slices of bologna, and when the counterman gave her the wrong change she gave him a tongue lashing that had him whining apologies before she relented. Storming back to the house, flushed with satisfaction, she shouted back at me—I always seemed to be five feet behind and running to catch up with her—"You've got to give these cheap chiselers a good piece of your mind."

It was Aunt Pat who first stirred my love of newspapers. A hopeless news junkie, she was powerless to resist when a newsboy came up the street yelling, "Extra! Extra! Read all about it!" Rushing onto the sidewalk, surrendering two pennies for the paper, she stood there staring in wonder at the wet black headlines.

"Jesus, Mary, and Joseph!" she cried if the news was sensational enough, and when I asked what was wrong she patiently explained the news and why it was grave.

"Jesus, Mary, and Joseph!"

"What's it say, Aunt Pat?"

"Somebody sent Dutch Schultz a red rose."

Dutch Schultz was Newark's most notorious gangster. But a red rose?

"It means they're going to bump him off," she explained. "When a gangster is going to bump off another gangster he sends him a red rose to warn him." For days afterwards I waited for an "Extra" about the bumping off of Dutch Schultz, but it did not come in my time.

Days when there were no news sensations the newsboys lived by their wits. Rushing out with her two cents one day at the cry of "Extra! Extra! Read all about it!" Aunt Pat unfolded the paper

71

and studied the front page in puzzlement. There was no wet black headline, only the routine daily humdrum.

She shouted at the newsboy speeding off up the street.

"Hey, what's the big news?"

"Barney Google just shot Sparkplug," the boy yelled back.

Barney Google was a comic strip character and Sparkplug was his racehorse, a stolid square-cut hay burner to whom Barney was devoted. Aunt Pat eagerly opened the paper to the comic strips, then showed it to me. Sparkplug was as sound as ever, and Barney was chatting peaceably with him.

"Barney Google didn't shoot Sparkplug," I said.

"No, dear," she said. "Your Aunt Pat's been played for a sucker." She laughed and laughed at that, and when Uncle Allen came home she told him the story and Uncle Allen laughed too.

Except for Aunt Pat, my transition to city life was a series of agonies. The apartment to which she and Uncle Allen welcomed us was in a declining row house on Wakeman Avenue. There was a kitchen in the basement, where we ate, and on the first floor a parlor and two bedrooms. Everything was slathered over in a depressing dark green paint. A brass chandelier hung from the parlor ceiling, and a naked light bulb illuminated two overstuffed chairs, a lumpy brown sofa, and a glistening black table on which sat an Atwater Kent radio. We had the use of a narrow backyard, enclosed by board fences, in which soil as hard as rock produced nothing but a sickly crop of weeds.

On my first day in Newark when I went out front to play and stepped off the curb, a car came within inches of killing me. The driver cursed me violently, leaped from his car, and carried me howling to the door. The screech of brakes had brought Aunt Pat on the run, and when the driver made the mistake of screaming at her, too, Aunt Pat gave him a piece of her mind and sent him packing, but days passed before I dared step out front again.

The sidewalk swarmed with streetwise children. One, a girl of ten or so, lured me into her house one afternoon by promising me a piece of cake. She towered over me and seemed authoritative and maternal, so I did not object when she said before I could have

72

any cake she would have to take off my pants. Being only five years old, I still wore short pants, and since authoritative maternal women had been removing my pants all my life, I let her have her way. I was uneasy though when, having dropped the pants to my ankles, she stepped back and asked if I wanted her to remove hers, too.

I had the timid five-year-old's desire to be agreeable and must have said yes, for she was out of her underwear in a twinkling and standing before me with her petticoat raised to her shoulders. The passion that wakened in me was anger, for I knew then that she had duped me. I knew then that her promise of cake was false, that there was no cake. She had promised it only to trick me into playing this silly girl's game. Angrily I buckled my trousers and hurried home to report the fraud to Aunt Pat. Aunt Pat smiled as I started to relate how I had been cheated, but the smile faded as I elaborated details.

"Jesus, Mary, and Joseph!" she roared.

After that I was forbidden the sidewalk without supervision and sentenced to confinement in the backyard with Doris. I hated that backyard. I hated the ugly board fence, I hated the sickly weeds, I hated the stone and brick walls and dirty windows that glowered down at me when I searched for the sky, and I hated the laundry that dangled from the overhead clotheslines as far as I could see.

I especially hated the cod liver oil, a nauseating goo tasting of raw liquefied fish, which was spooned twice a day down my gullet and Doris's. It was good for us, it would ward off dreadful diseases, or so Aunt Pat had persuaded my mother. There were plenty of diseases. Scarlet fever, mumps, chicken pox, and whooping cough floated in the air. Polio was around too, killing and crippling. Every neighborhood had a child with a twisted stick of a leg encased in metal braces. Cod liver oil was the defense.

"It's good for you," Aunt Pat declared sweetly twice each day, advancing into the backyard with her potion of bottled fish oil in one hand and tablespoon in the other.

"I hate it. It makes me throw up."

73

"Be a good boy now. You don't want to get infantile paralysis, do you? It's good for you."

It had the viscosity of axle grease. It did no good to gulp it down quickly, because it coated the lining of mouth and esophagus like a thick layer of glue. It did no good to vomit it up either. Aunt Pat did not become angry when this happened. She did not give me a piece of her mind, but simply poured another tablespoon full and smiled sweetly. "Come on now, it's good for you."

The cod liver oil failed, and there was more misery. Both Doris and I came down with whooping cough. The Newark health authorities nailed a quarantine notice on the front door to warn the neighborhood against us. The whooping cough passed, but humiliation lingered on. The authorities forbade us to go outside without wearing broad yellow arm bands marking us as disease carriers.

I hated the yellow arm band that made me a figure of shame. Very soon I hated the entire Newark health department. This bureaucracy, for reasons still obscure, had decided that my posture was a disgrace and had to be corrected. Accompanied by my mother, I was hauled before bureaucrats and stripped naked, pummeled, poked, and photographed by white-clad posture experts. There were worried scowls from doctors, nurses, and photographers studying the photographs.

"Something has to be done about this posture," the doctor said.

If not corrected immediately, well . . . Various consequences were mentioned. The most dreadful was "curvature of the spine." A corrective gymnastic program was proposed: somersaults, headstands, backflips, vigorous exercise on the chinning bar, flying rings, parallel bars. These would straighten me up.

I resisted, for I already knew I could not do a somersault, much less a headstand or cartwheel, and I sensed that I would never be anything but a ludicrous spectacle at gymnastics.

"Young man, do you want to grow up and get curvature of the spine?" The doctor opened a drawer and produced a book. There was a photograph of an adult case of advanced curvature of the spine. Was that what I wanted to look like when I grew up?

It was not for me to answer. My mother had seen enough. I began reporting to a gymnasium to be saved from curvature of the spine. I hated that gymnasium. My God-given physical graceless-ness immediately made me an object of derision among the other boys, most of whom had the agility of chimpanzees and found it hilarious that my efforts should always end in a clatter of crashing bones.

After months of this torment, parents were invited to a gymnastic exhibition. My mother brought Aunt Pat. When it was over and we were walking home Aunt Pat congratulated me on a wonderful performance. Not my mother. Lying was not in her.

"I think it'd be better if you learned to play baseball, Buddy," she said. A few days later she went to Woolworth's and bought a bat, a ball, and two gloves for Doris and me to use in the backyard. She never took me to the gymnasium again.

While I was experiencing the routine miseries of childhood, my mother was discovering the Depression. She quickly learned that her hope of finding a job and renting a place of her own was foolish. There were no jobs to be found.

She hoped to resume teaching. The school administrators told her Virginia credentials were no good in New Jersey and no jobs were likely to be available even if she qualified. The story was the same everywhere. No jobs. No jobs for saleswomen in the department stores. Department stores were firing, not hiring. No jobs in the factories. Factories that weren't laying off workers en masse were shutting down entirely. All that year she walked the streets, combed the classified ads, sat in offices waiting to talk to possible employers, and always heard the same refrain: No jobs.

In December she found temporary holiday work in a Newark five-and-dime store. Twelve hours a day, $18 a week. It was good pay; any pay was good pay by then. It enabled her to contribute to the budget for Wakeman Avenue, and that was good for her self-respect, but there was no longer any deceiving herself about becoming independent.

Of course there was always the chance she could marry again.

As 1931 went from bad to worse the possibility of another marriage began to seem her best hope of salvation. Tucking me into bed one night, she lingered an unusually long time, then asked out of the blue, "Do you think Oluf would make a nice father?"

It was a troubling question, and she must have noticed my uneasiness because she immediately said, "Oluf is a good man."

This was her official seal of approval, for there were few "good men" in her catalogue. "Papa" of course had been a "good man," and Uncle Allen was a "good man," but there weren't many others.

I was vaguely aware of Oluf. He came to the house now and then, arms filled with bags of pastries which he jovially pressed on Doris and me. I knew he and my mother occasionally went out together for walks. Beyond that I paid him little attention. To me he was little more than a jolly stranger with a funny way of talking. He was certainly not my idea of a father.

Uncle Allen had met him while selling oleomargarine. Oluf was a skilled baker who had graduated to traveling salesman. With his sample cases full of margarine he traveled through the northeastern states demonstrating and selling his goods in large plants and small neighborhood shops. Uncle Allen brought him home one evening and introduced him to my mother.

He was a Dane, a big, yellow-haired, outgoing man in his late forties, and a widower. He had emigrated to the United States after his wife's death. There was a son who was married and living in western Pennsylvania. Oluf had the venturesome business spirit my mother admired. He had borrowed from the banks to buy three or four houses in Pennsylvania and considered himself a developing American success story. He was a man of high good humor, well-pressed double-breasted suits, manicured nails, and glossily polished shoes. He had risen above the labor of bake ovens, traveled from city to city, talked business deals with bankers. My mother, looking at him, saw a man with a future.

And though I did not know it at the time, she loved him.

I did not. Though I liked Oluf's jovial spirits and ate his pastry with gusto, the possibility of having a new father scared me. My great terror then was of losing my mother. I had constant nightmares, ghastly nightmares in which she was dead and Doris and I were left alone. Her marrying, I thought, would be another way to lose her, though I never told her so.

Oluf's work kept him on the road much of the time. During his absences he wrote two or three times a week to my mother. The graceful flourish of his handwriting contrasted oddly with the fractured grammar and exotic spelling of his prose. Still, his discomfort with the mysteries of English did not diminish his power to make himself felt when he took up the pen. Through the comical spelling, eerie grammar, and devil-may-care punctuation a distinctive voice emerged, full of sweetness, despair, earnestness, love, and loneliness, all expressed in a graceful Scandinavian lilt.

The first note of fear was sounded in a letter he wrote her from Boston May 9, 1932. He had visited his home office that day. Back at his hotel that night he wrote her about it.

"Dear Elizabeth," he began. "Today I have been together with our Manager all day, and he told me that it look like I will have to go June first. Business is so bad and getting worse for us, he let four salesmen go here May first so now there is only seven left. Last year there was seventheen. Well it don't help to worrie, like you said, I have to start a bakery somewhere, do you want to help me if I get one?"

The following week he called on customers in Providence and Newport, then came back to Boston and began his letter with bad news.

May 21, 1932:

"Dear Elizabeth: Just was at our office, they showed me letters they had written to Swift trying to keep me, but Swift said no, so I am out."

He was answering a letter from her in which she said Aunt Pat was going to find her a job.

"How in the world could Pat get a job for you? You know jobs today don't hang on trees."

And then, the abrupt switch to a more pleasant subject that typified his instinct to look on the bright side:

77

"New Port is the nicest place I ever seing."

And in the next sentence, the relapse into fear:

"Do you know Elizabeth down in Baltimore is a baker who wanted me affoul bad last time I was there maby I will take the job for a while, how would you like that, would you come and see me, or I come and see you. Business is affoul bad, now they are going to stop this office and only keep three Salesmen, last Summer they hat 32 men here, how people are getting over next vinter, I can't untherstand. Again thanks for your letter you are a sweet Girl, I will Kiss you when I see you, how is that, love to you and the Children from Oluf."

By the summer of 1932 President Hoover's mere "depression" had become "the Depression" with a capital D. Campaigning for reelection, the President declared, "Prosperity is just around the corner." Oluf, however, was adjusting his goals downward.

May 26, 1932:

"Dear Elizabeth, I will try to see that Baker in Baltimore on Monday June 6, today I was offered a job here with a Baker he would pay me 45 dollars per week, I told him I would think it over but oh how working in a Bakeshop in the Summer months is hard work."

Then, a burst of romantic teasing:

"That Widow in Pittsburgh has heard about I loosing my job, now she offers me all there is in this world if I will come and run her shop, but I dont think it will be so great, do you, no I know, you say no, oh how worm it is here this days, and today we hat a Storm a bad one to, a Cann of Blue Berries exploted today in a shop and I got it all over my Close, how is that—not so good,

"Love to you and the Children from Oluf."

My mother was writing back to him letter for letter. She kept his stored away for years, not because she realized they constituted a personal history of the Depression, but because she valued them among her most precious treasures. What she said in her letters to him is all lost except for echoes and resonances in his replies. It was not a conventional lovers' correspondence, despite Oluf's frequent attempts to strike the chord of passion. He in growing fear, she in

78

her mid-thirties, impoverished, widowed with small children, both were using the mails to shelter them against loneliness.

Earlier that year Aunt Pat had her first child, a daughter she named Kathleen. By mid-June Oluf had retreated to his properties in western Pennsylvania and wrote a "Dear Friends" letter to the whole family:

"Pat you are an affoul bad Girl, not to write me any before, you know I am out of work, and have been for some time, nearly all Echerson Co is out, and soon Swift and all their large Packing Co will be out, I never know how hard times is till when I got back to this town trying to borrow mony, I am glad Allen is working, be sjure to hang on to it, Pat I told you a Child is word a Berl of Gold. . . ."

He had a job though: "demonstrating and selling Pomosin, a New Product from Germany." He had also traded his car for an old Buick—"a Buirich Carre"—and was about to set out in it on a selling trip with his son Niels.

"Not working, do you know I am lost, and now all the Insurence People down here comes to see me, they all thinks I am full of mony or somthing, I say full of Balony, but now I will try this job first, I may land on the poor House but then I wont be the first, nor the last."

Two weeks later:

"Dear Elizabeth, Monday morning Niels, my Son and I started out selling Flavors and Speices, we made during the week 37 dollars, but we spent 34 dollars you know what I mean, Hotels and Meals, so I wouldent say it was so good. . . . The worst truble is this Bakers think I am going cracy, coming down selling Speices, this morning in Pittsburgh a Baker we called on there, said when he seing me, say what is this World comming to, now Oluf comes and wont to sell Speices, I felt so bad about it, so I said to Niels come on lett us go Home. . . ."

July 9, 1932:

"Dear Elizabeth, I got Home last Night late, and I sendt in my Resignation. That job was no good, by selling that Stuf I would have spoiled my Name amongst the Bakers. . . ."

79

They had not seen each other for three months.

"Yes I would have liked to see you now but I will later on, and then you and I will make up for all lost time, then I will be kissing you till you tell me, oh Oluf you are good will you do that? you better say yes, because I am almost sjure of it . . . tell me in your letters all the news, I like to hear it from you, oh all the Taxces and Bills I got to paid and have no Mony, but then I don't worrie, love to you and the Children from Oluf."

He was having trouble now meeting the mortgage payments on the houses he had bought, and he hoped to solve the problem by selling one. It was August, nearly five months since they had last seen each other. The long stretch of joblessness had started him reflecting philosophically about friendship.

August 11, 1932:

"Dear Elizabeth, Thanks very much for your letter I received today, yes I wich I was down near you, and we would go out for a ride, I am sjure it would make you cool, here it is wery neice Weather, and cool at Night, oh how I sleep when I am here at my Home, you know it is so quiet, compared with when I use to be in the Citys all noise, and so worm, I don't hear from anybody but you, how funy People are, only when they thinks they can get something out of a Person then they are, or I mean they let on to they are Freinds, but they soon change, you remember some days I received up to twenty letters, and now, not any, only you stick to me, you are a good Girl. . . .

"I begin to think I was going to sell a House this morning, but the Party diddent have any mony, now I have three Houses empty, nothing coming in, and Taxes to be paid, well it will come out OK, I hope so, I always tell People not to worrie, so I won't eather, now good Night with love to you and the Children from Oluf."

Well it will all come out OK, I hope so.

With the country reaching the modern equivalent of the Dark Ages, "Well it will all come out OK, I hope so" was a declaration of boundless optimism. It was a season of bread lines, soup kitchens, hobo jungles, bandits riding the highways. Suicide was epidemic among men who felt their manhood lost because they could

no longer support their families. Unemployment stood at 25 per-
cent of the work force. There were 85,000 businesses bankrupt,
5,000 bank failures, 275,000 families evicted from their homes.

President Hoover's campaign slogan—"Prosperity is just
around the corner"—had become a sardonic national joke. Even
among people like Oluf who wanted to believe it, enthusiasm was
muted down to, "Well it will all come out OK, I hope so."

October 6, 1932. It was now seven months since they had seen
each other:

"Dear Elizabeth, Thanks very much for your letter I received
yesterday, I see you were feeling a little blue that evening, yes I
wich I could have been with you, I am sjure you would have feelt
alright. Yes I will be down there for your Birthday unless something happening, there was a man here today he wonted to hire
me, to call on Bakers in Pittsburgh, but it was all on Commission
and no salary, so I said no. . . .

"I got a wery neice letter from the People today where Niels
rents his House from, they asked me to paid Nielses rent from
August so on til next Spring, but I am not even going to answer
that letter, they said in the letter that you Mr. Oluf is the cause of
Niels being in this World, and it was up to me to take care of him
and his Familie, say I wonder who is to blame for I being here in
this World, who ever it is, never helpt me, and who is to blame for
you Elizabeth being here,—say that is what I call Balony, but that
it what the Vorld is fuld of."

During their long separation their letters were creating an
intimacy between them far deeper than they had known when
they walked out together in Newark. There their relationship had
been entirely correct and according to the canons of courtship.
The most passionate moment, to which Oluf alluded now and
then, occurred during a walk that took them near the neighborhood hospital, when they seem to have kissed.

"We are having such a neice Day," he wrote in the autumn
of 1932, "just like Spring, I went out for a warlk this morning, do
you remember when you and I went for a warlk, I mean to the
Hospital. . . ."

81

Distance and loneliness encouraged hopes of a more passionate relationship when they met again, yet Oluf's most romantic compositions were constantly being interrupted by cries of terror.

In October:

"If I don't come to your Birthday this year, please don't worrie, because when I do come I will kiss and love you that much more, yes I will keep on till you put your Arms rown me and tell me I am good, can I love you to much? You better say no, tell Pat I will answer her letter when I get to feel a little better, what makes me sick is all this jobs I am to have, but never gets any, I was up to see my Dochtor to day, he tells me I am OK, in very good Health I know I am, if I only could get a job."

The election of Franklin Roosevelt in November did not raise his spirits.

November 11, 1932:

"Precident elesktion came out I think OK, it don't matter if it is Republican or Democrate in times like this. . . . Butter Prices are down where they were a year ago, and till they go back up rown 30 cents pr lbs, they never will hire me to demonstrate Margarine, now I am down and out again, and I don't like to keep on borrowing Moony from the Banks, because I got to paid it back sometimes sooner or later."

Desperate to pay his bankers, he went back to the bake ovens that month.

November 19, 1932:

"Dear Elizabeth. . . . I wont to come to you wery, wery bad, and I will, and when I do come you will be so glad with me, I know you will, but I borrowed doring the Summer over 1,000 Dollars from the Banks and was down and out again, then Metz came along, and told me about this job, and I went and got it, but oh how I dont like it, it is absolutely no good, to much work, I mean to long hours, we got to go to work tomorrow Sunday all day, and again Monday morning, and every morning at one A.M. til next day rown two or three Afternoon, but I must stand it for a while. . . ."

Two days later:

". . . this hours, it is day and night, work all the time, Yester-day we work all day till ten last evening then we started again at two this morning, now it is three Afternoon I just got home, now Elizabeth don't worrie, get along the best you can, and always think and say, someday Oluf will come, and I will. . . ."

These lines were the closest to a promise of marriage he had written. She wrote back immediately urging him to look for an easier job more fitting for a man of his age and achievements.

November 25, 1932:

"No, Elizabeth I tried all over to get a job, I vill bet you I spendt over five Dollars on Stemps, sending letters to every one of this Bakers, who offered me jobs with big mony when I was travel-ing, but only one of them answered, no there was two, one in Newark and one in Boston, but they said they diddent have any-thing just now, the rest of them wouldent even spend a two cent Stamps on me, and they all were my Freinds, well such is Life, no you musent think I would stay here in this dumpe one day ef I could get an other Job. . . . now it is three a clock Afternoon, and we got to go to work at elleven this evening, isint it some Life, vell I hope soon vill change to something better . . . I will get to you some day, don't worrie, love to you all from Oluf."

Five days later he had good news.

"Yesterday I received a Box of Cigares from a wery good Baker in Philladelphia, so maby my Freinds begin to come rown again, I wrote him to day and Thankt him, and said ef he needed a man lett me know and I would come down there."

Ten days later:

"I got a letter from that Baker in Philadelphia to day, but it was the same story, he like very much to have me, but not now, vell there vill be something comming soon, I think so. . . .

"Say isent it funny doing a Persons Life all there comes up, one thing after an other, and then it is nothing, as long as we have our Health. . . ."

In the middle of December she wrote that she had sent him a Christmas present.

"You shouldn't send me any Precent, not in times like this," he replied. "I am sending a litle so you can by something for the Children for Christmas and I hope you vill all have a neice Christmas, and I wich I could be there with you, but I will someday, good Night with love to you all from Oluf."

Her gift arrived December 20.

"Dear Elizabeth, Thanks wery much for your letter and the Packets I received today. I wont open up for it til Christmas I never du with any Precent, My Wife used to open up for everything before the day and I always scoled her, say you are a sweet Girl now Elizabeth, the way you write me, and I like it, you vill see when I come down to you, we know each other, and we vont be afraid, now I never was of you, but you was a little of me, and you should be them days becouse you diddent know me, but now you do, and I can almost feel how sweet it vill be when I put my arms rown you. . . ."

He also had good news.

"To day a man came in our shop from Gumbert Co in New York, he said to me, vhat in the World are you doing here Oluf, I told hem, then he said, write to our Company and I think they vill heire you, so that is vhat I vill do, and I hope I vill get a job, but it vont be til in January, vell again I wishes you a Mery Christmas and Thanks for all your kindnes to me. . . ."

January 4, 1933:

"I got a letter from this People in New York to day, but the same Story, they vould like very much to have me, but the Depression is on, oh how I do wich it soon vill be better so I can get a job, but rown here it is getting worce insted of better. . . ."

Four days later his spirits were high and he was counting his blessings.

"This job here has been a great experience for me, you know vhat I mean, I use to be a Baker but it is eight years ago since I was working at it and a Fellow forgot all about working in that time, but now I am fearly good ad it again, I am loosing in waith now, I can feel it when I get dressed up on Sundays, but that is OK, because I was to fatt, don't you think? Elizabeth isent it

84

funny all a Person goes tru during a Life time you have going tru lots, but I think I a litle more, because I am older, but again as long as we have our Health everything is OK, and we shouldent complain. . . ."

In mid-January another job prospect failed.

"That Baker never answered, and I spoce never will, it is funny how it goes."

The end of January:

"I did write Jelke Co, and hat an answeer, I did write Echerson Co, but it is the same Story, they sjure would like to have me, but the Depression is on, it is affoul, I wont to come down to you, and you wont me to come and here I am more than 400 Miles away, and it is all from that Depression."

February 1, 1933:

"Business is getting worce insteadt of better. . . ."

February 9:

"That Baker in Baltimore never answered yet, it is funy, he is the one who offered me 125 Dollars per week ef I only whute come to hem, and it is not much over a Year ago, now he wont even spend a three cent Stamp on me, I mean telling me he cant use me, or something, the same day I wrote to hem, I wrote to one in Boston, he offered me 50 Dollars per week a Year ago, but I dont think he will spend a Stamp on me, well such is Life, I think I wrote over fifty Letters to differens Bakers about a job, but only two answered me telling how sorry they where they couldent use me. . . ."

The following week the gloom lifted at last. After so much despair, everything was turning out OK, after all. Life really was "funy" with its "cracy ups and downs." He was exuberant.

February 15, 1933:

"Dear Elizabeth, Can you imagien I received a letter to Day from Mr. Echerson in Jersey City telling me that Rice's Bakery at Baltimore wont to gett me at least for two weeks, and for ever if I am not to expensive, so I wrote them right now, I don't know who they are, but who ever they are, they must be OK, I mean becouse they wont me, so maby our dreams at last will come true, say it is funy, here I give up all this Bakers, and they send for me. . . . now I hope it soon will be over with and then I will come to you, are you glad? Love to you all from Oluf."

Was she glad? She was delighted. She immediately wrote urging him not to sell himself too cheaply to Rice's Bakery. His reply to her was an epitaph for their entire generation.

"Dear Elizabeth, Thanks very much for your letter I received Yesterday, and Thanks very much for your Advice, but Elizabeth the War is over with, the good times is over with, them days we did seat a Price on ourself, but to day we just take what we can get and must be satisfact,—am I not right? So I diddent put any Price on, only told them what I am getting here, but what ever the wages are for a man like me down there I vould take. . . ."

Franklin Roosevelt was inaugurated March 4, 1933, but his sonorous cadences designed to revive the national spirit failed to stir Oluf. The great Baltimore opportunity seemed to be vanishing.

"Dear Elizabeth, Do you know Elizabeth I am feeling wery blue, I never heard from Rices Baking Co yet, and I begin to think it will go the same way as the others, now I have been seathing here all Day listening to Rosevelt being installed as our new Precident, well I do hope some of all this neice tings they told us over the Radio will come true, Elizabeth I am very Radicall, my idea would be to day ef I was to be the Precident, to jump on a Freight Train going to Washington, and say here I am ready to go to work, what they done there today will cost over 10 Million Dollars and we all know it would have helped many poor People out spending that mony giving us work, but perhaps I am funny the way I look at such tings. . . ."

Four days later:

"Yes, I got a letter from Rices Baking Co, saying *no.*"

He had been trying to rent his houses, but without success. It was becoming harder to meet the payments on their mortgages. He was also having trouble paying the taxes. His letters were increasingly melancholy.

Lucy Elizabeth in 1933.

March 26, 1933:

"No, I dont do any thing, just seat rown or warlk up Town, and listening to People telling me how Lucky I am has lots of Mony, I always say, yes it is great, tomorrow I got to put in a new Hot Water Tank in a House, well there is always something. . . ."

On April 14 he confided that he was $1,000 in debt.

"I talk to the Caschier in our Bank to day, asking him to lett me have 1500 Dollars, he said, not now, but come in here middle of next month, I think then you can have it, ef I do I will come to you, ef I could have got it to day, I would have been down with you tomorrow night. . . ."

April 19, 1933:

"Dear Elizabeth, Thanks very much for your wery sweet letter I received to day, Thanks for telling me all the neice things, I do know now we can be free to each other, not afraid, when we see each other again, not like it was when I was down there, I know I was always looking at you when I was at your House, but you never seemed to be interested in me, I know you beginn to be the day we went to the Hospital, am I right? . . ."

His next letter, written on April 24, was a hammer blow.

"Dear Elizabeth, Thanks for your letter I received to day, I am sorry, but Please dont write me any more.

"Yours truly

"Oluf"

She wrote back immediately. Had she said something that offended him?

April 30, 1933:

"Dear Elizabeth, Thanks for your letter I received the other day, no you have not done anything to me, but the Deprescion has the City took everything I hat for Taxes, so I am down and out that is why I don't want you to write me any more, I came to like you tru your letters, and I thought maybe some day we would come to know each other Personly, but not now, I wont be able to borrow any mony, any more, I am trying to gett anof so I can go to Danmark, and Perhaps stay there, so Please forget all about me, I am lost and going, ef I ever got back again, and you are not married, then ef I can help you I will, but please try to feind a man good anof for you, and forget all about your ever seing Oluf."

She wrote again and had no reply. Then again, and no reply. She sent a registered letter and the Post Office sent her his signed receipt for it, dated May 18.

On May 19 he wrote "Dear Elizabeth" for the last time:

"Thanks for your letters, yes I received them all, but as I told you vhat is the use to keep on writting, I was in hope someday to come to know you, by getting a job down there, but now I never can come down, I am like I told you before, lost. I tried to raice anof mony so I could go over Home, but so far I diddent, this Town is going down and out, so I am asking you to stop writting to me, becouse I am not interested in anything any more, love to you all from Oluf."

The war was over with, the good times were over with.

"Well it will all come out OK, I hope so" had become "I am lost and going and not interested in anything any more."

Oluf disappeared into the Depression. My mother's hopes for finding love and security vanished with him.

CHAPTER SEVEN

UNCLE Allen moved us out of Newark and up to Belleville in 1932. I liked Belleville. There were big grassy lawns and streets canopied with trees. We lived on the first floor of a two-family house across the street from Public School Number 8. The landlady lived on the second floor. Aunt Pat detested her for being a landlady. The propertied classes ranked high in Aunt Pat's catalogue of natural enemies.

Coming in from play one evening at dusk, I heard Aunt Pat shouting in the kitchen.

"She's got her nerve!"

Uncle Allen tried his customary soothing refrain. "Calm down now, Pat. Just calm down."

"Calm down! Not with that thing on the front door! Jesus, Mary, and Joseph, Allen! What are the neighbors going to think?"

I tiptoed outside to see what terrible thing was on the front door. In fact there were two front doors side by side. One opened directly into our parlor, the other opened onto a staircase that led up to the landlady's quarters. Our front door looked the same as always, but fixed to the landlady's door was a large head-and-shoulders portrait of a genial-looking man with hair parted down the middle.

There was printing under the picture. I could read easily now. My mother had spent so much time teaching me to read that the principal at P.S. Number 8 had agreed to let me skip second grade and go on to the third, which didn't satisfy my mother, who thought I should have been skipped at least to the fourth. Reading the material under the picture gave me no trouble, but I couldn't understand why it should anger Aunt Pat.

It identified the man in the picture as Herbert Hoover. It said something to the effect that he should be reelected. I studied the picture carefully and was impressed by the gentleness of Herbert Hoover's expression. He had round, chubby cheeks that reminded me of babies. He certainly didn't look like a man to make your blood boil. I went back in the house, where Uncle Allen was trying to focus Aunt Pat's mind on making supper.

"How can I cook with that damn thing on the front door?" she cried.

My mother was sitting at the table smiling and enjoying the excitement. As meekly as possible, I asked her, "What's wrong about Herbert Hoover?"

"Great mother of God!" cried Aunt Pat. "You poor child!" And she told me what was wrong about Herbert Hoover. He was destroying America, that was one thing wrong about him.

"Now just a second, Pat—"

But Uncle Allen's plea for calm was lost in the gale. People were starving because of Herbert Hoover. My mother was out of work because of Herbert Hoover. Men were killing themselves because of Herbert Hoover, and their fatherless children were being packed away into orphanages—Aunt Pat's dread of orphanages made this the worst offense of all to her—because of Herbert Hoover.

"Now, Pat, be fair—"

"I'll be fair. I'm going to tear that thing off the front door."

91

She was in motion now. Uncle Allen stepped between her and the parlor. "You can't do that, Pat. It's her house. She has a right to put up a poster if she wants."

"We pay the rent that keeps her, it's our house too," Aunt Pat roared, but for the first time she seemed ready to defer to Uncle Allen's sense of what was right.

Seeing that he had averted a crisis for the moment, Uncle Allen adopted the foxy-grandpa style he sometimes used when he wanted to win a point by persuasion. Taking a toothpick out of his vest pocket, he chewed it thoughtfully for the longest while, a gesture we all recognized. He was thinking; he had an idea a-borning. When all was silent, he smiled a canny smile and spoke in his deepest down-home southern drawl.

"Waal, Pat, I'll tell you," he said. "Down in Lancaster Court House where I come from, we always liked to settle things peaceable. Kind of keep the blood cool, y'know. I remember one time old Mr. Charlie Nickens had a fight with a fellow down there whose cows kept getting into his orchard"—Uncle Allen remembered nothing of the sort. He was making it up out of the whole cloth, hoping to get Aunt Pat soothed sufficiently to get on with making the chipped-beef gravy for supper—"and old Mr. Nickens swore he was going to shoot the next cow he caught in there eating his apples off the ground, because he fed those apples to his hogs, you know. But I had a better idea. 'Lord, Mr. Nickens, you don't want to shoot that man's cows,' I told him. 'A hole in the fence is a two-way street. If his cows come over to your side, why don't you encourage your hogs to go over to his side and wallow around in his vegetable garden?' I think that's what we ought to do about *Mr.* Hoover out front."

"I don't get it," said Aunt Pat. I didn't either.

"We've got a front door too," Uncle Allen said. "It's a two-way street. Instead of tearing down her Hoover poster, why don't we get a Roosevelt poster and stick it up right alongside hers on our own door?"

Aunt Pat was delighted with the idea. She headed for the door. "Where are you going, Pat?" he asked.

"To talk to the Dunleavys," she said. "I want to find out where to get a Roosevelt poster."

"Can't it wait till after supper?"

It couldn't. Aunt Pat headed out to canvass the neighbors. The Dunleavys, the O'Connells, the Quinns, the O'Learys. They were all rabid Democrats. One of them would guide her to the source of Franklin Roosevelt posters. We had no telephone; telephones were luxuries for the rich. She traveled from neighbor to neighbor in search of someone wise in the mechanics of politics and came back with the address of a storefront campaign office where posters were available free.

The office lay a mighty distance, down on Washington Avenue, and we had no car. Cars were also luxuries for the rich. That was all right; Aunt Pat would walk.

"Supper," Uncle Allen pleaded.

My mother could cook the chipped beef, Aunt Pat said, and have it ready on her return.

"It's dark," Uncle Allen said. "It's too far to go alone."

By now I was totally involved. I too wanted to save America from Herbert Hoover. I wanted to defeat the landlady upstairs who lived off Uncle Allen's money. Above all I wanted to be part of the excitement. "I'll go with her," I cried.

Off we went. The walk seemed endless, the trip back even longer, but when we returned and Aunt Pat taped the picture of Franklin Roosevelt to our front door I forgot exhaustion. I felt like a hero of liberty. I had discovered the joys of politics. If I had lived upstairs with the landlady I would probably have become a hard-money Republican, but chance had put me on the lower level where the Depression stirred such passion that even a child could not resist. In my first venture into politics, I became a Roosevelt Democrat.

I was much too young to sense what the Depression was doing to people like my mother and Oluf, or to realize what a heroic feat Uncle Allen was performing simply by keeping us all fed and sheltered. Having known nothing but hard times, I had no sense of the hopes that were being destroyed or the fear in which adults lived or the defeat my mother felt at Oluf's farewell words, "I am lost and going and not interested in anything any more."

If anyone had told me we were poor, I would have been astounded. We ate well enough. There was always a bowl of oatmeal at breakfast, a bologna sandwich for lunch, and a cup of coffee to wash it down with. For supper the standard menu was chipped-beef gravy on bread, or macaroni and cheese. Canned salmon sold at eleven cents a can, and Aunt Pat splurged now and then and served fried salmon cakes. At Sunday dinner, the big meal of the week, we feasted on chicken and might even have dessert if Uncle Allen was in the mood to make sweet-potato pudding. This treat he produced by mashing a sweet potato to pulp and adding sugar, vanilla extract, and evaporated milk.

By 1933 I was free of the melancholia that had made me so miserable in Newark, and I was full of contentment with Belleville. With so many idle hours at her disposal my mother was focusing all her schoolteacher's energies on perfecting the education I would need to make something of myself. As a result I was always well ahead of most of the class at school and basked in a steady flow of A's and gold stars. I think she was already preparing me for the day when Oluf would secure our future and I would be sent off to college.

When this hope came crashing down that summer, I was totally unaware that anything terrible had happened to her. It had been a year or more since I had last seen Oluf. I knew nothing of what had been growing between them in the mails. I had forgotten Oluf existed, and when he ceased to exist for my mother, too, she gave me no outward sign that her life had come to another turning point.

At this moment, in her defeat, however, she was already laying plans for another campaign, a longer, harder struggle to come up from the bottom without help from the sort of Providence Oluf had represented. In this long, hard pull, I was now cast as the central figure. She would spend her middle years turning me into the man who would redeem her failed youth. I would make something of myself, and if *I* lacked the grit to do it, well then *she* would

94

make me make something of myself. I would become the living proof of the strength of her womanhood. From now on she would live for me, and, in turn, I would become her future.

The results of this decision began to appear immediately, though I was only vaguely sensitive to them. Since coming to New Jersey she and Doris and I had slept together, all of us in my father's bed which she had brought from Morrisonville. That summer she put me out of her bed. "It's time you started sleeping by yourself," she said. After that I slept on a couch in the parlor.

She began telling me I was "the man of the family," and insisting that I play the role. She took me to a Newark department store and bought me a suit with knickers, a herringbone pattern that must have represented a large fortune on her meager resources. But a suit and a necktie and a white shirt weren't enough; she also insisted on buying me a hat, a junior-scale model of the gray fedora Uncle Allen wore.

"You're the man of the family now," she said. "You have to dress like a gentleman."

The suit and hat were only for special occasions, of course. Like church. Men who wanted to make something of themselves went to church, and they went well dressed. Each Sunday she rolled me off the couch to put on the suit and accompany her to the Wesley Methodist Church on Washington Avenue. Her "Papa" had been a Methodist, and he had been a good man. She would start me out as a Methodist, and never mind that my father and all his people had always been Lutherans.

On the journey to church she instructed me in how a proper man must walk with a woman. "A gentleman always walks on the outside," she explained, maneuvering me to the curb edge on the sidewalk. If in childish excitement I dashed ahead of her and ran through a door she called me back for another lesson in manhood: "The man always opens the door for a woman and holds it so she can go first."

In her urgency to hasten me into manhood my mother did not neglect Doris, but I was aware that Doris was not expected to take up the heavy burdens someday that I was. It was enough for my mother to enroll Doris in dancing classes. Dancing was an asset for a girl. Eventually it might help her find the husband a woman needed for survival. Doris was taught the arts of housekeeping: washing dishes, setting the table, making beds, dusting.

It was at this time that my mother decided to acquaint me with work and obtained my job selling the *Saturday Evening Post*. In typical weeks my magazine sales earned me twenty-five to thirty-five cents. She took a dime of this to deposit in a bank account she had opened for me. "A man has to get in the habit of saving for a rainy day." As "the man of the family," I was expected to contribute another nickel in support of the household. The remaining ten or twenty cents was mine to squander on vices of my choice, which were movies, Big Little Books, and two-for-a-penny Mary Jane bars.

The making of a man, even when the raw material was as pliable as I, often seemed brutally hard without the help of a father to handle the rougher passages. There was the awkward problem of punishment. Small, not prepossessing, certainly not strong, she was wedded to the old saw "Spare the rod and spoil the child" and feared that unless my misbehaviors were corrected with corporal punishment my character would become soft and corrupt.

Before declaring me "the man of the family" she had never spanked me, and by that time, when I was eight, I was too large for spanking. It was her notion, picked up I know not where, that boys my age needed "a good thrashing" when they misbehaved. These she administered with my belt, often for what seemed to me like trivial offenses such as coming home late for supper because I was having a good time sledding on the hill. A man had a responsibility to meet his social obligations on time. Small as she was, she could still make the snapping belt sting when it lashed across my bared legs, but I hated the indignity of these beatings so much that I refused to satisfy her with a discreetly faked show of tears.

I had no real tears in me at that time. I hadn't cried since my father's death, not even on the day early in 1933 when my mother called me into the house and said, "I've got something to tell you now, and I don't want you to cry," and told me my grandmother had died in Morrisonville. In spite of my mother's words I knew I was expected to cry for Ida Rebecca, but I couldn't and didn't even want to. If in playing I tore my knee on a nail or one of the boys straddled me on the ground and pounded my face with fists until I was spitting blood, I did not cry because of the pain. I found myself thinking, "This hurts"; or if I was being beaten in a fight, I stared at my assailant in silent rage, thinking, "Some day I'll get you back for this," and when it was over limped homeward dry of eye, holding a bloody nose.

My failure to cry during her "thrashings" enraged my mother, and I knew it. Tears would be evidence that I had learned the lesson. My sullen submission to her heaviest blows intensified her fury. If she had been a man she would have been able to make me weep for mercy, but because she was not, and because I did not weep, she struck all the harder.

I knew that faking the tears would gratify her and end the punishment, but I refused. The injustice and humiliation of being beaten rankled so powerfully that I deliberately accepted the worst she could deliver to show my contempt. Sometimes, to goad her with proof of my contempt, I gritted my teeth and, when the belt had fallen four or five times, muttered, "That doesn't hurt me." In these moments we were very close to raw hatred of each other. We were two wills of iron. She was determined to break me; I was just as determined that she would not.

In the end she was the one who always cried, and then, when she had flung the belt aside and collapsed on a chair weeping quietly, the anger and hatred instantly drained out of me, and, overcome with pity and love, I rushed to embrace and kiss her, saying, "It's all right, Mama, it's all right. I'll never do it again. I promise, I'll never do it again."

Late that summer, after two and a half years of searching, she finally found full-time work. The A&P grocery chain ran a laundry in Belleville for cleaning and repairing their employees' work clothes. She was hired to work a sewing machine, patching worn grocer's smocks. The salary was $10 a week, and there was a piece-work bonus for workers who exceeded their daily quota; by working at top speed she could raise her weekly pay to as much as $11. Coming home Friday nights from the laundry with so much money, she liked to share her pleasure with Doris and me. The salary was packaged in a small brown envelope. She sat at the kitchen table and showed us the envelope.

"Guess how much money I made this week?"

Then she poured the treasure on the table. It was usually in one-dollar bills and coin. To Doris and me a dollar was an unbelievable sum of money, and the sight of ten dollars all on one table left us goggle-eyed. So much wealth, and she let us count it. First Doris counted it, and then I counted it, and when we had finished my mother said, "That's right—ten dollars and eighty-five cents. Now what do you think Mama should do with it?"

"Go to the movies," was my usual answer.

I was teasing her with this spendthrift suggestion because I knew she was happy and would enjoy being teased a little, though there was always the chance she would accept the idea and take me down to Newark to one of the great first-run movie houses—Loew's State or the Branford or Proctor's—that charged twenty-five cents for admission.

Very little of it went for idle pleasures, though. Part of it she paid to Uncle Allen as her contribution to the common welfare. Part was earmarked for the bank to finance the next big phase of her long-term program. This was to establish "a home of our own" where she and Doris and I would at last live in independence from Uncle Allen's charity.

"A home of our own"—that was her great goal. She talked about it constantly. If Aunt Pat and I crossed swords—and sometimes we did, for with my mother away at work all day Aunt Pat had the mother's task of enforcing discipline—my mother said, "Just be patient, Buddy, and one day we'll have a home of our own."

Aunt Pat was also beginning to yearn for a home of her own. We had come into her house in the dawn of the Depression for what my mother thought would be a few months with Pat and Allen until she could rent her own place. Now, at the pit of the

98

Depression, the few months had become three years, and the way the world was going it looked as if it might become fifty before Aunt Pat and Uncle Allen regained their privacy.

That winter, with the birth of their second daughter, their household expanded again. With his $30 a week and the few dollars my mother contributed from her salary, Uncle Allen was, now supporting a wife and two baby daughters, his older sister, and his niece and nephew. Uncle Charlie was also with us now, and Uncle Charlie was jobless and penniless. There was more to come. Just around the corner was not prosperity, but Uncle Hal.

Chapter Eight

Uncle Hal arrived in the night with three boards. This was after Uncle Allen had moved us to New Street, just off Belleville Avenue. We had an entire two-story house there, Uncle Allen and Aunt Pat sleeping downstairs in the dining room, which they'd turned into a bedroom, and Doris, my mother, and me sprawled luxuriously over two bedrooms on the second floor. There was a pool table in the cellar, a good big professional-size pool table. Aunt Pat had bought it for $5 from a bankrupt pool parlor, along with the billiard balls and a handsome set of cue sticks. She and Uncle Allen and my mother and Uncle Charlie were in the cellar playing pool when Uncle Hal arrived.

Doris and I had gone to bed on the second floor, Doris in my mother's bed, me on the daybed in the room that had the radio in it and my father's old rocking chair from Morrisonville. We called that room our "private parlor" because of the radio and because the daybed converted into a couch after I got up in the morning, allowing the three of us to sit in there and read or listen to the radio.

I had just dropped off to sleep when the racket started out front.

"Damn it, boy, careful with that board! Careful!"

Looking out the window I saw a flatbed truck drawn up in front of the house and two black men in overalls lifting off a plank while a third man shouted at them. He issued orders in an awesome voice.

"Steady there, steady! Watch what you're doing, damn it!"

The two black men put the plank on the grass and started unloading a second.

"Put it down easy! Easy! That's right. That board's worth a fortune."

He was talking loud enough to be heard all the way to Belleville Avenue. I went out into the hall. Doris was up too in her nightgown. I was always timid about taking action in a crisis, but not Doris.

"What do you think we ought to do?" I asked.

"I'm going to tell Aunt Pat," she announced, heading for the cellar.

In the cellar they hadn't heard the ruckus. There was clatter on the porch now. The doorbell rang. Up out of the cellar came Aunt Pat, trailed closely by Doris. Ready to give somebody a piece of her mind, Aunt Pat strode to the front door and flung it open. She was staring at a tall, stooped, sandy-haired man with a bushy mustache and no teeth. ("No teeth at all, just his lip flapping in the breeze," she said afterwards.)

Before she could ask, he stepped forward with outstretched hand and told her: "Hi, Pat, I'm Hal."

"Jesus, Mary, and Joseph!" she cried to the others, who had filed out of the cellar behind her and stood clustered in the hallway. "Let's make a pot of coffee!"

Making a pot of coffee was the automatic reaction to every event at New Street, and after effusive greetings and cries of "Good Lord, it's Hal!" and handshakes and embraces and kisses, somebody went off to fire up the pot.

Spotting me at the top of the stairs my mother said, "Come down here Russell and meet your Uncle Hal."

I did and he shook my hand authoritatively.

"What's your name, son?"

"Russell," I murmured.

"Speak out, boy. Don't be afraid to speak out."

"Russell," I repeated a little more firmly, but I had already lost his attention. He was talking big money to Uncle Allen.

"I've got three walnut boards outside that are worth a fortune," he said. Turning to the black men who stood silently at the door, he shouted, "Don't just stand there! Bring those boards in here and put 'em on the floor!"

The black men went into action.

"Leave any scratches on them and I'll sue you for every cent you're worth," he growled.

Doris and I were sent back to bed then, but I knew I had seen an important man. With Uncle Hal's commanding manner toward hired help and his impressive mustache and his fortune in lumber lying in the downstairs hallway, it was like having Daddy Warbucks come for a visit. I failed to notice that Uncle Hal had brought only one small suitcase, and I did not know he was toothless because he didn't have enough money to buy a set of false teeth.

To my mother and Uncle Allen, Hal was the big brother, the oldest of Papa's nine children, rightful heir to Papa's mantle of authority, the one whose duty in life was to restore the family to the glory it had known before Papa's death.

In the old days before the First World War, Papa had traded in the walnut veneer business. Since Hal had no interest in going to college, Papa had taught him the walnut veneer trade, and this had been his calling ever since. His home for the past ten years had been Richmond. Arriving at New Street unannounced in the night, he created the impression of mystery and grandeur which movies had taught me to expect in men of great affairs.

When they all gathered in the kitchen over coffee that first night, he explained that he was up from Virginia to swing a large deal in New York. Had important business appointments scheduled over there. Thought he might as well take the opportunity to visit his sister and little brothers.

Wouldn't he stay a while? Aunt Pat asked.

Well . . . Why not? Some things were more important than business. Things like family. He didn't get a chance to be with the family that often. Why not stay a couple of days and talk over old times? No, of course he didn't mind sleeping on the couch in the parlor. Didn't mind at all. Not at all.

Next evening when Uncle Allen came home from his sales route and my mother from her sewing machine and me from my *Saturday Evening Post* route, I sat at the kitchen table long after supper listening to Uncle Hal talk about corporate giants with whom he was dealing in New York, and about the skill he would need to keep them from outwitting him in the big walnut-veneer deal. The boards in our hallway were cut from a forest full of walnut of the finest, rarest quality. Its location was known only to him. He would need great cleverness to keep New York businessmen from wheedling its location out of him, but he wasn't worried. *He* knew how to handle such men.

I noticed that they referred to Uncle Hal as "the Colonel" and sometimes called him "Colonel" instead of Hal. I also noticed that while my mother and Aunt Pat seemed excited by the Colonel's talk, Uncle Allen ate his macaroni and cheese as calmly as ever and didn't seem much moved by the festive spirit infecting the rest of us.

He smiled agreeably now and then during the Colonel's talk about the big walnut-board deal, but seemed genuinely interested only when asking about Virginia relatives he hadn't seen for many years. Now and then Uncle Allen tried to extract certain dull business information about the lumber deal, but Uncle Hal, ten years his senior, brushed aside these questions with a wave of the hand. I could see that business on Uncle Hal's scale of operations was far beyond Uncle Allen's understanding.

Uncle Hal obviously knew it too. The only time he gave

Uncle Allen much attention that night was when he noticed Uncle Allen drinking coffee. In stern parental terms he told Uncle Allen he would ruin his health by drinking coffee.

Uncle Hal was an authority on many things, including stomach ulcers. He had undergone surgery for ulcers and predicted Uncle Allen would too, unless he gave up coffee and drank a quart of milk a day.

During the following days I noticed that Uncle Hal seemed to enjoy spoiling Uncle Allen's meals by telling him he was "digging your grave with your own teeth." One night at dinner Aunt Pat served candied sweet potatoes, one of Uncle Allen's favorite dishes, and when Uncle Allen was well into his helping, Uncle Hal said, "Eating candied sweet potatoes is digging your grave with your own teeth, Allen."

Uncle Allen smiled his agreeable smile and ate the rest of them anyhow while the Colonel explained at length that there was no food more likely to cause stomach ulcer than candied sweet potatoes. Unless it was fried chicken. Fried chicken was Uncle Allen's favorite Sunday dinner.

"Eating that fried chicken," Uncle Hal told him in the middle of one Sunday dinner, "is like digging your grave with your own teeth."

From his first supper at New Street Uncle Hal insisted on the life-prolonging benefits of a good after-supper belch. After gumming his food he asked Aunt Pat to bring the bicarbonate of soda, spooned some into a glass of water, and delighted himself a few moments later with a magnificent eruption. "There's nothing better for you than letting those poison gases out," he said.

Uncle Hal's business coup took longer than anticipated. His "couple of days" visit became a week's visit, then developed into a month's stayover. One month stretched into two. In the daytime he usually left the house explaining he had "appointments." Maybe he did. We had no telephone; maybe he arranged his appointments on the pay phone at Zuccarelli's drugstore.

Gradually his visit turned into a residency. His boards lay in the hallway for weeks, then months, and became a permanent part of the furniture. He left the house less and less frequently and spent more and more time in the cellar playing pool.

When he first arrived my mother thought he might be an agent of salvation. She confided to me that Uncle Hal had promised to help us set up "a home of our own" after his lumber deal went through. "When Uncle Hal gets his business going he's going to take us to Baltimore and help us have a nice place," she told me a few nights after his arrival. As the months passed and the boards gathered dust in the hallway, she no longer talked about the wonderful day when Uncle Hal's deal would go through but began speaking of a time "when Uncle Hal's ship comes in." And then, "*if* Uncle Hal's ship comes in."

Everybody was waiting for his ship to come in. It was a sad, bitter phrase used even by children to express the hopelessness of hoping. In the schoolyard we said, "When my ship comes in, I'm going over to New York and see the Yankees play." Meaning that we never expected to be rich enough to sit in the Yankee Stadium. Now as the months passed, if I was out with my mother and an acquaintance asked about Uncle Hal, she replied, "Oh, he's still waiting for his ship to come in."

After Uncle Hal had stayed long enough to feel at home, he began to take his big-brother duties seriously and to apply his mind to reorganizing the family's life. He saw that Aunt Pat was increasingly unhappy running a commune for Uncle Allen's impoverished relatives and began devising plans for moving them out. The immediate task he set himself was getting rid of Uncle Charlie.

There was bad blood between Uncle Hal and Uncle Charlie. Hostility between them went back to childhood and had many roots, some of them possibly sinister, others quite natural. For one thing, Charlie was the baby of the family and had always been indulged and coddled. For another, Uncle Charlie was the embodiment of everything Uncle Hal disliked.

"That weakling," he called Uncle Charlie one day while I was eavesdropping on him and Aunt Pat. I was shocked and offended by that. I was fond of Uncle Charlie. Uncle Charlie was the only person in the house who talked to me as one adult to another.

Admittedly, Uncle Charlie did look weak. He was even shorter than Uncle Allen and skinny to boot. He came to visit us in Morrisonville once when I was a toddler, and afterwards my grandmother marveled, "Hasn't got an ounce of meat anywhere on him, wouldn't make a meal for a hummingbird." His eyes were palest blue, his hair bright yellow, his skin so white and transparent you could see the blue veins pulsing underneath. He had a long sharp nose, a pointed chin, and thin lips that curled up at the corners to make his happiest smile look like an elegant sneer.

Since for years Uncle Charlie had refused to leave the house for any purpose whatever, his wardrobe consisted of Uncle Allen's hand-me-downs and things Aunt Pat picked up for him at the dry-goods store. They were always a couple of sizes too big. Swathed in billows of excess shirt and trouser material, all cinched tightly around his tiny waist with a belt, he looked like a child wearing a man's clothes.

Uncle Allen had supported him almost constantly since 1923, though he did not take him in permanently until after my mother, Doris, and I came to Newark. Uncle Charlie had not worked since, nor looked for work, and it was taken for granted by everybody that he would never work again nor look for work. When Uncle Hal began planning to deport him, he was thirty years old and had already enjoyed several years of happy retirement.

My mother loved him dearly, but nevertheless held him up to me as a tragic example of the sluggard's life. If she caught me idling when I should have been peddling magazines, it was: "Do you want to grow up to be like Uncle Charlie?" Preparing to give me "a good thrashing," she cried, "You're not going to be another Uncle Charlie as long as I've got anything to say about it."

Uncle Charlie, they all said, was "brilliant."

"Almost a genius," Uncle Allen told me. "With a mind like that he could have done almost anything."

Why hadn't he?

"Laziness," Aunt Pat told me. She said it as though laziness were a disease, a bad heart or failed kidneys, for which he was not to be blamed. "Uncle Charlie is lazy, dear," she said.

106

My mother spoke of the affliction in sorrow. "Poor Charlie," she sighed one day when I asked why she and Uncle Allen and I had to work while Uncle Charlie never did. "He's the laziest man God ever put breath into."

It puzzled me that she considered my own laziness curable with a few whacks of the belt but tolerated Uncle Charlie's with sorrow and love. Old enough now to study adults and their world with a skeptical eye, I began to suspect there was some secret about Uncle Charlie which they were hiding from me.

One evening when Uncle Charlie was in his bedroom reading and I was in the kitchen with Uncle Allen, Aunt Pat, and my mother, I probed for fuller explanations. "Didn't Uncle Charlie ever work?"

Uncle Allen was in one of this twinkling moods. "Waaaal, I'll tell you, Russ," he said. "He worked until the Moe Simon business began to get him down."

"He was a newspaperman," Aunt Pat said. "When we all lived in Brooklyn. He worked for the—what's the name of that paper, Allen?"

"The *Brooklyn Eagle.* Yeah, he was working for the *Brooklyn Eagle.*"

"Who's Moe Simon?"

Uncle Allen poured himself another cup of coffee and leaned back in his chair. "You mean to say nobody ever told you about Moe Simon?"

"Oh, it was a terrible thing for Charlie," Aunt Pat said.

Between them they told the story.

The problem began the first day Uncle Charlie reported for work at the *Eagle.* His editor looked at him curiously and called over one of the reporters. "Does this fellow look familiar to you?" the editor asked.

"Yeah, he looks just like Moe Simon," the reporter said.

"That's what I thought," said the editor. Then to Uncle Charlie, with suspicion: "Are you related to Moe Simon?"

Uncle Charlie said no, he had never heard of Moe Simon.

A few days later Uncle Charlie was eating his soup in a

Brooklyn lunchroom when an evil-looking fellow slid into the chair across the table, looked around as if to be sure no police were eavesdropping, and whispered, "I got the stuff, Moe."

In his Virginia drawl Uncle Charlie explained that he was not named Moe.

Persuaded by the southern accent, the man muttered, "Jesus Christ! You look enough like Moe Simon to be his twin brother," and departed swiftly.

The Moe Simon resemblance began to prey on Uncle Charlie. Walking to work one day he was hailed by a stranger on the far side of the street. "Look who's back!" the man cried to two other men with whom he was idling on the street corner, and all three of them waved jovially for Uncle Charlie to come over and join them.

Uncle Charlie did so.

"You been doing time lately, Moe?" one of the men asked.

"My name is not Moe," Uncle Charlie said.

The men apologized: "Sorry, pal, but you're a dead ringer for Moe Simon."

Coming out of a Brooklyn subway not long afterwards, Uncle Charlie was stopped by a passing pedestrian.

"Hey," said the man, "you look just like Moe Simon."

Uncle Charlie dove back into the subway and rode to shelter at Uncle Allen's place, where he reshaped his life so he would never have to go into public again.

Such was the story Uncle Allen, Aunt Pat, and my mother told me that night. They were all fanciful yarn spinners, of course, especially late in the evening when the coffee was being reheated, and not above weaving a comic fiction out of a single thread of fact, but I accepted the story as Gospel and secretly envied the way Uncle Charlie had rebuilt his life.

Uncle Charlie had four pastimes. He slept, read, smoked, and drank coffee. He was the only person I'd ever seen who, if asked his occupation, could have honestly answered, "Sleeping." Eleven or twelve hours under the blankets presented no challenge at all to Uncle Charlie. It merely whetted his appetite for more, and after a few hours off the mattress he often slipped back for a restorative nap. He usually slept until about one o'clock in the afternoon, then rose, made a pot of coffee, rolled a cigarette from his bag of Bull Durham, and settled down to read. His reading consisted mostly of biography and works on history, government, and politics. Aunt Pat, who went to the public library two or three times a week for the murder mysteries she consumed like fodder, kept him supplied with books. His one passion was politics, and to feed it he consumed the daily newspapers Uncle Allen brought home, listened intently to the radio newscasts, and studied the *Saturday Evening Post* and the *Literary Digest*.

Alone in that house full of New Deal Democrats, Uncle Charlie was a totally committed Republican. He regarded the 1932 defeat of Herbert Hoover as a disaster for the Republic and looked forward happily to the 1936 elections, when, the *Literary Digest*'s famous poll assured him, Roosevelt would be easily beaten.

Uncle Charlie gave me my first real education in politics. From Uncle Charlie I first heard the word "socialism," a doctrine so evil, he gave me to understand, that it could destroy our country. America, he told me, had been built with initiative and hard work. Socialism, he told me, discouraged hard work and destroyed initiative. And socialism was what Franklin Roosevelt was practicing. Didn't I ever look at the newspapers, for God's sake? Didn't I realize that millions of people were being given money by the government for doing no work at all?

Devoted to Roosevelt, I made the usual New Deal arguments children picked up on the streets.

"You'll live to curse the day Franklin Roosevelt was born," he told me.

Afterwards I shouldered my magazines and trudged off to work, and Uncle Charlie poured himself another cup of coffee, rolled a new cigarette, and stretched out on the sofa to reread *The Federalist Papers*. For the longest time I thought of Republicans as people who rose from twelve-hour stretches in bed to denounce idlers and then lie down with a good book.

Uncle Charlie, of course, only wanted to improve my

education. It pained him to see me wasting good reading time on Zane Grey's westerns and the Oz tales. His own favorite book was *The Autobiography of Benjamin Franklin*. It was one of three books that made up the parlor library, the other two being a Funk & Wagnall's dictionary and the Bible, and Uncle Charlie reread the *Autobiography* frequently.

Catching me one day in the parlor reading *The Land of Oz*, he spoke to me angrily, which was very rare. "For God's sake, Russell, you've got a good mind and you're destroying it reading that trash. Here"—and he thrust Franklin's *Autobiography* at me—"read something worthwhile." I read until he left the room, then put it aside in boredom.

The hostility Uncle Hal nursed toward Uncle Charlie had nothing to do with politics but a good deal to do with *The Autobiography of Benjamin Franklin*. It's doubtful Uncle Hal had ever read a book from cover to cover. He was a man of large entrepreneurial vision. People who pursued the intellectual life as single-mindedly as Uncle Charlie outraged his belief that it was a man's duty to make something of himself by scoring big in business.

Talking was Uncle Hal's chief entertainment, and talking to Uncle Charlie was out of the question. When Uncle Hal wanted to talk, Uncle Charlie was in bed. Or worse, Uncle Charlie had his nose buried in a book. Idled for weeks, alone for endless hours with nothing to do but roam the sidewalks and prowl the house, Uncle Hal needed Uncle Charlie to listen to him talk, and Uncle Charlie was deaf to his need. If he listened at all, it was with impatience or maybe a curt sneer—"Quit talking baloney, Colonel"—for Uncle Charlie was contemptuous of Uncle Hal's great plans.

In the kitchen one afternoon I heard Aunt Pat complaining to Uncle Charlie about so many cracks in her dishes. "Maybe the Colonel will buy a new set when his deal goes through," she said.

Uncle Charlie snorted. "Don't get your hopes up," he said. "That guy's been a faker all his life."

I began noticing that Uncle Charlie's eyes became hooded and that he rubbed his chin with his fingertips when Uncle Hal launched on his suppertime stories. I'd learned to recognize the hooded eyes and the chin rubbing as signs that Uncle Charlie thought I was talking nonsense when I discussed Roosevelt with him. Now I saw that he thought the same thing about Uncle Hal's stories. I began listening to Uncle Hal's stories in a different way, the way Uncle Charlie must have been listening to them. Watching Uncle Charlie measure his big brother, I was myself learning to measure older men with a more complex gauge than I had used before.

I began to perceive that Uncle Hal's stories always portrayed him as the soul of manly chivalry. One evening at supper he told a story illustrating his refusal to tolerate the insolence of the lower classes. Its villain was a tough lout in Richmond who had spat insultingly in the dust at Uncle Hal's feet. The man was a brute, not worth a gentleman's thrashing with fists, though Uncle Hal said he could have given him a thrashing easily enough.

"I've taken boxing lessons, you know. From a retired prize-fighter, and he showed me how to kill a man with my fists."

This was not a case for extreme punishment, though.

"I didn't do a thing but take off my belt—"

Rising from the table, Uncle Hal yanked his belt off to illustrate.

"—and doubled it up in my hand like this—"

He showed how to turn the belt into a weapon.

"—and then I laid that belt across the side of his head like that—"

A mighty whack against the kitchen wall.

"—and he took off running. Not a word out of him, by God. He knew, by God, I'd kill him if he so much as turned around and looked at me."

I had been changed by Uncle Charlie's influence. Under its power, I was losing childhood's innocent credulity and beginning to realize that adults had weaknesses too. That night I knew there wasn't a grain of truth in Uncle Hal's story.

Uncle Hal, who was nobody's fool after all, must have seen all along that Uncle Charlie knew he'd been "a faker all his life." It must have been hard to forgive Uncle Charlie for knowing that and for showing that he knew it.

Coming in from school one afternoon I walked into the parlor and saw Uncle Hal towering over Uncle Charlie in a rage. "Get on your feet if you call yourself a man, because I'm going to beat the Goddamn living hell out of you." It was an astonishing scene in our house. Everything associated with Uncle Allen's house was opposed to violence and abusive language.

Uncle Charlie, seated in an armchair, had been rereading *The Autobiography of Benjamin Franklin*, which now lay on the floor where it had landed when Uncle Hal knocked it out of his hands just before I came in. I had heard the thud. It was hard to tell what had provoked him. He was in the prizefighter's crouch now, fists ready and moving.

"Get up out of that chair, you little weakling. I'm going to give you the beating of your life."

Uncle Charlie did not rise. He had seen me enter the room quietly behind Uncle Hal, and he spoke calmly.

"What do you want, Russell?"

Startled, Uncle Hal turned, saw me, dropped his fists, and departed quietly, obviously embarrassed because I had caught him behaving childishly. I judged that my entrance saved Uncle Charlie, for he weighed scarcely half as much as Uncle Hal and had been training too long on Bull Durham and coffee to have much of a chance against the Colonel.

Never mind. Uncle Hal had a plan to get rid of Uncle Charlie once and for all. He would ship Uncle Charlie so far that he would never be able to come back. San Francisco was the place he had in mind. In San Francisco there was yet another brother. This was my Uncle Willie. I had never met Uncle Willie. He was two years older than my mother, and as children she and Uncle Willie had been especially fond of each other. "Of all the boys at home," my mother told me, "Willie was always my favorite. Willie was fun."

Uncle Willie had "disappeared" in 1924 and stayed lost to the family until 1935. After a brief, tumultuous marriage in the early 1920s, he had walked out on his wife one day in Washington and told nobody his whereabouts. Eleven years later my mother finally traced him to San Francisco, where he was living alone and working for a California state tax agency. He proved to be as fond of my mother as she was of him, and when he learned how things were with her and Uncle Allen he began sending her a regular monthly share of his salary.

Upon learning that Willie was prosperous enough to share his income, Uncle Hal decided that Uncle Willie should do even more. He wrote him a letter detailing the burdens Uncle Charlie's joblessness placed upon Uncle Allen. In his role as senior brother and administrative director of the family, Uncle Hal suggested it was Uncle Willie's duty to relieve Allen of that burden. In short, since Willie was living alone it would be easy for him to house his baby brother and help him find work. He, Hal, would put Uncle Charlie on the westward Greyhound as soon as Uncle Willie gave the go-ahead.

Uncle Hal let too much of his bile toward Uncle Charlie seep into the letter and disclosed too much about what he considered Uncle Charlie's antisocial character. "If Charlie is entirely dependent on Allen," Uncle Willie wrote back, "he is certainly not in a position to give rein to a temperamental or neurotic disposition. . . . If he is sound how can he be content to do nothing and see his widowed sister getting by on her own efforts? If I had anything I would be much more inclined to give it to Allen for all he has done for Lucy and Russell and Doris during the past five years. I believe that any normal person should rely on his own resources after reaching maturity."

Uncle Hal wrote again. Uncle Willie's reply this time courteously avoided asking why Uncle Hal didn't himself remove the intolerable Charlie burden from Uncle Allen. "Coming to California would merely make matters worse, I believe," he said. "The help I am giving Lucy takes all of my spare money. . . . I think Charlie would be much better situated in a small town than in a large city such as this. Lucy seems to be getting by on her own power, and if I remember correctly Charlie is thirty years old. It's time he was doing something for himself."

That was the end of another of the Colonel's plans.

Rebuffed from the west, he began hatching a scheme to ship Uncle Charlie south. Baltimore was the new place he had in mind, but this would be a more complex operation. It involved moving my mother, Doris, and me to Baltimore too. Uncle Hal had an idea to accomplish that. If he could establish a lumber company for himself with a branch office in Baltimore, he could encourage my mother to move and take Charlie with her by making her an officer of the company.

Baltimore—there was the solution. But to form his company he would require capital. The necessary sum, he thought, was about $150. Where could such a sum be found?

In my mother's bank account, of course. She was now earning better than $12 a week at the A&P Laundry and had been banking a little of her income for the past three years. Willie was also sending her money. Yes, she had money in the bank, all right. Perhaps as much as $150. That money was the key to everybody's future happiness. Pat and Allen could be free at last, Hal's new lumber company could spring into being, Uncle Charlie could be shipped south to start a productive life—if only Lucy could be persuaded to take her $150 from the dead hand of thrift banking and convert it into investment capital.

He began talking to her again about Baltimore. "It's time you and the children had a home of your own," he said.

He knew what her weakness was.

Chapter Nine

O FTEN, waking deep in the night, I heard them down in the kitchen talking, talking, talking. Sitting around the table under the unshaded light bulb, they talked the nights away, reheating the coffee, then making fresh coffee, then reheating the pot again, and talking, talking, talking. I would lie on my daybed half awake listening to the murmur of voices, the clatter of cups, the splash of water in the sink, the occasional burst of laughter, the warning voice saying, "Hold it down, you'll wake the children."

Now and then I could make out a distinct phrase or two. "Lucy, remember the time old Mr. Digges . . . ?" This was Uncle Charlie addressing my mother. "—reminds me of the time the cops arrested Jim over in Jersey City." This was Uncle Allen retelling a story I'd heard many times. Uncle Hal's mellow drawl would come in: "—so I didn't do a thing but tell that dirty scoundrel, 'Man, don't you ever try—' " And I would drop off to sleep again, lulled by the comforting familiarity of those kitchen sounds.

At New Street we lived on coffee and talk. Talking was the great Depression pastime. Unlike the movies, talk was free, and a great river of talk flowed through the house, rising at suppertime, and cresting as my bedtime approached before subsiding into a murmur that trickled along past midnight, when all but Uncle Charlie had drifted off to bed, leaving him alone to reheat the pot, roll another cigarette, and settle down with his book.

If my homework was done, I could sit with them and listen until ten o'clock struck. I loved the sense of family warmth that radiated through those long kitchen nights of talk. There were many chords resonating beneath it, and though I could not identify them precisely, I was absorbing a sense of them and storing them away in memory. There was longing for happy times now lost, and dreaming about what might have been. There was fantasy, too, which revealed itself in a story to which they returned again and again, about the time Papa made his wonderful trip to England in search of the family's great lost fortune.

Nothing I heard in the kitchen astonished me more than the story of the great lost fortune, for if the story was true it meant that we were all rightfully entitled to be rich. I heard it told over and over again until I knew it thoroughly. How the Robinson family—Uncle Allen's family, my mother's family, *my* family—descended from a fabulously rich old Bishop of London back in the time of Marlborough and Queen Anne. How the bishop had willed his fortune to his Virginia kin, and Papa was the direct descendant.

For some reason—they were always vague on this point—nobody had got around to collecting the fortune from England until two hundred years later when Papa thought of it and went to England to recover it.

"How much do you think it was worth, Allen?" Aunt Pat asked one night when the story was being retold.

"Probably a million dollars in today's money," he said. "It would have been sitting there for hundreds of years just accumulating."

"More like fifty or sixty million," Uncle Hal said.

"Well, it's all water over the dam now," my mother said. Of all of them, she was the least inclined to mourn for life's might-have-beens. "If the Lord meant me to be rich, he'd have made me rich," she told me when I commiserated with her once about the great lost fortune.

It was lost all right. After making inquiries in London, Papa was told it had "reverted to the Crown" and become the property of King and Empire.

"Reverted to the Crown, my eye!" Aunt Pat snorted.

None of them doubted that the family fortune had been finagled into English bank accounts by British connivers. The British were heartily disliked and distrusted at New Street. Uncle Charlie spoke for all when he said, "Those dirty cusses are always out to hoodwink an American."

My excitement about the great lost fortune was dampened by Doris when, grousing one evening about having to sell magazines, I said, "If Mama's father had got the family fortune, I wouldn't have to work."

"You don't believe that baloney, do you?" she replied.

I quit believing it then and there. No nine-year-old girl was going to beat me at skepticism. After that I always smiled inwardly when they started talking about the great lost fortune, and for the first time I began to feel superior to them in a small way. The tale of the great lost fortune was only a minor ingredient in their talk, though. Usually I listened uncritically, for around that table, under the unshaded light bulb, I was receiving an education in the world and how to think about it. What I absorbed most deeply was not information but attitudes, ways of looking at the world that were to stay with me for many years.

Sometimes their talk about the Depression was shaded with anger, but its dominant tones were good humor and civility. The anger was never edged with bitterness or self-pity. Most often it was expressed as genial contempt toward business, labor, government, and all the salesmen of miracle cures for the world's ailments. Communists were "crackpots" and "bomb throwers." Father Coughlin and Huey Long were "rabble-rousers." The German-American Bund with its Nazi swastikas, "a bunch of sausage stuffers." Benito Mussolini, "the top Wop." Not even the New Deal escaped. In Belleville, men on the government's W.P.A.

payroll were usually seen leaning on shovels. The initials W.P.A., Uncle Allen said, stood for "We Poke Along."

Besides politics, they talked about movies, philosophy, and morals. Methods for banking a coal furnace. How to outwit the electric company by putting in meter "cheaters." About their high-school Latin teacher, Professor Brent, who'd known Woodrow Wilson. About Wilson himself, who was "a good man, but an idealist." About the rotten deal Herbert Hoover had given the boys who fought in France. They debated the relative merits of crooners—Bing Crosby v. Rudy Vallee. They spun humorous tales about relatives long dead. Argued about baseball. Joked about Roosevelt's "brain trust." Reminisced about the time ancient Aunt Henrietta was mistaken for a ghost by two carpenters and scared them so badly they jumped out the second-floor window.

They also talked about Cousin Edwin who had made something of himself in a big way.

"I hear Edwin's making $80,000 a year," Uncle Allen said one evening. "I always knew he'd amount to something. Edwin had sort of a way about him."

"Edwin was the worst tease I ever knew," my mother said. "And mean! He could say the meanest things to you."

"Edwin had plenty of nerve though," Uncle Allen said. "Did you ever hear how he got his first newspaper job? It was a paper in Pittsburgh, I think, and Edwin went in for an interview with the editor. The editor looked at him and said, 'Young man, how do I know you're not a damned fool?' And Edwin said, 'That's a chance we'll both have to take.' They gave him the job on the spot."

Edwin was their first cousin. Though he'd grown up near them in Virginia, they hadn't seen him in twenty years and didn't expect ever to see him again. He had achieved success on the monumental scale. "Edwin's no more going to visit his poor relatives than I'm going to walk on water," my mother said.

"You've got to realize, Lucy, Edwin's a big man," said Uncle Allen, who had no envy in him.

By New Street measures, Edwin was a big man indeed. Since

Edwin James, at the dawn of his career.

1932 he had been managing editor of the *New York Times*. I was only slightly impressed. I had seen the *New York Times*. Uncle Allen loyally bought it every Sunday because it was Edwin's paper. It was the dullest excuse for a newspaper I'd ever seen.

"Why doesn't it have any funny papers?" I asked one Sunday after declining Uncle Allen's offer to look at it.

"Because it's a real newspaper," he said. "All it prints is the news, and funny papers aren't news."

Cousin Edwin wrote a column on affairs of state which ran every Sunday in the *Times*. One Sunday Uncle Allen opened to Cousin Edwin's column and beckoned to me. "Look here," he said. "When you get your name printed there like your cousin Edwin you'll be able to say you've made something of yourself."

There, over a mass of gray print I read that great name set down in large bold type: "By Edwin L. James." On Sunday afternoons, Edwin's column was a leaden family duty that filled the parlor. Aunt Pat, bustling in from the kitchen, would ask Uncle Allen, "Have you read Edwin's column yet, Dad?"

"Not yet. I gave it to Charlie."

Uncle Charlie had always read it. My mother never had. "I'll get to it later. Let Hal read it," she said.

Uncle Hal, the sense of family obligation sitting strong upon him, would pick it up and after a paragraph or two say, "Edwin always had a good way of expressing himself," and lay it down casually and say, "I remember the time Aunt Sallie brought Edwin over to visit Mama and . . ."

Then, interrupting his reminiscence, he handed the paper to Aunt Pat, saying, "Here, Pat, take it out in the kitchen with you and read it while you're making dinner."

"Oh, you read it first, Lucy," Aunt Pat would say to my mother.

"I'm too busy right now," my mother would say, "but don't lose it."

In this way Cousin Edwin's column passed from hand to hand unread by all but Uncle Charlie, until, late in the afternoon, Uncle Allen settled himself in his favorite chair, opened the *Times* wide and began to read. If Doris or I spoke too loudly Aunt Pat said, "*Sh*, dear, Uncle Allen's reading Edwin's column."

It was hard for me to see what Uncle Allen was doing behind the wall of newspaper, but I suspected there was little reading. One Sunday I watched the paper fall gently back over his face, then saw it rise and fall gently in rhythm with his breathing, and after a few moments heard a satisfied snore rumbling under the newsprint. Awakened by his own snoring, Uncle Allen let the paper fall to his lap and, seeing me grinning at him, gave me a small guilty smile.

"Edwin's a big man," he said, "but he sure can write some dull stuff."

When my mother talked of me making something of myself, Cousin Edwin was one of the models of success she had in mind. Her childhood memories of Edwin were not formidable.

"Edwin James wasn't any smarter than anybody else," she assured me, "and look where he is today. If Edwin could do it, so can you."

If she really believed this, I did not. I was eleven years old and consumed with timidity and a sense of my own incompetence. I attributed my success at school entirely to my mother's school-teacher insistence on good grades and her constant help with my studies. My career selling magazines had convinced me I had no future in business enterprises, and I had recently had a brief fling at music which had shattered my self-confidence.

A door-to-door salesman had come to the house one day selling banjo lessons at bargain prices. For a trivial sum, he told my mother, he would rent me a banjo and enroll me in a new academy of musical instruction being formed in the neighboring town of Nutley. My mother was not naive enough to imagine that music could lead to riches, but my business skills had been fully tested and found wanting by now, and it wouldn't cost much to gamble on an outside chance. The salesman wanted a down payment of one dollar on the banjo rental. Lessons would be fifty cents each. Well, every civilized man ought to know a little something about music, she reasoned.

I took my rented banjo to the Nutley musical academy. It was a small single-family house. The rooms were empty except for two dozen folding wooden chairs. Eight or nine other students turned up, we took our seats, and a burly red-headed man sat on the parlor windowsill and illustrated the use of the banjo pick. It was a humbling experience.

I had expected the banjo to sound like a guitar. I knew what a guitar sounded like, because Aunt Pat listened every day to a radio show called "Tito Guizar and His Spanish Guitar." I'd thought that after a few lessons in Nutley I'd be strolling around the house making guitar music and singing the way Tito Guizar did about Conchita, the fair senorita, and moonlight over Granada. Lessons were given once a week. After the first half dozen I knew the banjo and I were hopelessly mismated.

One evening at home somebody asked to hear a little banjo music. Uncle Allen, who had a passion for the Grand Ole Opry, was especially persistent. I argued that it was too soon for a public performance, but my mother refused to listen. There was no getting out of it. I sat on a kitchen chair and began stabbing the banjo pick at the strings. Now and then I hit one.

When the performance was over, Aunt Pat, speaking very softly, murmured, "Sweet mother of God!"

Uncle Allen didn't say anything, but his mouth was firmly locked in the shut position to keep him from bursting into laughter. My mother didn't say anything either. For a long while she seemed to be thinking. Then she said, "Buddy, don't feel bad. There's more to life than playing the banjo."

But what?

At this time I had decided the only thing I was fit for was to be a writer, and this notion rested solely on my suspicion that I would never be fit for real work, and that writing didn't require any. My mother didn't try to discourage me, though writing was not a career just then that many ambitious parents encouraged their children to plan for.

"Writing runs in the family," she said. And it seemed to. Her mother had written poetry in the manner of Tennyson. One of her uncles had written for the *Baltimore American;* with a little more luck Uncle Charlie might have had a career on the *Brooklyn Eagle;* and Cousin Edwin was proof that writing, when done for newspapers, could make a man as rich as Midas.

"Look where Edwin James is today. If Edwin could do it, you can do it." I heard those words again and again while we toiled together over seventh-grade English homework. She pounced like a tigress if she spotted an error in spelling or grammar, and she spotted many. I was not a sparkling writer. Once, assigned to write a composition about farm produce, I chose to write about wheat. In seventh grade they were always assigning you to write about things like farm produce. I chose to write about wheat, maybe because it seemed less boring than turnips and was easier to spell than rutabagas. My mother examined the finished product in despair.

"You can do better than this, Buddy," she said.

I didn't know how. Wheat was not Carl Hubbell pitching against Dizzy Dean at the Polo Grounds or James Cagney walking the last mile to the electric chair—subjects which fascinated me. Wheat was just—wheat. But she was insistent. She found an old geography book preserved from her teaching days for just such an emergency as this. It contained a fine discussion of wheat. I cribbed it furiously, but still failed to satisfy her. She scratched out lines, changed words, added a paragraph or two of her own, then had me rewrite it neatly. The result contained hardly a word or thought from my version.

The teacher was delighted with it. She read it aloud to my classmates. They were unmoved, but I preened shamelessly in the honor of having it read aloud as my own work. The teacher was so pleased she sent it to the *Belleville News* for possible publication as an example of the fine work being done in the school system. Several weeks later, buried inside the newspaper under the one-word headline WHEAT, this composition ran on for five or six paragraphs. At the top were the words "By Russell Baker." It was my first appearance in print. It had been ghost-written by my mother. She bought several copies of the paper, clipped out "Wheat," put

123

a few copies of it in the mail to distant relatives, and stored two in her trunk. She had produced a budding contender for Cousin Edwin's crown of glory.

"Look where Edwin James is today—"

I did look now and then. Edwin was in New York, and from certain places in Belleville I could look out and see the top of the New York skyline piercing the far horizon. I lacked artistic inclination and had no eye for beauty, but, making my magazine rounds on roller skates, when I reached a hilltop vista which looked far out over the Hackensack Meadows, I loved to sit and stare at that fantasy rising miles and miles away through the mists. From that distance it seemed to me as dreamlike as the Emerald City of Oz. I was sitting there daydreaming late one autumn afternoon when Walter came along to beat me up.

I had been beaten up three or four times in the past by Walter for not being Irish. On the first occasion he'd caught me on St. Patrick's Day not wearing a green necktie and bruised my ribs. Since then he'd fallen into the habit of beating me up whenever our paths crossed. The second time, figuring he hated me for not being Irish, I tried to buy peace by telling him my Aunt Pat was Irish, but it didn't satisfy him. He seemed to feel a patriotic Hibernian duty to bully me whenever we accidentally met. The result was I hated Walter and had begun to hate everything Irish, though I made an exception for Aunt Pat.

The strange thing about Walter was that he was an absolute loner. Usually you didn't have to worry about being beaten up unless you ran afoul of a whole gang. Gangs seemed to lust for battle, but a boy you didn't know never gave any trouble if he was traveling alone. Except for Walter. Walter always traveled alone. He hadn't a friend in the world so far as I could make out. I never saw him playing with a crowd on an empty lot or heading off to the movies with a pal. He went to the Catholic school in Belleville, and I had some friends there too, but I never saw them in company with Walter. Short, red-haired, not much taller than a fireplug but just as solid, he prowled the streets, taciturn and alone, looking for blood. Now, finding me sitting on the hilltop admiring the Manhattan skyline, he said, "Get up and fight."

It was no use trying to jolly Walter out of it. I'd tried that, too, but genial talk didn't interest him. He didn't seem to have any talk in him, just grunts and a few basic lines he'd picked up from movies about tough guys. Still, I didn't get up off the ground. It was dishonorable to hit a man while he was on the ground.

I tried wheedling. "What'd'ya always want to fight for?"

"I don't like your looks," he said.

This was a line I recognized from many tough-guy movies. "I got skates on," I said. "You can't fight with skates on."

Walter bent over, grabbed me by my shirt, pulled me upright, and punched me in the stomach, and I went down again. Since he had now knocked me down from the standing position he was entitled to fall on me and pummel away, and he did, but only around my ribs and stomach. Walter had never punched me in the jaw, nose, or face, which was another strange thing about him. Most street fighters wanted to blacken your eye or bloody your nose. Not Walter. He preferred punishing the torso. I concentrated on trying to push him off me, but he was solid rock. Suddenly I felt his weight being lifted away.

Looking up, I saw my three best friends—Frankie, Nino, and Jerry—taking Walter in hand.

"What's the idea hitting a guy with skates on?" Frankie demanded. "You ought to have your teeth knocked out for that kind of fighting."

Any one of them could have done it, too, even to Walter. Or so I thought, for I envied their rippling muscularity. Sons of Italian immigrants, they'd befriended me in the classroom, taken me home to meet their parents, placed me under their protection in the schoolyard, and even engineered my election as president of our homeroom class. Aunt Pat referred to them when they weren't around as "Russell's beloved wops." The slur angered me toward her, but it was true that the affection I felt for them was close to love. Their friendship had brought me to a love of all things

Italian, as Walter's bullying had caused me to hate all things Irish.

Just now, though, I had a serious problem. Although they had Walter under restraint, there was no possibility they would do what I wished they'd do and beat him senseless. This would violate the code of honor, just as Walter had violated it by hitting me with my skates on. Frankie, Nino, and Jerry weren't there to avenge me by pounding Walter black and blue but to see that the rules of honor were observed.

"We'll hold him while you get your skates off, then we'll see if he can fight clean," Frankie announced.

This was grim news. I knew too well how effectively Walter could fight, even fighting clean. I didn't mind being beaten, I was used to that with Walter, but I hated the idea of being humiliated in front of my friends. Still, Frankie was our leader, and his decision was law. I didn't dare let him see I was too timid to fight Walter.

The truth was, I was always too timid to fight. I hated fighting and did it badly because I lacked the appetite for inflicting pain. I couldn't bear to cause pain. This weakness went back to my earliest childhood in Morrisonville, when, climbing on the back-yard fence one day, I stepped to the ground without looking and crushed a newborn chick under my foot. I'd screamed at the horror of it and wept for an hour in spite of my mother's assurances that it was all right, I didn't mean to do it, there were plenty of other new chicks, it happened all the time.

I'd developed a loathing for violence that made me an easy victim for the world's Walters. Now Frankie's interference meant I would have to go at Walter with the violence necessary to make it a good fight or be thought a sissy by my friends. Hating Walter's taciturn Irish stupidity for getting me into this, I unstrapped my skates, got to my feet, and balled my hands into fists.

"You ready now?" Frankie asked.

"Yeah, let him loose."

Frankie shoved Walter at me and stepped back. Freed, Walter raised his fists and started to circle as we'd seen actors do in movies about boxers. Then he dropped his fists.

"Not fair fighting four against one," Walter said.

"We're not fighting," Nino said.

"We're just watching," Frankie said.

Walter looked at the three of them.

"It's not fair watching," he said.

"Fight!" Frankie commanded, and gave him another push.

"Watching's not fair," Walter howled.

"What'r'ya, yella?" Jerry shouted.

"Not yellow," said Walter, and he got his fists up again and looked at me with an expression I'd never seen before when he was calmly beating me. Then we had been punisher and victim locked silently in idiot's solitude. Now he was plainly scared as sick as I was.

We circled each other listlessly, and one of them—Nino or Jerry—yelled to me, "Hit him! He's yellow!" and for the first time I knew the pleasure of feeling like the brute in battle. I lunged forward and swung as hard as I could at Walter's face. My fist caught him across the mouth and nose. He cried out. There was blood on his mouth and chin.

"All right," he shouted, "all right," and dropped his fists in the recognized signal of surrender. Still, certain words had to be spoken.

"You give up?" I asked.

"Give up," he said.

The code also required certain civilities once the fight was over.

"Somebody give him a handkerchief," Frankie said. "His nose is bleeding."

I gave him mine. Walter clamped it over his nose and walked off the field alone and silent. I didn't tell Frankie, but I knew Walter could have whipped me easily if they hadn't destroyed his solitude. After that, though, he never waylaid me again.

My mother didn't like my being so close to Italian boys. For one thing, friendship with Italians wasn't likely to help me make something of myself, since in Belleville Italians stood at the bottom of society. Their community, clustered on "The Hill" at the top of the town, was made up mostly of poor immigrants from southern Italy and Sicily. Though most of my classmates were native-born Americans and spoke English in the streets, they spoke Italian in their homes to parents who clung to the dialects of Naples, Calabria, and Palermo. When I first began to be accepted on The Hill, I marveled that people could talk and understand each other in sounds as meaningless to me as hen cackles. It seemed wonderful that Frankie and Nino could shift so easily from English into a language that was totally beyond me. To my mother this was not a miracle but cause for alarm.

"My God, Russell, they don't even speak the English language up there," she said once when I told her I'd been visiting on The Hill.

We quarreled off and on about the Italian problem. She never forbade me to run with Frankie or Nino or Jerry or Carmen or Joe, but for the longest time she tried by wily arts to break those friendships.

If I was off to the Saturday movies with Frankie and Nino she might say, "Why don't you ever go with any nice boys?"

I knew what she meant by "nice boys"—boys who were not Italian—and the sly knife-thrust of her bigotry infuriated me. Still, I was not cheeky enough to come back at her with the question that had formed in my mind: "How can you go to church every Sunday and talk about loving your neighbor when you hate my friends because they're Italian?"

Instead I took the mild tack—"I'm sorry you don't like my friends"—which produced another twist of the knife:

"I'm not saying I don't like your friends, Buddy. You've got a right to pick your own friends, but remember—a man is known by the company he keeps."

Most likely she didn't actually hate my friends because they were Italian; she was probably just angry at me for choosing friends who couldn't pass muster in the world of people who had made something of themselves. Maybe, in a way she didn't understand, she was angry at them, too, for being as poor as we were and so far down on the social ladder. In this quarrel, though, I had detected for the first time a flaw in her character. I didn't know the word "hypocrisy," but this was the crime I silently charged her with. She insisted we go to church to improve my character, and it angered me that she should slip disgracefully from the gospel of brotherly love after the Sunday singing and praying were over and brotherly love was put to the test of daily life. Until now she had done all the improving on me; now I tried my hand on her. Determined to bring her around on the Italian question, I found ways of luring my friends to the New Street house when I knew she'd be home. This was not easy, but gradually I persuaded Nino and Frankie to come by and sit on our porch steps, and after a while I got them to enter the house.

Their introduction to my mother was a triumph. Frankie, whose manly power to charm women was always impressive, received the highest accolade in my mother's power. "He's just like Tom Sawyer," she said. Frankie had won her over by telling her I was the smartest person in school.

I envied his skill at manipulating women. When he was eleven he was already a seducer of women. In the schoolyard at recess one day Nino and Jerry took me aside for thrilling news: Frankie had made a date to kiss Katherine Filler after school in Belleville Park. Katherine was no wanton trull but a lean chestnut-haired beauty, and smart to boot. It was Katherine, not I, who was the smartest person in school. That this beautiful brilliant creature could offer herself for kissing was more than I could believe. I marveled that Frankie even had the nerve to ask her. Nevertheless, it was the honest-to-God truth, he whispered to me as we lined up to go back to class. He had asked and she had said yes. She would meet him at four o'clock that afternoon on a park bench in a secluded grove where the kiss would take place.

Nino and Jerry had asked if they could watch, and Frankie had said yes. I could watch too, he said. Well before the agreed time, the four of us arrived at the rendezvous point.

"I don't think she'd go for it if she knows you guys are looking," Frankie told us while we all hovered over the bench. "It'd be better if you hide in the bushes."

There was good cover in the bushes. Nino, Jerry, and I burrowed in to wait. After a while, sure enough, Katherine came along the path and joined Frankie at the park bench. They didn't speak a word. Katherine sat down and Frankie sat beside her. Still not a word out of either one of them. They sat very still for what seemed a long time, then Frankie abruptly placed an arm around her shoulder, and she turned to face him and offered her lips. A second later she rose and walked briskly away.

We hadn't been able to see from our position whether the kiss had actually happened, but when Frankie told us it was safe to come out, he swore it had.

"What's it like? I asked.

"It tastes like chewing gum," Frankie said.

I admired Frankie's courage but was shocked that a nice girl like Katherine would engage in lovemaking. In the movies women were always making love, but I never thought of movie women as real. The things they did had no connection with life as I knew it. The idea that a real girl of my own age, a girl I'd always admired, might actually want to make love—that was a revelation hard to absorb.

The one phase of my education my mother had not pressed vigorously was sex. How, after all, could a woman take the man of the family aside and tell him about the birds and the bees? With her old-fashioned Protestant views of life, sex was not a subject civilized people discussed openly around the house. It was hard enough for a father to explain these things to a son. For a mother of her character it was simply impossible.

I heard in school from friends whose parents had told them about sex, and I had picked up enough information about it to realize it would be terribly embarrassing to have to listen to an explanation from my mother. I dreaded the possibility she might try. When she called to me from another room, as she often did, and said, "Come in here, Russ, there's something I want to talk to you about," I was in terror that this was the awful moment when she was going to tell me about sex.

I was saved by Aunt Pat's brother, a young man named Jack

who lived in Hoboken but came to New Street frequently for visits of two or three days. "Uncle Jack," I called him, and I admired him outrageously. He was dark, handsome, athletic, and led a life, I thought, of romantic swashbuckling. He had boxed professionally in preliminary three-rounders over in Hoboken and told me he was billed as "The Hoboken Tiger." He'd taken me to Hoboken a couple of times and introduced me to people he knew on street corners, suggesting they were dangerous men. He'd thrilled me by saying, after we'd passed the time with one such street-corner bunch, "Those guys are killers."

Aunt Pat cautioned me not to believe anything Uncle Jack told me, but I admired him anyhow.

"Uncle Jack is really tough, isn't he?" I said one day.

"He's not tough, he just needs a shave," Aunt Pat replied.

This was probably true, for he usually did need a shave, and about this time he had given up boxing and was trying to sell vacuum cleaners door-to-door on commission.

An evening when he, my mother, Aunt Pat, and I were in the kitchen, the conversation came around to a neighbor who had just had a baby. I made the mistake of saying something that indicated I was curious about where babies came from. Uncle Jack looked at my mother.

"Doesn't he know about *that* yet?" he asked.

No, she said, she hadn't gotten around to *that* yet.

"Why don't I take him upstairs and tell him?" he suggested.

She must have felt an immense sense of relief. "I think it's about time somebody did," she said.

Uncle Jack looked at me gravely. "Go upstairs," he said. "There's something I want to talk to you about alone."

I went. I was in a dreadful state of mind. The awful moment had come at last. I was going to be told "the facts of life." That was how everybody referred to sex—"the facts of life." Nobody ever called it "sex." To call it "sex" was to talk dirty. Upstairs I dropped onto the daybed to await the worst.

Uncle Jack was slow in arriving, and, when he finally did come up, he didn't seem to be too easy in his own mind. He looked at me and then walked across the room and looked out the window. Then he paced silently for a minute or two.

Finally: "You think the Giants can win the pennant this year?" he asked.

"Well, they've got Carl Hubbell, who's the best pitcher in the League, and if Mel Ott hits .350, and if . . ."

And on and on I went in a happy torrent of arcane baseball speculation.

"Yeah," Uncle Jack said, "but it don't make any difference who wins in the National League because nobody's going to beat the Yankees in the World Series."

"Don't be so sure. Who've the Yankees got as good as Mel Ott?"

"They've got Lou Gehrig, they've got Bill Dickey, they've got this kid DiMaggio, they've got . . ."

We were slowly exhausting baseball. Uncle Jack went back to the window and looked out again, then turned to face me.

"Look here," he said, "you know how babies are made, don't you?"

"Sure," I said.

"Well that's all there is to it," he said.

"I know that," I said.

"I thought you did," he said.

"Sure," I said.

"Let's go on back downstairs," he said.

We went downstairs together.

"Did you tell him?" my mother asked.

"Everything," Uncle Jack said.

I could have fainted with relief. Uncle Jack probably felt the same way. So did my mother, I'm sure. That was my formal sex education. My informal education had begun the afternoon in Belleville Park when I discovered that girls were wantons willing to sneak away to shaded glades to be kissed. It was to continue for many years to come, but not in Belleville.

My time in Belleville, where I was happy and made good friends and learned that adults were also flawed, was coming to an end. Uncle Hal, who needed my mother's capital to help fund his projected lumber company, had her mesmerized now with the prospect of "a home of our own" in Baltimore.

Yes, she told him, she was dying to get out of Belleville, and Baltimore was the place that called her, Baltimore was the place of possibilities she remembered from her childhood. When she was a girl in Virginia, Baltimore had always been the great city at the end of the steamboat trips Papa took from Merry Point. Papa and Mama had been married in Baltimore. Once or twice she had ridden the steamboat with Papa to Baltimore and walked among those glittering lights and swirling crowds holding Papa's hand and gaping at the wonder of it.

Now there were people she knew living in Baltimore. Several of my father's people, people she had known in Morrisonville, had made the Depression migration from farm to town and found work in Baltimore. Among them was my father's sister. My mother had always liked her. Her name was Selba, but no one had called her by that name since her infancy. The only daughter among twelve sons, she had been "Sister" from earliest childhood and seemed to have no other name. To me she was "Aunt Sister." My mother had twice taken the Greyhound to Baltimore to visit Aunt Sister. They found they liked each other. Aunt Sister was particularly fond of Doris, and during the past two summers my mother had sent Doris to Baltimore to spend vacations with her.

Uncle Hal designed a plan to catch my mother's fancy. She would move Doris, me, and Uncle Charlie to Baltimore. Aunt Sister would find an apartment for us. With Uncle Charlie to handle the household chores and look after Doris and me, my mother would be free to take a job temporarily. Uncle Hal would go to Richmond and set up his company funded with her capital. He would make her an officer of the company; her income from the investment would supplement her other earnings until the company generated enough profit to let her quit working. After the lumber business began to prosper—Easy Street.

To start his company Uncle Hal wanted her to put up $100 from her bank account. She wasn't totally credulous about Uncle

133

Hal's ability to put us on Easy Street. A student of human frailty, she probably knew deep in her soul that he was one of life's losers. Still, she wanted that "home of our own" so desperately. She took a huge gamble. If he was asking for $100, she reasoned, he could probably make do with $75. That's what she gave him.

The Colonel instantly launched plans to proceed to Richmond and set up business. Before leaving, he sat in the parlor at New Street and wrote her his receipt for $75, "same to be invested by me, B. H. Robinson, in walnut timber, in the name of E. Baker & Co. of Belleville, N.J., which sum she is to receive . . ."

It went on and on, finally stating that if he died she was to receive "all proceeds" accruing to the company, "both gross and net."

In Richmond he plunged into action by ordering stationery. The letterhead said:

The Robinson Lumber Company
Dealers in Figured Walnut and Exporters
of Walnut Logs
B. H. Robinson, President & Treasurer

There was no mention of E. Baker & Co. of Belleville, N.J., but my mother didn't mind. She was too delighted about the prospect of "a home of our own." Arriving home from the A&P Laundry one October evening in 1936, she wrote him:

"Russell just said to me, 'Mama, don't you ever get tired? You keep going all the time,' and it's certainly true, but I have lots of pep and I'm working hard because I feel as though I have something to work for now. I pray for you each and every day and I'm hoping with all my heart that you succeed for your own sake as much as my own. I've often said the happiest day of my life would be when I knew I had punched that old card in the A&P Laundry for the last time, and it begins to look as if that time is not so far distant. I'm hoping and praying we can go to Baltimore soon and have a home of our own once more. Oh, let it be soon!"

A month passed. Instead of an answer to her prayers, he wrote saying he needed another $25. She wrote back apologizing but insisting she didn't have it to send. By early December he had bad news. His plans had hit a snag. She would have to hold off the move to Baltimore, but she wasn't to worry. It was just one of those delays you ran into in business. He still hoped to meet her in Baltimore early in January.

Her patience with him was already exhausted.

"I don't understand your business," she wrote, "but I really don't see how you can hope to be able to go to Baltimore by the first of the year now. I have to do something and do it soon, so I'd like to know: if you don't find out anything definite by Christmas, could you let me have the $75 by the first of the year so I'd know I could depend on it. I'm getting out of here by the first of the year if I live and nothing happens."

Nothing happened in Richmond. He wrote her an apology. He was terribly pinched for money. Didn't have the full $75 to send her, but here was a little something—$10. "Well, every little bit helps," as she constantly said. And he hadn't cleaned her out completely. She had held back some money in her bank account. That December she told Uncle Allen we would be moving to Baltimore at the end of January.

Uncle Allen found an amiable neighbor named Walter who owned a rickety flatbed truck and would move our furniture to Baltimore for $20. He arrived after work on a Saturday to start the loading. My mother, Doris, and I were to take the overnight Greyhound and get to Baltimore early Sunday morning. Aunt Sister had already put the deposit down on an apartment.

I was tremendously excited by the prospect of an overnight bus trip to a new city and a new home, a home of our own, and especially happy about being rid of my job with the *Saturday Evening Post*. I had taken a last roller-skate tour of the old town. Frankie, Nino, Jerry, and Carmen came to the house to say their good-byes while Walter and Uncle Allen loaded our things on the truck and tied a sheet of canvas over them. When the truck lumbered away we still had hours to wait until time to go to the bus station in Newark. I put on my good clothes—a man dressed properly when he traveled—and stood outside the house eager to get away.

A few months earlier Aunt Pat had bought a badly used piano for a few dollars and put it in the parlor, on the theory that every civilized house ought to have a piano in the parlor, though neither she, Uncle Allen, nor Uncle Charlie played. I was standing on the sidewalk in the darkness when I heard piano music inside. Curious, because I'd never heard the piano played before, I went inside. Aunt Pat, Uncle Allen, Uncle Charlie, and Doris were sitting in the parlor, and my mother was at the piano wearing her dark suit and a small dark hat with a little veil that fell over her eyes, and she was playing "Rock of Ages."

I hadn't known she could play the piano. She wasn't playing very well, I guess, because she stopped occasionally and had to start over again. She concentrated intensely on the music, and the others in the room sat absolutely silently. My mother was facing me but didn't seem to see me. She seemed to be staring beyond me toward something that wasn't there. All the happy excitement died in me at that moment. Looking at my mother, so isolated from us all, I saw her for the first time as a person utterly alone.

Suddenly I hated to leave that house. Suddenly I realized I had been happy there. It had been six years since my mother had brought us to Uncle Allen and Aunt Pat to live for a few months until she could set up a home of our own. Now her youth had passed without a single triumph. She was in her fortieth year.

Chapter Ten

UNCLE Harold was famous for lying.

He had once been shot right between the eyes. He told me so himself. It was during World War I. An underaged boy, he had run away from home, enlisted in the Marine Corps, and been shipped to France, where one of the Kaiser's soldiers had shot him. Right between the eyes.

It was a miracle it hadn't killed him, and I said so the evening he told me about it. He explained that Marines were so tough they didn't need miracles. I was now approaching the age of skepticism, and though it was risky business challenging adults, I was tempted to say, "Swear on the Bible?" I did not dare go this far, but I did get a hint of doubt into my voice by repeating his words as a question.

"Right between the eyes?"

"Right between the eyes," he said. "See this scar?"

He placed a finger on his forehead just above the bridge of his nose. "That's all the mark it left," he said.

"I don't see any scar," I said.

"It's probably faded by now," he said. "It's been a long time ago."

I said it must have hurt a good bit.

"Hurt! You bet it hurt."

"What did you do?"

"It made me so mad I didn't do a thing but pull out my pistol and kill that German right there on the spot."

At this point Aunt Sister came in from the kitchen with cups of cocoa. "For God's sake, Harold," she said, "quit telling the boy those lies."

People were always telling Uncle Harold for God's sake quit telling those lies. His full name was Harold Sharp, and in the family, people said, "That Harold Sharp is the biggest liar God ever sent down the pike."

Aunt Sister, Ida Rebecca's only daughter, had married him shortly after my mother took Doris and me from Morrisonville. He'd spent sixteen years in the Marines by then, but at Aunt Sister's insistence he gave up the Marine Corps and the two of them moved to Baltimore. There they had a small apartment on Hollins Street overlooking Union Square. Our place was a second-floor apartment on West Lombard Street just across the square. It was easy for my mother to stroll over to Aunt Sister's with Doris and me to play Parcheesi or Caroms or Pick-Up-Sticks with the two of them, but the real pleasure of these visits for me came from listening to Uncle Harold.

It didn't matter that my mother called him "the biggest liar God ever sent down the pike." In spite of his reputation for varnishing a fact, or maybe because of the outrageousness with which he did the varnishing, I found him irresistible. It was his intuitive refusal to spoil a good story by slavish adherence to fact that enchanted me. Though poorly educated, Uncle Harold somehow knew that the possibility of creating art lies not in reporting but in fiction.

He worked at cutting grass and digging graves for a cemetery in West Baltimore. This increased the romantic aura through which I saw him, for I had become fascinated with the Gothic

Uncle Harold in Paris.

aspects of death since arriving in Baltimore. In Baltimore, disposing of the dead seemed to be a major cultural activity. There were three funeral parlors within a one-block radius of our house, and a steady stream of hearses purred through the neighborhood. I had two other distant relatives from Morrisonville who had migrated to Baltimore, and both of them were also working in cemeteries. In addition, there was a fairly steady flow of corpses through our house on Lombard Street.

Our landlord there, a genial Lithuanian tailor who occupied the first floor, lent out his parlor to a young relative who was an undertaker and sometimes had an overflow at his own establishment. As a result there was often an embalmed body coffined lavishly in the first-floor parlor. Since our apartment could be reached only by passing the landlord's parlor, and since its double doors were always wide open, it seemed to me that instead of finding a home of our own, we had come to rest in a funeral home. Passing in and out of the house, I tried to avert my eyes from the garishly rouged bodies and hold my breath against inhaling the cloying odors of candle wax, tuberoses, and embalming fluid which suffused the hallway.

When Uncle Harold came over for an evening of card playing and found a corpse in the parlor, his imagination came alive. On one such evening I went down to let Aunt Sister and him in the front door. Noting the coffin in our landlord's parlor, Uncle Harold paused, strode into the room, nodded at the mourners, and examined the deceased stranger with professional scrutiny. Upstairs afterwards, playing cards at the dining-room table, Uncle Harold announced that the old gentleman in the coffin downstairs did not look dead to him.

"I could swear I saw one of his eyelids flicker," he said.

Nobody paid him any attention.

"You can't always be sure they're dead," he said.

Nobody was interested except me.

"A man I knew was almost buried alive once," he said.

"Are you going to play the jack or hold it all night?" my mother asked.

"It was during the war," Uncle Harold said. "In France. They were closing the coffin on him when I saw him blink one eye."

The cards passed silently and were shuffled.

"I came close to being buried alive myself one time," he said.

"For God's sake, Harold, quit telling those lies," Aunt Sister said.

"It's the truth, just as sure as I'm sitting here, so help me God," said Uncle Harold. "It happens every day. We dig them up out at the cemetery—to do autopsies, you know—and you can see they fought like the devil to get out after the coffin was closed on them, but it's too late by that time."

Uncle Harold was not a tall man, but the Marines had taught him to carry himself with a swaggering erect indolence and to measure people with the grave, cool arrogance of authority. Though he now shoveled dirt for a living, he was always immaculately manicured by the time he sat down to supper. In this polished man of the world—suits pressed to razor sharpness, every hair in place, eyes of icy gray self-confidence—I began to detect a hidden boy, in spirit not too different from myself, though with a love for mischief which had been subdued in me by too much melancholy striving to satisfy my mother's notions of manhood.

Admiring him so extravagantly, I was disappointed to find that he detested my hero, Franklin Roosevelt. In Uncle Harold's view, Roosevelt was a deep-dyed villain of the vilest sort. He had data about Roosevelt's shenanigans which newspapers were afraid to publish and occasionally entertained with hair-raising accounts of Rooseveltian deeds that had disgraced the Presidency.

"You know, I suppose, that Roosevelt only took the job for the money," he told me one evening.

"Does it pay a lot?"

"Not all that much," he said, "but there are plenty of ways of getting rich once you get in the White House, and Roosevelt's using all of them."

"How?"

"He collects money from everybody who wants to get in to see him."

"People have to give him money before he'll talk to them?"

"They don't give him the money face to face. He's too smart for that," Uncle Harold said.

"Then how does he get it?"

"There's a coat rack right outside his door, and he keeps an overcoat hanging on that rack. Before anybody can get in to see him, they've got to put money in the overcoat pocket."

I was shocked, which pleased Uncle Harold. "That's the kind of President you've got," he said.

"Do you know that for sure?"

"Everybody knows it."

"How do *you* know it?"

"A fellow who works at the White House told me how it's done."

This was such powerful stuff that as soon as I got home I passed it on to my mother. "Who told you that stuff?" she asked.

"Uncle Harold."

She laughed at my gullibility. "Harold Sharp is the biggest liar God ever sent down the pike," she said. "He doesn't know any more about Roosevelt than a hog knows about holiday."

Through Uncle Harold I first heard of H. L. Mencken. Mencken's house lay just two doors from Uncle Harold's place on Hollins Street. Uncle Harold pointed it out to me one day when we were walking around to the Arundel Ice Cream store for a treat. "You know who lives in that house, don't you?"

Of course I didn't.

"H. L. Mencken."

Who's H. L. Mencken?

"You mean to tell me you never heard of H. L. Mencken? He writes those pieces in the newspaper that make everybody mad," Uncle Harold said.

I understood from Uncle Harold's respectful tone that Mencken must be a great man, though Mencken's house did not look like the house of a great man. It looked very much like every other house in Baltimore. Red brick, white marble steps. "I saw

Mencken coming out of his house just the other day," Uncle Harold said.

It's doubtful Uncle Harold had ever read anything by Mencken. Uncle Harold's tastes ran to *Doc Savage* and *The Shadow*. Still, I could see he was proud of living so close to such a great man. It was a measure of how well he had done in life at a time when millions of other men had been broken by the Depression.

He had left home in 1917 for the Marines, an uneducated fifteen-year-old country boy from Taylorstown, a village not far from Morrisonville, just enough schooling to read and do arithmetic, not much to look forward to but a career of farm labor. Maybe in the Marines he even became a hero. He did fight in France and afterwards stayed on in the Marines, shipping around the Caribbean under General Smedley Butler to keep Central America subdued while Yankee corporations pumped out its wealth. For a man with negligible expectations, he had not done badly by 1937 standards. Full-time cemetery labor; a one-bedroom apartment so close to a famous writer.

My first awe of him had softened as I gradually realized his information was not really intended to be information. Gradually I came to see that Uncle Harold was not a liar but a teller of stories and a romantic, and it was Uncle Harold the teller of tales who fascinated me. Though he remained a stern figure, and I never considered sassing him, I saw now that he knew I no longer received his stories with total credulity, but that I was now listening for the pleasure of watching his imagination at play. This change in our relationship seemed to please him.

Over the Parcheesi board one evening he told a story about watching the dead in Haiti get up out of their shrouds and dance the Charleston. Aunt Sister and my mother had the usual response: "For God's sake, Harold, quit telling those lies."

His face was impassive as always when he issued the usual protest—"It's the truth, so help me God"—but I could see with absolute clarity that underneath the impassive mask he was smiling. He saw me studying him, scowled forbiddingly at me for one moment, then winked. That night we came to a silent understanding: We were two romancers whose desire for something more fanciful than the humdrum of southwest Baltimore was beyond the grasp of unimaginative people like Aunt Sister and my mother.

Still, it took me a while to understand what he was up to. He wanted life to be more interesting than it was, but his only gift for making it so lay in a small talent for homespun fictions, and he could not resist trying to make the most of it. Well, there was nothing tragic about his case. Our world in Baltimore hadn't much respect for the poetic impulse. In our world a man spinning a romance was doomed to be dismissed as nothing more than a prodigious liar.

It was common for the poorest household to contain a large dictionary, for conversation was a popular Depression pastime and Americans were passionately interested in words. Uncle Harold consulted his dictionary regularly looking for jaw-breaker vocabulary to give his tales more weight. One evening when my mother was there he made the mistake, when she spilled her cocoa, of saying that the spilled cocoa was "super-flu-us." Always the schoolmarm when it came to words, my mother chided him for ignorance. The word "superfluous," she pointed out, was ridiculously misused when talking about fluid on the tablecloth and, in any case, was not pronounced "super-flu-us."

Uncle Harold was often subjected to these small humiliations and accepted them without anger or sulkiness, at least when they came from women. Ungallant behavior toward a woman was not in his nature. This probably accounted for the happiness of his marriage, because Aunt Sister had inherited Ida Rebecca's disposition to be a commander of men. Like her mother, Aunt Sister was tall, angular, tart, and forceful. Uncle Harold may have been the Marine by profession, but Aunt Sister was born and bred to be commandant of the household corps.

She had no patience for what she called Uncle Harold's "foolishness": his love of fiction, his habit of giving her romantic presents like filmy nightgowns and Evening in Paris perfume. She stored the cosmetics in a closet for use on special occasions which never arose and folded the lingerie away in chests where it lay forgotten. "Aunt Sister is too practical sometimes," said my mother, who thought Uncle Harold "a good man" despite his frailties, and therefore a man who deserved more indulgence than Aunt Sister granted him.

If she was "practical," though, Aunt Sister had none of Ida Rebecca's sternness. Quite the opposite. Somehow in the 1920s the "flapper" spirit had seeped into Morrisonville and infected her with the licentiousness of the jazz age. She had rolled her stockings below the knee when it was flapper chic to do so and defiantly smoked cigarettes and chewed gum in front of her mother. Now in Baltimore she still smoked, chewed gum, and outraged Uncle Harold's and my mother's sense of decorum by crying, "Oh shit!" when provoked by some mishap in the kitchen. She enjoyed scandalizing my mother by taking her aside to tell the latest dirty joke. Off-color humor embarrassed my mother. Aunt Sister knew that, and embarrassing my mother tickled her as much as the joke itself.

Without children of their own, Aunt Sister and Uncle Harold had chosen Doris to love as dearly as the child they would never have. During the Belleville years they had twice kept Doris with them in Baltimore during her summer vacations. These summers Uncle Harold stuffed Doris with ice cream and watermelon, rode the Ferris wheel with her at street carnivals, and entertained her with stories of gigantic serpents he'd fought in tropical jungles and cars he'd rolled over at a hundred miles an hour on the highway without denting a fender or ruffling a hair on his head. They also arranged a reunion with Audrey.

Uncle Tom and Aunt Goldie had legally adopted Audrey after my mother surrendered her, but they had kept the promises made in Morrisonville when they took her away. They'd told her from the beginning that Doris and I were her brother and sister. To Audrey, Uncle Tom was "Daddy" and Aunt Goldie was "Mother." When she was old enough to grasp such complications, though, they explained adoption and told her that Doris's mother and mine—the woman Audrey called "Aunt Betty"—was her natural mother. They also encouraged her to know Doris and me in hope of creating a sense of family between us. With Audrey growing up in Brunswick, and Doris and me living in faraway New Jersey, this was impossible. But Baltimore was more easily reached from Brunswick. When Aunt Sister and Uncle Harold, during Doris's first Baltimore summer, suggested that Audrey come for a visit, it was immediately arranged.

Reports from Brunswick had it that Uncle Tom and Aunt Goldie treated Audrey like a princess, dressed her in clothes from the finest stores in Washington, kept her perpetually scrubbed and so thoroughly combed that she dazzled the eyes. It was said that Audrey even owned a fur coat to protect her from cold weather. Such were the stories that reached me in Belleville, at any rate, and Uncle Harold and Aunt Sister had heard them too. And so, to prepare for the great meeting, they flung themselves into the spit-and-polish task of making Doris shine.

This wasn't easy, for Doris was at the age in which her favorite pastime was playing with mud. Aunt Sister had nicknamed her "Dirty." The day of Audrey's visit, they soaked Doris in a tub, washed her hair, swabbed out her ears, and scoured out under her fingernails. Her wardrobe consisted of plain, sturdy clothes my mother had bought for endurance rather than beauty. Aunt Sister laundered her fanciest dress and Uncle Harold polished her shoes to a presentable state. They finished off by splashing a little cologne behind her ears.

Doris was on the slight side, thin and not very tall for her age, with dark brown hair and dark skin inherited from her father, a pert upturned nose and an ear-to-ear grin that gave her the expression of a contented cat. My mother, who was not sensitive to such things, had never told her she was pretty. To my mother, physical beauty was not something that deserved compliments. You were born to be pretty, or plain, or ugly, and there was nothing you could do about it one way or the other. It wasn't like making something of yourself, which took work and character. Uncle Harold's gentler nature gave him a better understanding of a girl's needs. That summer he'd begun telling Doris she was pretty, and she liked hearing it. Now, scrubbed and sparkling, combed and wearing her finest dress, she had never felt so beautiful.

The great moment's arrival was announced by the doorbell.

"Look who's here!"

It was Aunt Goldie. She and Uncle Harold exchanged greetings that Doris was too stunned to hear. She was staring at the most spectacular vision of elegance she had ever seen outside a movie palace.

"This is your sister, this is Audrey," Aunt Sister was saying.

"Aren't you going to kiss your big sister?" Aunt Goldie was saying to Audrey.

Doris scarcely heard any of it, or knew afterwards whether she had spoken herself, or whether Audrey had spoken to her. She was only aware of a humiliating sense of shabbiness and plainness. Staring at Audrey's serene blond beauty, dazzling dimpled smile, and splendid dress and coat and shoes, Doris was overwhelmed by something close to shame. Now it seemed to her that Uncle Harold had been deceiving her, for compared to Audrey, she thought, she was not beautiful, nor even pretty.

In spite of this awful moment, the visit was a huge success. Though Audrey looked like a princess, Doris quickly discovered that she was only a sweet-tempered six-year-old eager to be liked and delighted to be with the big sister she had heard about so often and was determined to love. That day they became friends for life.

Uncle Harold, however, had seen and understood everything during those first moments when the door opened and Doris stared across the room at Audrey. Next evening he did not come directly back from work but dug into his wallet and went to West Baltimore Street to do some shopping. Arriving home, he called Doris in and handed her a box to unwrap. It held a new, brightly colored cotton bathrobe.

"You're going to have pretty things, too," he told her.

Doris's heart belonged to Uncle Harold ever afterwards. Long after this time when he was young and she was a child, she was to discover that the ability of the true liar, which is the ability to lie to yourself, was not in him. He was to suffer a series of heart attacks so severe that only Aunt Sister and Doris were allowed at his hospital bedside. One night, trying to cheer him, Doris said,

"The doctors say you're doing wonderfully. You'll be out of here and up and around in a couple of weeks now."

The true ability to lie was not in him. "You know it's no use," he said, which was the truth. He died two days later.

But that was in a time far beyond those years when he was showing me the pleasures to be had from setting imagination— even a limited imagination—free to play. To me he was the man playing Parcheesi and drinking cocoa in a two-room flat so close to H. L. Mencken, the man who infected me with the notion that there might be worse things to do with life than spend it in telling tales.

To me he was the man who could remember being born. He told me about it one night while Aunt Sister was out in the kitchen making cocoa. He could remember the very instant of birth. His mother was pleased, and the doctor who delivered him—Uncle Harold could remember this distinctly—said, "It's a boy." There were several people in the room, and they all smiled at him. He could remember their faces vividly. And he smiled back.

Chapter Eleven

The thrill of a new life in a home of our own in Baltimore was short-lived. The only job my mother could find was selling magazine subscriptions door-to-door. There was no salary, just commissions on her sales. There were a few weeks when she sold nothing and there was no pay.

Uncle Hal's lumber company collapsed quietly in Richmond. He turned up at West Lombard Street to sleep on the couch and sell magazine subscriptions too. In accord with Uncle Hal's master plan, Uncle Charlie had come to live with us as soon as we'd moved in. He handled the housekeeping while my mother and Uncle Hal were on the streets ringing doorbells, but he didn't last long. The funerals down on the first floor were more than he could take.

Coming in from school one afternoon, I found him in low spirits over his coffee. A corpse had been delivered downstairs while I was at school. "Is something wrong?" I asked Uncle Charlie.

"They've got another one of those Goddamn stiffs downstairs," he said, "and I can't stand the smell of that shrimp."

The landlord's funeral activities were always marked by the

powerful odor of boiling shrimp. These were for guests who would be attending the wake. I had never eaten, seen, nor smelled shrimp. Until Uncle Charlie told me what the odor was, I'd thought it was something associated with the burial business, like the smells of candle wax, flowers, and after-shave lotion on the undertaker.

"They've been cooking it all day," Uncle Charlie said. "I could tell what was up the minute I smelled it."

Sure enough, an hour or two after the odor began to seep upstairs Uncle Charlie had heard the undertaker bringing another coffin through the front door.

"Are you scared having dead people in the house?" I asked him.

"Don't be foolish, Russell. Dead people don't hurt you. It's the shrimp that get me down."

A few days later Uncle Charlie took the Greyhound back to Belleville and was gone for good. Uncle Hal was not far behind. After a few months of pounding sidewalks, trying to talk his way into the parlors of suspicious housewives so he could spread his magazine samples on the floor and start his spiel, he heard of a promising business opportunity in Richmond, packed his bags, and went south.

I was too busy trying to learn the arts of survival in a big city to realize my mother was having a hard time making ends meet. On the third or fourth day at my new school I was authoritatively beaten up by a boy named Pete. It wasn't gentleman's combat such as I'd known in Belleville, but a savage, murderous beating. The playground at that school was a small fenced yard paved with brick. Pete flattened me on my back, straddled me and pounded my head into the brick with his fists while a hundred other boys, all strangers to me, cheered him on. My nose was bloodied, my lips split, my eyes blackened, and my face swollen for days afterwards. When a teacher finally pulled him off we were both hauled to the principal, who terrified me by threatening to expel us both from school if we were ever brought before her again.

Pete was not chastened. When we left the principal's office

under orders to go immediately to our classes, he grabbed my arm and said, "Let's go outside and finish this right now."

"You already won," I said.

"Come on, we'll go outside and finish it," he said.

I was horrified. He wanted to kill me and was willing to risk expulsion from school to do it. "No," I said.

"Anytime you want to finish it, I'll be waiting," he said.

We went our separate ways to different classrooms. When I walked into mine the class had already begun. The teacher, a man admired by the students for his wit, interrupted the lesson to glance at me, then turned to the class and said, "Well, if it isn't 'Battling Baker.'" The class erupted in laughter. I hated that teacher, hated the school, and, above all, hated and feared the terrible Pete.

After that I felt like hunted prey. I feared that Pete was stalking me, looking for an opportunity to finish me off. I adjusted my habits to avoid him. At lunchtime I never went into the schoolyard, where he could trap me, but sat inside pretending to be absorbed in unfinished homework. I learned where Pete lived and was careful never to walk within two blocks of the place. I noted the route he walked to school and worked out another for myself that would keep me off his path. Even in areas where I felt reasonably safe, I developed the habit of knowing always who was behind me on the sidewalk and studying intersections ahead for the slightest hint of danger. Learning the same jungle moves that quarry use to avoid their predators, I was developing the reflexes necessary to survive in cities.

Soon I learned other dangers peculiar to city streets at night. At my twelfth birthday my mother had got me a job delivering the *Baltimore News-Post* and *Sunday American*. The *News-Post* was an afternoon paper, but the *American* didn't come off the presses until long after midnight and had to be delivered before dawn on Sunday. Usually I set my alarm clock for two A.M. on Sundays and tiptoed out of the house to avoid waking my mother and Doris. It was always an eerie experience: streets dark and abandoned, silences so deep that I jumped in fear at the sudden screech of a cat.

151

Waking on one such morning, I felt lower in spirit than usual, for it was one of those times when we had a coffin in the downstairs parlor, and the funeral fumes, complete with the smell of yesterday's boiled shrimp, lay heavily in my bedroom.

To brace my spirit for the moment when I'd have to pass the coffin, I headed back toward our kitchen for a glass of milk from the icebox. Flicking on the kitchen light, I panicked battalions of cockroaches and watched them skitter for cover behind the loosened wallpaper. After the glass of milk, I was still unprepared to brush past the dead houseguest, so I busied myself emptying the icebox pan and studying the blueprints for a balsa-wood airplane model I'd started to build on the dining-room table the night before. Thinking of airplanes was almost as pleasant as thinking of Christmas, for I was developing a lurid imagination and could lose myself delightfully by flying an imaginary Spad on the dawn patrol against the deadly Baron von Richthofen.

Charging my brain with the roar of aerial combat, I pocketed the wire cutters I used to open bales of newspapers and slung a long webbed strap over my shoulder. With the strap I could balance forty pounds of Sunday newspapers on my hip and walk easily. Down the stairs and into the first-floor hallway I went. The double doors to the landlord's parlor were wide open. A dim orange light seeped into the hallway. I always tried not to look as I scurried past, but always did anyhow. This time I saw a mourner sprawled dozing in an armchair. The coffin was open. Its occupant, an elderly gentleman with a huge gray mustache, lay absolutely motionless.

Outside, the bracing cold air lifted my spirits, though there was nothing inspiring in the landscape. Baltimore was the dullest place to look at I'd ever seen. Miles and miles of row houses, all with red brick facades, flat rooftops, four or five marble or sandstone steps. It was a triumph of architectural monotony, illuminated at night only by dim little globes of light that came from gas street lamps. Still, it was always exciting to rip open the bundles of fresh newspapers and be the first in the neighborhood to know tomorrow's news. Lately it had been more and more abou'

Hitler, Mussolini, Chamberlain, and Stalin. The chanceries of Europe. War in the air, and so forth, and so on.

This morning, however, there was a bloodcurdling revelation. Page one was half filled with a picture of several parcels, crudely wrapped in newspapers, lying on a police-station table. The story said they were pieces of a human body which had been dissected by an insane killer and discarded in the Baltimore sewer system. I scanned the story rapidly and felt a little better to learn that all the human parts so far recovered had been found in East Baltimore, a full two miles from West Lombard Street. Police had still not found the victim's head, however, and what was worse, the insane dissector was still at large.

A few months earlier Baltimore movie theaters had shown *Night Must Fall*, a terrifying film about a killer who carried his dismembered victim's head around in a hatbox. I had seen this film. So, apparently, had the reporter writing this morning's story. It was possible, the story said, that the Baltimore madman was wandering the streets carrying his victim's head. The *American* was a Hearst newspaper, and I knew Hearst papers sometimes tried to make a good story better than it actually was, but at that hour of the morning, alone on the streets of southwest Baltimore, I was incapable of mustering any reassuring skepticism. Still, the newspapers had to be delivered, no question about that, and I would do it, but I didn't want to meet anybody on those abandoned streets this morning while I was getting it done.

With a tonnage of Sunday papers held to my hip by the web strap, I set off up the Lombard Street side of Union Square. This was the best part of the route. There was good street light, and all the customers paid their bills every Saturday. Twelve cents for six afternoon papers and a nickel for the Sunday. Seventeen cents a week. Everything was quiet on Lombard Street and around on Gilmor Street, too. Not a sound stirring, not a shadow moving.

Out of papers, I went back to the drop point for a second bundle. This part of the route took me to Pratt Street, where half my customers were slow payers, wanting me to carry them three or four weeks until the bill ran up to 51 or 68 cents. When I finally threatened to cut off their service, they might come up with seventeen or maybe thirty-four cents and promise to pay in full next week. The worst part of Pratt Street was that the houses were cut up into small apartments and the customers expected me to come inside buildings, climb steps, and leave papers at their doors. Often there was no hallway light, which meant groping around in the darkness on tricky staircases and maybe falling over somebody's roller skate and spilling my whole load of papers. Trying to recover fifteen or twenty Sunday papers in a pitch-black hallway was no picnic. I always walked in these places like a soldier in a mine field.

This morning I had no intention of going inside those houses. Delivering news of a mad dissector and the missing human head, I was in no mood to grope around on dark staircases. If I'd touched something human in there, which was possible since every once in a while I stumbled across drunks sleeping it off in unlit hallways, I might have died of fright. So I left the papers in downstairs hallways, deciding to let the customers howl next payday when most of them weren't going to pay anyhow.

When I went back to the drop point for the third bundle I was tired, and I sat down for a break to treat myself to the funny papers. I knew the natural sounds of the city at this hour—the clang of a distant trolley car, the clatter of a dog rooting in a garbage can, the faint wail of fire engine sirens far away. I could detect the unfamiliar sound—and therefore the potentially dangerous sound—at considerable distances. This was what I heard now while I was looking at "The Katzenjammer Kids." It was the sound of footsteps, a man's footsteps. One man, and coming toward me from the east.

I saw his silhouette a block away, down at Calhoun Street. Quickly hoisting a bundle of papers, I rammed them under the strap and set off at a right angle to his line of march. It was dark in this direction. Halfway down the block there was an alley with two outlets. If he'd seen me and followed, I could dump the papers and run. I ducked into the alley and waited. No footsteps. Peeking around the corner, I saw why. He had stopped at the intersection I'd just abandoned and seemed undecided which way to go.

When he started to walk again it was not in my direction, but towards Union Square. I'd had a good look at him while he stood under the gaslight at the corner. He was short, wore a dark overcoat with the collar turned up around his neck, and was hatless. Under the light, his hair looked silvery gray. He was not carrying a hatbox.

My imagination had got the best of me. He was probably a drunk out too late, I thought. I saw drunks like that now and then on these Sunday mornings. Sometimes they bought a paper, gave me a quarter, and told me to keep the change. I'd probably missed a bonus by running away from this one. I resumed the work, feeling relaxed now that the bad moment was over. I finished the third bundle and was almost finished with the last when I turned the corner at McHenry and Stricker streets and found myself face to face with a man in a black overcoat. The collar was turned up around his neck. His hair looked silvery gray.

"Good morning," he said.

I was beyond speaking. I still had a few papers left to deliver and, like an automaton, headed toward the houses where they belonged.

"Mind if I walk along with you?"

Terror made me speechless.

"It must be lonely with nobody to talk to," he said.

I shook my head. No, it wasn't lonely.

"It's cold this morning. Aren't you cold?"

With the combination of exertion and fear, I was sweating.

"I'm lonely too," he said.

I'd been mechanically dropping newspapers on doorsteps, and now as I dropped the last and turned from the doorway I was facing him under a good light. I'd never seen a man who looked so elegant. Certainly not in southwest Baltimore. He was from another, fancier section of town, I thought. His shoes glistened like patent leather. His overcoat seemed to have been finely tailored, as if molded to his body. The face was soft, sallow under the dim

155

gaslight, but the eyes were piercing. The hair, I could now see, was not silver but yellow gone to gray. It was fastidiously barbered and slicked back with an unguent. I could smell a faint perfume.

"I've got to get home now," I said, sliding the strap off my shoulder. It was fitted with a heavy metal buckle. When doubled up so that the buckle was at the end of the loop, it made a weapon of sorts.

"You don't want to go home yet, it's early," he said, striding along beside me. "I know where there's a party. Would you like to go to a party?"

It was now around four-thirty in the morning.

"I'm too tired," I said.

"Don't you like parties? There'll be girls there."

"Not tonight," I said. We were getting closer to Lombard Street. I groped in my pocket for the door key.

"You'll like these girls," he said. "They're the kind of girls who let you do things to them."

I didn't believe that. Even if I had it wouldn't have tempted me to set off with him. I'd begun to have fantasies about such girls, but fantasy girls and real girls were not the same. I was scared in the presence of real girls, but I was not stupid about them. I knew that the kind of girls who let men do things to them weren't going to pass time with somebody like me at four-thirty on a Sunday morning.

We'd finally reached Lombard Street, just a few doors from home.

"Come on," he said. "I've got a nice girl for you. She likes to do things and she's fourteen years old. She knows what to do."

"I don't like girls," I said.

I had my key out now. With a quick bound I was up the steps and had the key in the lock, but he was just as fast, and he was up the steps leaning against me with his hand slammed down over the key before I could turn it. I twisted aside to free the hand that held the web strap and swung it as hard as I could, but in such close contact I couldn't get any momentum into the blow and the strap whacked him harmlessly across one shoulder.

The hostility of the blow, though, cooled him a bit, and he backed down two steps and studied me.

"Come on, you'll have a wonderful time," he said, speaking very low now, almost whispering.

"No."

He took one step back toward me. I brought the strap around as hard as I could and heard it slash across the side of his face and saw him back off holding his hand to his jaw. I twisted the key in the lock, pushed the door open, slid into safety, and slammed the door behind me. I stood in the vestibule, soaked with perspiration, my hands shaking violently. Inside, the house was silent, the mourner still slept soundly in his armchair, and the old gentleman in the coffin was still motionless.

When I woke around noon I decided against telling my mother, or anybody else, about the man with the silvery hair. A few days later when the madman who dissected his victims was arrested, the pictures of him in the *News-Post* showed a squat and shabby longshoreman with matted black hair who had lost his temper in a lover's quarrel and, panicked by what he had done to his love, dismembered her with a butcher knife. For months afterwards I spent the dark hours before Sunday dawn on guard against the man with the silvery hair, just as I spent the daytime hours on guard against Pete, but I never saw him again.

The paper route earned me three dollars a week, sometimes four, and my mother, in addition to her commissions on magazine sales, also had her monthly check coming from Uncle Willie, but we'd been in Baltimore a year before I knew how desperate things were for her. One Saturday morning she told me she'd need Doris and me to go with her to pick up some food. I had a small wagon she'd bought me to make it easier to move the Sunday papers, and she said I'd better bring it along. The three of us set off eastward, passing the grocery stores we usually shopped at, and kept walking until we came to Fremont Avenue, a grim street of dilapidation and poverty in the heart of the West Baltimore black belt.

"This is where we go," she said when we reached the corner of Fremont and Fayette Street. It looked like a grocery, with big plate-glass windows and people lugging out cardboard cartons and bulging bags, but it wasn't. I knew very well what it was.

"Are we going on relief?" I asked her.

"Don't ask questions about things you don't know anything about," she said. "Bring that wagon inside."

I did, and watched with a mixture of shame and greed while men filled it with food. None of it was food I liked. There were huge cans of grapefruit juice, big paper sacks of cornmeal, cellophane bags of rice and prunes. It was hard to believe all this was ours for no money at all, even though none of it was very appetizing. My wonder at this free bounty quickly changed to embarrassment as we headed home with it. Being on relief was a shameful thing. People who accepted the government's handouts were scorned by everyone I knew as idle no-accounts without enough self-respect to pay their own way in the world. I'd often heard my mother say the same thing of families in the neighborhood suspected of being on relief. These, I'd been taught to believe, were people beyond hope. Now we were as low as they were.

Pulling the wagon back toward Lombard Street, with Doris following behind to keep the edible proof of our disgrace from falling off, I knew my mother was far worse off than I'd suspected. She'd never have accepted such shame otherwise. I studied her as she walked along beside me, head high as always, not a bit bowed in disgrace, moving at her usual quick, hurry-up pace. If she'd given up on life, she didn't show it, but on the other hand she was unhappy about something. I dared to mention the dreaded words only once on that trip home.

"Are we on relief now, Mom?"

"Let me worry about that," she said.

What worried me most as we neared home was the possibility we'd be seen with the incriminating food by somebody we knew. There was no mistaking government-surplus food. The grapefruit-juice cans, the prunes and rice, the cornmeal—all were ostentatiously unlabeled, thus advertising themselves as "government handouts." Everybody in the neighborhood could read them easily

158

enough, and our humiliation would be gossiped through every parlor by sundown. I had an inspiration.

"It's hot pulling this wagon," I said. "I'm going to take my sweater off."

It wasn't hot, it was on the cool side, but after removing the sweater I laid it across the groceries in the wagon. It wasn't a very effective cover, but my mother was suddenly affected by the heat too.

"It is warm, isn't it, Buddy?" she said. Removing her topcoat, she draped it over the groceries, providing total concealment.

"You want to take your coat off, Doris?" asked my mother.

"I'm not hot, I'm chilly," Doris said.

It didn't matter. My mother's coat was enough to get us home without being exposed as three of life's failures.

From then on I assumed we were paupers. For this reason I was often astonished when my mother did me some deed of generosity, as when she bought me my first Sunday suit with long pants. The changeover from knickers to long pants was the ritual recognition that a boy had reached adolescence, or "the awkward age," as everybody called it. The "teenager," like the atomic bomb, was still uninvented, and there were few concessions to adolescence, but the change to long pants was a ritual of recognition. There was no ceremony about it. You were taken downtown one day and your escort—my mother in my case—casually said to the suit salesman, "Let's see what you've got in long pants."

For me the ritual was performed in the glossy, mirrored splendor of Bond's clothing store on Liberty Street. She had taken me for a Sunday suit and, having decided I looked too gawky in knickers, said, "Let's see what you've got in long pants." My physique at this time was described by relatives and friends with such irritating words as "beanpole," "skinny," and "all bones." My mother, seeing me through eyes that loved, chose to call me "a tall man."

The suit salesman displayed a dazzling assortment of garments. Suit designers made no concessions to youth; suits for boys were just like suits for men, only smaller. My mother expressed a preference for something with the double-breasted cut. "A tall man looks good in a double-breasted suit," she said.

The salesman agreed. Gary Cooper, he said, looked especially good in double-breasted suits. He produced one. I tried it on. It was a hard fabric, built to endure. The color was green, not the green of new grass in spring, but the green of copper patina on old statues. The green was relieved by thin, light gray stripes, as though the designer had started to create cloth for a bunco artist, then changed his mind and decided to appeal to bankers.

"Well, I just don't know," my mother said.

Her taste in clothes was sound rather than flamboyant, but I considered the suit smashing, and would have nothing else. The price was $20, which was expensive even though it came with two pairs of pants, and upon hearing it I said, "We can't afford it."

"That's what you think, mister," she said to me. "It's worth a little money to have the man of the house look like a gentleman."

In conference with the salesman, it was agreed that she would pay three dollars down and three dollars a month until the cost was amortized. On my attenuated physique, this magnificent, striped, green, double-breasted suit hung like window drapes on a scarecrow. My mother could imagine Gary Cooper's shoulders gradually filling out the jacket, but she insisted that Bond's do something about the voluminous excesses of the pants, which in the seat area could have accommodated both me and a watermelon. The salesman assured her that Bond's famous tailors would adjust the trousers without difficulty. They did so. When finally I had the suit home and put it on for its first trip to church, so much fabric had been removed from the seat that the two hip pockets were located with seams kissing right over my spine.

My mother was dazzled. With visions of a budding Gary Cooper under her wing, she said, "Now you look like somebody I can be proud of," and off to church we went.

She was a magician at stretching a dollar. That December, with Christmas approaching, she was out at work and Doris was in the kitchen when I barged into her bedroom one afternoon in search of a safety pin. Since her bedroom opened onto a community hallway, she kept the door locked, but needing the pin, I took the key from its hiding place, unlocked the door, and stepped in. Standing against the wall was a big, black bicycle with balloon tires. I recognized it instantly. It was the same second-hand bike I'd been admiring in a Baltimore Street shop window. I'd even asked about the price. It was horrendous. Something like $15. Somehow my mother had scraped together enough for a down payment and meant to surprise me with the bicycle on Christmas morning.

I was overwhelmed by the discovery that she had squandered such money on me and sickened by the knowledge that, bursting into her room like this, I had robbed her of the pleasure of seeing me astonished and delighted on Christmas day. I hadn't wanted to know her lovely secret; still, stumbling upon it like this made me feel as though I'd struck a blow against her happiness. I backed out, put the key back in its hiding place, and brooded privately.

I resolved that between now and Christmas I must do nothing, absolutely nothing, to reveal the slightest hint of my terrible knowledge. I must avoid the least word, the faintest intonation, the weakest gesture that might reveal my possession of her secret. Nothing must deny her the happiness of seeing me stunned with amazement on Christmas day.

In the privacy of my bedroom I began composing and testing exclamations of delight: "Wow!" "A bike with balloon tires! I don't believe it!" "I'm the luckiest boy alive!" And so on. They all owed a lot to movies in which boys like Mickey Rooney had seen their wildest dreams come true, and I realized that, with my lack of acting talent, all of them were going to sound false at the critical moment when I wanted to cry out my love spontaneously from the heart. Maybe it would be better to say nothing but appear to be shocked into such deep pleasure that speech had escaped me. I wasn't sure, though. I'd seen speechless gratitude in the movies too, and it never really worked until the actors managed to cry a few quiet tears. I doubted I could cry on cue, so I began thinking about other expressions of speechless amazement. In front of a hand-held mirror in my bedroom I tried the whole range of expressions: mouth agape and eyes wide; hands slapped firmly against both cheeks to keep the jaw from falling off; ear-to-ear grin with all teeth fully exposed while hugging the torso with both arms. These and more I practiced for several days without acquiring confidence in any of them. I decided to wait until Christmas morning and see if anything came naturally.

Christmas was the one occasion on which my mother surrendered to unabashed sentimentality. A week beforehand she always concocted homemade root beer, sealed it in canning jars, and stored it in the bathroom for the yeast to ferment. Now and then, sitting in the adjoining kitchen, we heard a loud thump from the bathroom and knew one of the jars had exploded, but she always made enough to allow for breakage. She took girlish delight in keeping her brightly wrapped gifts hidden in closets. Christmas Eve she spent in frenzies of baking—cakes, pies, gingerbread cookies cut and decorated to look like miniature brown pine trees and Santa Clauses. In the afternoon she took Doris and me to the street corner where trees were piled high and searched through them until she found one that satisfied our taste for fullness and symmetry. It was my job and Doris's to set the tree up in the parlor and weight it with ornaments, lights, and silver icicles, while she prepared Christmas Eve dinner. This was a ritual meal at which the centerpiece was always oysters. She disliked oysters but always ate them on Christmas Eve. Oysters were the centerpiece of the traditional Christmas Eve supper she remembered from her girlhood in Virginia. By serving them she perpetuated the customs of Papa's household.

She did not place her gifts under the tree that night until Doris and I had gone to bed. We were far beyond believing in Santa Claus, but she insisted on preserving the forms of the childhood myth that these were presents from some divine philanthropist. She planned all year for this annual orgy of spending and girded for it by putting small deposits month after month into her Christmas Club account at the bank.

That Christmas morning she roused us early, "to see what Santa Claus brought," she said with just the right tone of irony to indicate we were all old enough to know who Santa Claus was. I came out of my bedroom with my presents for her and Doris, and Doris came with hers. My mother's had been placed under the tree during the night. There were a few small glittering packages, a big doll for Doris, but no bicycle. I must have looked disappointed.

"It looks like Santa Claus didn't do too well by you this year, Buddy," she said, as I opened packages. A shirt. A necktie. I said something halfhearted like, "It's the thought that counts," but what I felt was bitter disappointment. I supposed she'd found the bike intolerably expensive and sent it back.

"Wait a minute!" she cried, snapping her fingers. "There's something in my bedroom I forgot all about."

She beckoned to Doris, the two of them went out, and a moment later came back wheeling between them the big black two-wheeler with balloon tires. I didn't have to fake my delight, after all. The three of us—Doris, my mother, and I—were people bred to repress the emotional expressions of love, but I did something that startled both my mother and me. I threw my arms around her spontaneously and kissed her.

"All right now, don't carry on about it. It's only a bicycle," she said.

Still, I knew that she was as happy as I was to see her so happy.

Chapter Twelve

I was fourteen when my mother began keeping company with a man she'd met at Uncle Harold's. It was strange to think of her "dating," because she hadn't gone out with men, except for me and my uncles, since Oluf's time. Still, I saw nothing ominous in it. They went to the movies occasionally and stopped at the ice cream parlor afterwards. Sometimes they brought back ice cream for Doris and me. Now and then they went to play cards with Aunt Sister and Uncle Harold, and drank cocoa. His name was Herbert Orrison, but my mother suggested I call him "Herb." He worked for the B&O Railroad and was financially well fixed, or so I judged from the evidence of his sporty 1934 Chevrolet and the fact that he always wore a suit, white shirt, necktie, and gray fedora when he came calling.

It never occurred to me that Herb was courting. I would have been alarmed if I'd thought so. Wasn't I long established as "the man of the family"? A competitor was inconceivable. I was also too deeply engrossed in myself to pay attention to peripheral people like Herb. It was the summer of 1939, and just before Labor Day the German army had invaded Poland and World War II was under way in Europe; but though I delivered the news every afternoon, even World War II seemed far away. I was hopelessly mired in the agonies of adolescence and too filled with inner uproar to sense the menaces that Herb and Adolf Hitler posed to my security.

Under my mattress was a heavily thumbed copy of *Spicy Detective* magazine which I'd recovered from a trash can while delivering newspapers. With racing pulse I read and reread stories in which some rock-jawed detective caught glimpses of milky white thighs through wisps of lace or embraced some "luscious tomato" and felt her bosom heaving hungrily against his chest. In every story there came a maddening moment at the very height of the bosom-heaving when some terrible distraction occurred—the luscious tomato was shot dead in the detective's arms, for example, leaving me to imagine what might have happened if the killer had been a few minutes late arriving on the scene. I hated these killers whose untimely interruptions ruined the sexual drama, and my imagination was on fire with guesses about what might have been.

My suffering was increased by my certainty that no tomato would ever let her luscious bosom heave against my chest. In the presence of girls I had paralyzing seizures of blushing embarrassment. I was in misery about my physical shortcomings. I was too skinny. My hair wouldn't stay combed. I couldn't dance. If a girl smiled at me I blushed and turned away, pretending not to notice her, powerless to smile back, incapable of speaking a single word.

My secret passion was Laraine. She hadn't much bosom to heave. Never mind. My appetite for her was not carnal but pure. She had glistening dark hair that swept to her shoulders, great blue eyes, and a manner so gentle and ladylike that it was impossible to imagine her bosom ever heaving against any boy, including me. She lived along my newspaper route and, I believed, shared my inner passion. Several times she looked me straight in the eye, fluttered her lashes, and gave me a dazzling smile. Always I pretended not to notice and stared past her. I was in high school and reading *The Idylls of the King,* and under Tennyson's influence I began to think of Laraine as a damsel to be rescued by a knight.

I reveled in fantasies in which I was that knight. I didn't wear armor, though. It was not horses that interested me, but airplanes, and so in my daydreams I wore pilot's goggles and a flowing white scarf and flew in an open cockpit in pursuit of lascivious devils who had kidnapped Laraine and were flying her to secret hideouts to have their brutal way with her. In these fantasies I always arrived in the nick of time and, after beating her kidnappers senseless, was always offered a kiss in reward. Always I refused it. Our passion was too pure to be defiled by kissing.

One day, needing to feel my beloved's name on my lips, I made the mistake of speaking it to Doris. In the most uninterested manner I could manage, I asked Doris, "Do you know a girl named Laraine?"

"You're not having anything to do with Laraine, are you?"

"Come on, you know I don't go for girls."

"Well stay away from Laraine. She's a cafe trotter."

This was staggering. My glistening damsel of the glorious eyes—a cafe trotter!

I didn't know what a cafe trotter was—I'd never heard the term before, never heard it afterwards, and never knew where Doris acquired it—but it sounded dreadful. I imagined my sweet fourteen-year-old Laraine late at night, after I was sound asleep, traveling the smoke-filled saloons of southwest Baltimore and permitting her bosom to heave against the chests of reeking beer drinkers. It was my first taste of the suffering a man invites by loving a treacherous woman.

This was only one of the many miseries that kept me too occupied with myself to see the menace of Herb. There was also my absorbing fear of public embarrassment. When my mother sent me to the drugstore with instructions to buy milk of magnesia one day, I dawdled for an hour before daring to enter the store. Milk of magnesia was a laxative. Laxatives had to do with bowels, and bowels were embarrassing. If I walked in and asked for milk of magnesia, everyone in the store would turn and stare at me, I thought, and start thinking about my bowels. It was painful to contemplate such humiliation. Finally, at the counter, waiting for the moment when no one else was in earshot, I spoke to the clerk in a whisper: "A bottle of milk of magnesia, please."

"What's that?"

To me he seemed to be roaring. A little louder I said, "A bottle of milk of magnesia."

He produced it, and I handed him money, and he gave me change, but I couldn't let it go at that.

"It's not for me," I said.

"Not enough for you? You want the bigger bottle?" he roared.

"No, no. I just said—this bottle—it's not for me. It's for somebody else."

He eyed me curiously as I slunk out, certain that he would now report my purchase to the whole neighborhood.

There wasn't much that could be done about my cadaverous physique except avoid all situations that required me to take off my shirt. This meant never going to beaches or swimming pools, which became impossible after I entered high school. I was appalled the first day there to discover it had an Olympic-size pool and required all students to take swimming instruction. I was doubly stricken to learn that everyone was expected to swim buck naked. There was no getting out of it either. The idea that my fellow students—it was an all-boys school—would now see me in all my skinniness and laugh about me behind my back was enough to make me ponder suicide. Instead I chose humiliation. When we were all lined up nude at the edge of the pool, nobody pointed at me and laughed, but I was certain that everyone was busily counting my plainly visible ribs. I spent so much time in swimming class worrying about my boney profile that despite four years of instruction in that pool I never learned to swim a stroke.

To make up for so many shortcomings, I flung myself furiously into the one thing I was good at, which was book learning, and found a little self-respect in the successful chase for high grades. In short order I developed intellectual arrogance. This was encouraged by the special program I was taking in high school, a four-year course for fast learners which, when completed, would supply me with enough credits to enter college at the second-year level. There was no possibility of my going to college, of course. Not on my mother's meager earnings. When she learned that the program was available, though, she insisted that I apply.

"At least you'll get a year of college learning out of high school," she said. "And who knows, maybe by the time you're through with high school something may come along."

Well, it was another opportunity to help me make something of myself, and she overlooked no possibility, no matter how remote. For me it meant early escape from the junior high school I hated; boys accepted in the program were freed from junior high after eighth grade and sent to do their ninth grade in high school. I leaped at the chance to change schools. If I'd known about the nude swimming I would have resisted. But then my mother would have forced me to apply anyhow. The school catering to us ambitious bookworms was called City College. Despite its name, which dated from the nineteenth century, when it had been a city college, it was merely a high school, though a very good one whose best graduates were equipped to enter the best universities in the country.

The program I entered was in the classical tradition. There was very little science, but by graduation you were expected to have mastered mathematics through elementary calculus. Grammar, rhetoric, and English literature were heavily emphasized, and the course included two years of German, three years of French, and four years of Latin, at the end of which we were expected to have read Caesar, Cicero, Virgil, Ovid, Horace, and Livy.

This was a far world from the rough and tumble of junior high, where you could have your brains beaten out in the schoolyard, and I took to the rarefied scholarly air with gusto. The school was located an hour's trolley ride from West Lombard Street in what seemed by comparison one of Baltimore's snootiest neighborhoods. It was a mammoth gray stone structure topped by a huge gray tower, the whole thing sprawling across the highest hill in Baltimore like some grim Gothic fortress heaved up to shelter civilization from the Vandals. My classmates came from all sections of the city. Most, I soon discovered, were just as formidable at the books as I was, and many were my betters at the grind. After the first year thinned our ranks of sluggards who couldn't keep the pace, some twenty-five of us survived as a small elite cadre of scholars, and when I realized that I was good enough to keep up with the best I began to view myself with extraordinary respect. I also began to look upon the common masses of humanity with pleasurable disdain.

When Doris asked for help with her arithmetic, I tore up her solutions in disgust while enthusiastically explaining that she would never be able to master the mysteries of trigonometry. Worse, I began to punish my mother. For years she had been my tutor in everything academic, the eternal schoolteacher forcing me to learn to read when reading bored me, watching over my shoulder while I did my homework, encouraging me when I complained it was too hard. "Just calm down and think it through, Buddy. You can get it if you try." And if I couldn't in spite of trying, she had always sat down beside me and helped me do it.

In the past I had been in awe of her education, her year of college where she had read Shakespeare and learned Latin. In my first year at City, when we were reading Caesar and I was having terrible trouble, she sat beside me long nights at the dining-room table on Lombard Street and helped me solve the puzzles of Latin declensions and conjugations. She was good at Caesar. But now, as I moved on into Cicero and Virgil, I realized that I was leaving her behind. I was like a swimmer in deep ocean waters pulling away from someone too weak to keep up. Nevertheless, she wanted to stay abreast of me, and many nights she still took her seat beside me at the table hoping to be helpful.

"What's the trouble, Buddy?"

"Cicero. I can't get this passage here," I said, showing her the book.

She looked at it silently for a long time, then tried to translate it. I knew her translation was far off the mark. Even my own, which was not very good, was better than hers. At this early stage I didn't yet have it in me to hurt her, and so would nod and say, "Thanks, let me try it that way and see if I can work it out."

Gradually she became glad to let me work out the Latin by myself, and I knew I was outdistancing her. The same progress took place in mathematics, and though she tried to help as she had always helped, her powers failed when we reached quadratic equations, and she left me to swim alone into trigonometry and analytic geometry. One of the oldest links in the chain binding us together had snapped. She was no longer my ultimate schoolteacher.

As my intellectual pride increased I began to take pleasure in the feeling that my education was superior to hers. For years I had heard about her year of college, her Latin classes, her schoolteacher's art, and now I was pleased to realize that despite all that, she could no longer keep up with me. One evening I yielded to an evil impulse to show her how little Latin she knew.

In school we were then reading the *Aeneid*. In class that day we had translated a difficult passage concluding with the line "*forsan et haec olim meminisse iuvabit.*" After great difficulty and with much help from the teacher I had worked this out to mean, "Someday we shall recall these trials with pleasure." While doing my homework that night I called her to the table and showed her the passage, pretending to have trouble with it. "You're the Latin expert around here," I said. "Can you translate this line for me?"

She sat down, took the book, and studied the passage, then began consulting the Latin dictionary. Knowing from my class that day how tricky the line was to translate, I was filled with inner giggles. Still, she made the effort, laboriously working out a couple of lines and getting them wrong and finally translating the last line to read, "Perhaps and this it will help to remember."

"It doesn't make any sense that way," I said.

She was apologetic. "I never got up to the *Aeneid* when I was in school," she said. I ignored this.

"Don't you think it makes more sense this way?" I asked, and read the entire passage as the teacher had helped translate it earlier, concluding, "Someday we shall recall these trials with pleasure."

"If you knew it already, why did you bother to ask me?" she said.

Herb.

"I thought maybe you could improve it," I said.

"Improve it for yourself," she said, and left the table.

Something else that had bound us together parted that night. It had been cruelly done, but I had issued my first declaration of independence from childhood.

How unprepared for independence I was, I did not realize until a few months later when I got in from school one afternoon and found she was out of the house. That wasn't surprising, but when I'd delivered my newspapers and got back at six o'clock she was still away. "Where's Mom?" I asked Doris.

"She and Herb went out somewhere," Doris said.

That wasn't surprising either. Maybe they would bring back some ice cream for supper. But they didn't. She came back alone. She was dressed in her good suit, which wasn't surprising. She usually wore her best when she went out with Herb. The surprise was the news she brought back. She said she and Herb had gone to Ellicott City that afternoon. Then she smiled at Doris and me and without further ado said, "Herb and I were married today."

She said it in such a matter-of-fact voice. She might have been telling us that she'd been to the grocery and cheese had gone up a penny a pound. "Herb and I were married today." She made it sound as though getting married were the most commonplace thing in the world. Nothing for Doris and me to get excited about. See? He didn't even come home with her after the ceremony. Well yes, of course he would be moving in with us in a day or two. Doris would have to give up her bedroom and sleep on the parlor daybed until the house was reorganized. Still, everything would be the same, everything would go on as it always had with us, except now there would be a man to help provide.

I was too stunned to speak. At a single stroke, without being consulted, without a word of warning, I had been replaced as "the man of the family." Our home, the home of our own which my mother had struggled so long to create, was no longer a home of our own, but a place in which a stranger I hardly knew would now be master. I had liked Herb well enough as an affable visitor dropping in occasionally with ice cream treats, but now my heart closed against him. Because I was too dumbstruck to speak, it was Doris who asked the inevitable question.

"Does this mean I'm supposed to call Herb 'Daddy'?"

"If you want to," my mother said.

"I'm not going to call him Daddy," I blurted. "He's not my father."

My anger must have shone in my voice and face. "Aren't you happy for Mama's sake, Buddy?" my mother asked.

"Sure," I lied. "Only—"

"He won't mind if you go on calling him Herb," she said. "Now let's have some supper." And she went to the kitchen and began cooking, and afterwards she and Doris washed the dishes together as they always did, as though a wedding day were the most routine day in the world.

Herb moved in the following morning. That was the day the Depression finally ended for us. During the afternoon a man rang the doorbell and asked my mother where she wanted the telephone installed. Herb needed the phone so the railroad could call him at any hour. When the man left, we were living for the first time in our lives in a house that had a telephone. The age of miraculous household gadgetry had begun. After nine years of hard times we had arrived on the shore of a new age. We were no longer on relief, and for my mother, though youth was behind her, the world seemed to be bending finally to her dreams of the future. It was not my dream of the future, though. I was seething with resentment and anger, and soon I was embarked on a campaign of remorseless hostility against my new stepfather.

Herb's first memory was of seeing his mother burn to death. That was in 1899. He was only five, the baby of the family, at home in a country kitchen with his mother on a June afternoon. She was doing something at the stove, something with kerosene. The child saw a brilliant flare of light. There was fire in her clothes flickering down the long full-length country woman's dress fitted tightly at the throat, fire sweeping down to the wrists, the ankles. The screaming—he could still hear that forty years later.

173

He was taken in by relatives. When he was ten they took him out of school and sent him to work in the fields. He brought his pay home on Saturday night, a few coins, sometimes maybe a full dollar for the week's work, and surrendered it to pay for his keep, and gradually he came to hate them and hate the drudgery.

It was not a fierce, rebellious hatred. He was a quiet boy, and inarticulate, and kept his thoughts to himself. There was a stolidity about him. He was full of silences and not much given to laughter or gaiety or outbursts of rage or rebellion. He could smile pleasantly enough. He was rather handsome, with thick, coarse black hair, a straight nose, broad jaw, broad athlete's shoulders. He was going to be a big man. He had the heavy broad bones for it, thick muscular thighs, big cornhusker's biceps and forearms.

The quietness masked a boyish impulse to do something romantic with his life. It was the age of the railroads. All over America boys lay awake in the night listening for train whistles echoing down long valleys and shimmering across the prairie. To boys imprisoned in lonely farms and dull backwater towns those whistles spoke of distant worlds where life was better. Lying in bed at night listening to those whistles, a boy could imagine the great locomotives thundering out to the ends of the continent and, at the controls, leaning out the cab window with his hair streaming back under the rushing wind, the ultimate figure of American romance: the locomotive engineer, the man who made the earth shake and walked in distant glittering cities. Herb dreamed of commanding those awesome engines, of leaning confidently out the cab window, of becoming one of the railroad knighthood.

Herb did join the railroad, though when he came to live with us he had still not made it all the way to the top; he was a fireman and had been for years. It was back-breaking labor which required shoveling as much as twenty tons of coal from the tender to the locomotive firebox for every run. The labor thickened a man's arms, blackened his face, and wore out his back, but it was the final stepping-stone to the ultimate job. If you survived, and if enough engineers on the seniority ladder ahead of you keeled over with heart attacks or came down with tuberculosis or were scalded to death in accidents, one day they would have to call you in and tell you that from now on you were going to be the man at the throttle. This was the stage at which Herb had arrived—waiting for the call —when he and my mother were married. He was forty-five years old. She was forty-one.

It was Herb's second marriage. His first had been brief and ended in divorce. I didn't know why. Aunt Sister told me his first wife was a woman who "liked a good time too much." Herb was not the good-time sort. For him a lively evening was a game of cards at a friend's house, followed by a cup of cocoa or a dish of ice cream. Then it was home to bed so he could rise refreshed when the B&O called him to duty. Living entirely for his work, he avoided all frivolity which could jeopardize his dream of becoming an engineer. He had no children from his first marriage, and his own Spartan childhood provided him no clue to the troubles awaiting him in trying to play the father to a fourteen-year-old like me.

The day Herb moved into Lombard Street with us I set out on one of those campaigns of silent resistance of which only adolescents and high-spirited nations under conquerors' occupation are capable. I gave no spoken sign of my dislike. I was too cunning for that. My policy was to ignore him as completely as possible. Without saying a word that could possibly offend him, I would let him know that so far as I was concerned, he did not exist. There were a hundred ways of doing this.

In meal conversations I addressed myself only to my mother or Doris, always managing to omit him from the circle. When he interrupted to say, "Pass the potatoes," I passed the bowl silently without looking at him while continuing to talk to my mother and Doris. When he addressed me directly with some pleasant remark about the food, such as, "Isn't that the best applesauce you ever tasted?" I murmured, "It's all right," or "Not bad," and without looking at him began speaking to my mother on some subject I knew would shut him out of the table talk.

It galled me that my mother should be married to a man with so little schooling, a man who licked the point of his lead pencil when struggling with the simplest mathematical calculation, a man who had never heard of Cicero, Virgil, or Shakespeare, a man who read nothing but the sports pages and moved his lips silently while trying to puzzle out some unfamiliar word in the baseball news. It was easy in those supper-table conversations to let him know how dense I thought he was. Cunningly, I started hundreds of conversations in which I knew he would be hopelessly lost.

One night, to my mother: "I'll bet you don't know the difference between a bicameral and a unicameral legislature." She did know of course, and I knew she would, but that wasn't the point. The point was that Herb didn't know, probably didn't even know what a legislature was, and my aim was to make him feel the depths of his ignorance, to let him know that he was not worthy of my attention.

The cunning lay in making him miserable without resorting to open insult. This would have given him justification for hitting me, and I knew that, big and powerful as he was, he could snap me like a string bean if given a good excuse to use corporal punishment. He must have wished often that I would give him that excuse, but I was too clever. My technique was aimed at withering his soul without giving him the slightest excuse for a refreshing outburst of violence.

He not only tolerated me with saintly patience, he also tried to befriend me. He knew I was rabid about baseball. Both of us were. One Sunday morning at breakfast he said, "Let's the two of us go over to Oriole Park and see the double-header this afternoon."

Nothing could have made me happier than a trip to Oriole Park, but not with Herb. He wasn't going to worm his way into my heart that easily.

"I've got too much homework," I said.

One evening, knocking at my bedroom door, then sticking his head in when I said, "Come in," he grinned and said, "I'm taking the car out for a little ride; you want to come along?"

"I'm too busy," I said.

"I'll teach you how to drive her," he said.

This was the ultimate temptation, for I desperately wanted to learn to drive, but I refused to succumb. "I'm too young to drive," I said.

"Well, why don't the two of us just walk over to the Arundel Ice Cream store and get ourselves a sundae?" he suggested.

I turned my eyes back to the book, pretending to be studying, and said, "I've got too much work to do," and kept staring at the book until I heard the door close behind him.

Herb had an oddly stiff walk; his upper torso tilted forward slightly from the hips with his back stiffly arched, as though he were afflicted with a lifelong backache. When he was not around I entertained Doris with what I thought were hilarious imitations of his bent and painful posture. Doris looked on Herb with more compassionate eyes. "If you'd spent your life shoveling coal into a steam engine you might walk funny too," she told me.

Unrepentant and amused by my ability to caricature Herb's walk, I did it one day for my mother's benefit. She was furious.

"That's just enough of that, Russell," she said. "Herb's been good to you, and I don't want you making fun of him. Herb's a good man. I want you to treat him right."

Being hailed as "a good man," Herb had my mother's highest accolade, one she bestowed on very few. Papa had been "a good man," even "a wonderful man." Uncle Allen was "a good man." So was Uncle Willie. Lately she'd begun to concede that Uncle Harold was "a good man" too. It wasn't easy becoming "a good man," but the few who succeeded were entitled to justice and were not to be ridiculed, even by a beloved son. In my mother's world "a good man" was entitled to "a good wife." Once Herb qualified for "good man" ranking, my mother wholeheartedly fulfilled her part of the contract. When the railroad phoned at three A.M. she rolled out of bed to make him a meal and pack his lunch. She baked the pies and cakes he loved, waged a gallant campaign against the cockroaches, kept the house spick and span, organized the household accounts, handled the bills, and even scowled at me if she caught me betraying my insolence.

Herb's patience with me was superhuman. Maybe he learned

that patience as a boy doing the farm labor, bringing the money home to his relatives, and biding his time with dreams of the big locomotives. Maybe he just understood how deep a boy's unhappiness could be. I don't know. Much later when I was older and we came to know each other and I grew to like and respect him, we never talked about those adolescent tortures I inflicted on him, and I never raised the subject or tried to apologize. He was never much good at talk like that. If I'd tried it, he would have smiled and dismissed the subject with a wave of his big hand and said, "Aw!" and then, to change the subject, "How about that Willie Mays! Isn't he something?"

Herb was finally elevated to the rank of engineer shortly after his marriage. He had no regular run but was subject to call at all hours of the clock. Keeping such irregular hours, he seemed perpetually tired. It was a constant struggle for him to get his rest. When the downstairs funeral wake turned noisy at ten P.M., Herb wandered out of his bedroom, miserable and hollow-eyed, complaining, "A man just can't get his rest around here." If he'd come in from work at suppertime, my mother would be in my room at six-thirty, asking me to turn off my radio, saying, "Herb's trying to get his rest." If Doris and I were quarreling on a Saturday afternoon, Herb would rise from his bed and interrupt us. "I'm trying to get my rest," he pleaded.

One morning when he'd come in from work after midnight the phone rang at two A.M., the saloon-closing hour in Baltimore. Herb climbed out of bed, lifted the receiver, and found himself speaking to an unlikely caller. "This is Benito Mussolini," the voice said. "It's time to get up."

It was one of the few times I saw Herb in a violent mood. He stormed out of the bedroom with a racket that woke me in my bedroom across the hall, and I stumbled out to investigate. Herb was standing in the hallway roaring, "Mussolini! Mussolini, my foot!" Herb never cursed; "my foot!" was the strongest oath in his vocabulary.

He was belting up his trousers for an assault on the landlord, whom he suspected of being the prankster since the landlord was

178

Lithuanian and "Mussolini" had spoken in a Lithuanian accent. My mother calmed him by pointing out that the landlord didn't have a telephone, so couldn't possibly have made the offending call. Herb pondered the logic of that for a moment, then let his rage dissolve into a grin. He wasn't a man for smashing furniture when he was angry. "Mussolini," he said to himself, shaking his head as if it had been a great joke after all. Then, loosening his belt and heading back for the mattress: "I've got to get my rest."

He was the gentlest of men despite his strength. He asked only that there be a choice of two or three home-baked pies on the table for Sunday dinner and that household noise be held down while he was listening to radio broadcasts of the Washington Senators baseball games. He was hopelessly addicted to the Senators, a team of monumental incompetence on the baseball diamond. A Senators victory lifted him to ecstasy, a defeat cast him into the pit of depression. For Senators fans there wasn't much ecstasy in life. Switching off the radio after the Senators had lost yet again, Herb looked like a man who'd glimpsed the afterlife and seen that Heaven was a fraud.

His only other vice was betting. Like most blue-collar Baltimoreans, he was a horse player, a $2 bettor placing phone calls to a mysterious and illegal bookie at the far end of a telephone wire. Once he was so thrilled by winning $40 that he told my mother about it. After lecturing him on the evil of gambling and admonishing him never to do it again, she demanded $35 of his winnings to put in the bank and let him keep $5. After that he kept news of his winning bets to himself.

Though he had a pint of rye whiskey concealed around the house, he used it rarely and then only for medicinal purposes. He worried a great deal about his innards and considered a nip of whiskey a curative for certain intestinal crises. At table he was a prodigious trencherman, capable of polishing off a huge mound of victuals, sending his plate around for a second helping of everything, and then finishing off with two varieties of pie rammed home with a slab of coconut or chocolate cake. I often saw him slumped in distress and moaning about "terrible gas" or heard him in dead of night tramping dark corridors and calling to my mother, "Betty! Where's the Bisodol?"

While I bullied him with subtle psychological torments, my mother took the direct approach and bullied him without finesse. Her natural instinct with a man was to push, and if he didn't budge, to push harder. If he failed to push back, she leaned on him full force. Herb pushed back a little at first, but he wasn't up to combat against a will like hers. When she discovered this, she took charge. She managed the bank account, handled his shopping, told him how she wanted him dressed for each occasion, and, in general, dealt with him very much as she had dealt with me all my life. At the very time I had begun to escape her control, Herb was becoming captive to it.

With wry humor, Herb began referring to her as "the Madam" in delicately mocking tribute to her authoritarian nature. One evening when the three of us were playing cards and I was winning consistently she became increasingly angry. She hated to lose at anything. It was a time when I enjoyed asserting my superiority over her, and I was having a fine time crushing her in hand after hand. After a half hour she excused herself briefly from the game. When she'd left the room Herb leaned across the table toward me, smiled a smile of great wisdom, and whispered, "Let the Madam win."

"Let her win?"

"It'll make her feel good," he said.

I saw that though Herb knew nothing about Cicero or Shakespeare his wisdom was far larger than mine. This explained several obviously stupid plays he had made earlier in the game. A little happiness for her would lead to peace of mind for him, as well as for me, and putting the Madam in good spirits was well worth a loss at cards. It was the first time I let Herb teach me anything, and when finally she rose triumphant from the card table to make us coffee and serve cake the evening was a total success.

By the summer of 1940 Herb gave up his effort to be a father to me. He no longer needed a surrogate child. At the age of forty-six he was at last to have a child of his own. That November, three days before my mother's forty-third birthday, she gave birth to her fourth and last child. It was a girl. They named her Mary Leslie after Herb's mother. Herb was launched on what was to be a lifelong career as doting father. My mother started all over again in the business of motherhood in which she now considered herself a skilled professional. This time, however, she had the resources to do things right, thanks to Herb's steady income.

Her first goal was to have her own house. For this purpose she began pressing Herb with arguments why an apartment on Lombard Street was an unsuitable place for a baby. Herb was uneasy about this at first. Buying a house was an immense financial burden, even for a railroad man. My mother ignored his objections and began canvassing the mortgage market, then sat down with him and explained about monthly mortgage and equity payments. As always, she had her way. In the summer of 1941 Herb signed papers committing himself to pay the breathtaking sum of $4,700 for a four-bedroom house in a bosky dale on the western edge of Baltimore.

I was sixteen and in my last year of high school when we moved out of Lombard Street. Though I still hadn't made my peace with Herb I was more than delighted to luxuriate in his new house. I'd never dreamed of living in such splendor. Besides its four bedrooms, it had a living room twenty feet long, a dining room more than ten feet in both dimensions, and a "sun parlor" that overlooked an expanse of green, tree-shaded parkland through which flowed a small stream. There was a front porch big enough to accommodate a glider. In the kitchen sat a gleaming white refrigerator that made its own ice cubes. I would never again have to worry about the icebox pan overflowing. The cellar floor was covered with blocks of inlaid linoleum tile. The house's most magnificent feature, however, was the bathroom, with lavender fixtures, green wall tiles, and—wonder of wonders—a shower over the bathtub. For the first time in my life I could take a shower right in the house.

For all this I had Mary Leslie and Herb to thank, but though I loved Mary dearly, my heart was still hardened against Herb, and, ignoring his responsibility for granting me such luxury, I felt only resentment toward him for being the agent of my happiness. I'd never seen my mother more radiantly happy than the day we moved in. The house was on Marydell Road in the Irvington section of Baltimore. For my mother it was that "home of our own" she had talked about from my earliest memory. It was the place of permanence, the permanence embodied for her in the word "home." She was to live there for the next thirty-five years.

CHAPTER THIRTEEN

"SOMETHING will come along."

That became my mother's battle cry as I plowed into the final year of high school. Friends began asking her what Russell planned to do when he graduated, and her answer was, "Something will come along." She didn't know what, and nothing was in sight on the horizon, but she'd survived so long now on faith that something always came along for people who did their best. "Russ hasn't made up his mind yet, but something will come along," she told people.

I saw no possibilities and looked forward to the end of school days with increasing glumness. It was assumed I would get a job. Boys of our economic class didn't ordinarily go to college. My education, however, hadn't fitted me for labor. While I was reading the Romantic poets and learning Latin syntax, practical boys had been taking shop, mechanical drawing, accounting, and typing. I couldn't drive a nail without mashing my thumb. When I mentioned my inadequacies to my mother she said, "Something will come along, Buddy."

If, gloomily, I said, "Fat chance," she snapped at me, "For

God's sake, Russell, have a little gumption. Look on the bright side."

I didn't mind the prospect of working. Having worked since I was eight, I had acquired the habit of work, but I was stymied about what kind of full-time work I might be fit for. That winter I was trying to muster enthusiasm for a career in the grocery business. Moving from Lombard Street to Marydell Road, I had lost my newspaper route. To make up the lost income I'd taken a Saturday job at a large grocery in the Hollins Market, which paid $14 for twelve hours' work. It was a "self-service" store, a primitive forerunner of the supermarket, the first expression of an idea whose time had not yet come. Situated in a dilapidated old building where groceries had once been sold, old-style, across the counter, it bore little resemblance to the bulging supermonuments to consumption that were to rise after World War II. There was no air-conditioning in summer and little heat in winter. Under the cellar's cobwebbed rafters an occasional rat scurried among sacks of cornmeal and hundred-pound bags of flour. As a stock clerk, I toted merchandise from the cellar, marked its price in black crayon, and stacked it on shelves for Saturday shoppers. The flour sacks were slung over the shoulder and lugged upstairs to be dipped from with an aluminum scoop on demand.

The manager was Mr. Simmons, a bawdy, exuberant slave driver who had learned the business in the days of over-the-counter selling, when a manager's personality could attract customers or turn them away. Simmons was a tall, square-shouldered man who affected the breezy style, as though he'd studied his trade under burlesque comedians. His head was as round and hairless as a cannon ball. He wore big horn-rimmed glasses and bow ties, and his mouth, which was wide and frequently open from ear to ear, displayed dazzling rows of teeth so big they would have done credit to a horse.

Throughout the day the store was filled with his roars, guffaws, shouted jokes, and curses. He romped the aisles in a Groucho Marx lope, administering tongue lashings when he discovered empty shelves where the canned tomatoes or the Post Toasties or the Ovaltine were supposed to be. Spotting a handsome woman at the meat counter, he might glide behind the hamburger grinder to whisper s. to voce some dirty joke at the butcher's ear, then glare at the woman, part his mouth from ear to ear, and display his magnificent ivory. The store was his stage, and he treated it as if he were its star, director, producer, and owner.

If there was a dull half hour he might creep up behind one of the stock clerks hoisting oatmeal from crate to shelf, goose him with both thumbs, then gallop away roaring with laughter. Many of the customers were black and poor and arrived late on Saturday nights hoping to have their paychecks cashed. With them Simmons played Simon Legree, examining their checks suspiciously, demanding identification papers, then rejecting some damp proffered document as inadequate. "That damn thing is so dirty I don't even want to touch it. You open it up and show it to me." Or, if the credentials were in order: "I don't know whether I'm going to cash this check or not. How much do you want to buy here?"

Simmons boasted of being a great lecher. In the cellar ceiling he had drilled a small hole through which he could look up the skirts of women customers standing at the cash register overhead. When a woman who pleased his fancy entered the store, he ostentatiously departed for the cellar with some such cry as "Hot damn! I've got to see more of this." Rolling his eyeballs and smacking his lips he plunged into the cellar and could be found there standing on a pile of flour sacks, one eye glued to his peephole.

I wasn't exhilarated by the grocery business, but at least I was getting experience I thought might help me get full-time work at it after high school. For this purpose I wanted to learn to work the cash register so I could become a checker, the most glamorous job in the store except for the manager's. Simmons withheld this prize. At some point I'd made the mistake of trying to show him I was fancily educated, thinking this would move him to promote me from cellar labor. Whether he took me for an overeducated young fool or whether he resented my failure to laugh loudly enough at his jokes, I don't know. Whatever the reason, I waited in vain for my chance to work the cash register. I knew I would never get it when Simmons, desperate one day for help at the cash registers, came down to the cellar, passed me by, and called on Earl to do the job. Earl was black, and black people were contemptible to Simmons but still preferable to me. It made me wonder if I was cut out for the grocery business. But on the other hand, what else was there?

The only thing that truly interested me was writing, and I knew that sixteen-year-olds did not come out of high school and become writers. I thought of writing as something to be done only by the rich. It was so obviously not real work, not a job at which you could earn a living. Still, I had begun to think of myself as a writer. It was the only thing for which I seemed to have the smallest talent, and, silly though it sounded when I told people I'd like to be a writer, it gave me a way of thinking about myself which satisfied my need to have an identity.

The notion of becoming a writer had flickered off and on in my head since the Belleville days, but it wasn't until my third year in high school that the possibility took hold. Until then I'd been bored by everything associated with English courses. I found English grammar dull and baffling. I hated the assignments to turn out "compositions," and went at them like heavy labor, turning out leaden, lackluster paragraphs that were agonies for teachers to read and for me to write. The classics thrust on me to read seemed as deadening as chloroform.

When our class was assigned to Mr. Fleagle for third-year English I anticipated another grim year in that dreariest of subjects. Mr. Fleagle was notorious among City students for dullness and inability to inspire. He was said to be stuffy, dull, and hopelessly out of date. To me he looked to be sixty or seventy and prim to a fault. He wore primly severe eyeglasses, his wavy hair was primly cut and primly combed. He wore prim vested suits with neckties blocked primly against the collar buttons of his primly starched white shirts. He had a primly pointed jaw, a primly straight nose, and a prim manner of speaking that was so correct, so gentlemanly, that he seemed a comic antique.

I anticipated a listless, unfruitful year with Mr. Fleagle and

186

for a long time was not disappointed. We read *Macbeth*. Mr. Fleagle loved *Macbeth* and wanted us to love it too, but he lacked the gift of infecting others with his own passion. He tried to convey the murderous ferocity of Lady Macbeth one day by reading aloud the passage that concludes

> . . . I have given suck, and know
> How tender 'tis to love the babe that milks me.
> I would, while it was smiling in my face,
> Have plucked my nipple from his boneless gums. . . .

The idea of prim Mr. Fleagle plucking his nipple from boneless gums was too much for the class. We burst into gasps of irrepressible snickering. Mr. Fleagle stopped.

"There is nothing funny, boys, about giving suck to a babe. It is the—the very essence of motherhood, don't you see."

He constantly sprinkled his sentences with "don't you see." It wasn't a question but an exclamation of mild surprise at our ignorance. "Your pronoun needs an antecedent, don't you see," he would say, very primly. "The purpose of the Porter's scene, boys, is to provide comic relief from the horror, don't you see."

Late in the year we tackled the informal essay. "The essay, don't you see, is the . . ." My mind went numb. Of all forms of writing, none seemed so boring as the essay. Naturally we would have to write informal essays. Mr. Fleagle distributed a homework sheet offering us a choice of topics. None was quite so simpleminded as "What I Did on My Summer Vacation," but most seemed to be almost as dull. I took the list home and dawdled until the night before the essay was due. Sprawled on the sofa, I finally faced up to the grim task, took the list out of my notebook, and scanned it. The topic on which my eye stopped was "The Art of Eating Spaghetti."

This title produced an extraordinary sequence of mental images. Surging up out of the depths of memory came a vivid recollection of a night in Belleville when all of us were seated around the supper table—Uncle Allen, my mother, Uncle Charlie, Doris,

Uncle Hal—and Aunt Pat served spaghetti for supper. Spaghetti was an exotic treat in those days. Neither Doris nor I had ever eaten spaghetti, and none of the adults had enough experience to be good at it. All the good humor of Uncle Allen's house reawoke in my mind as I recalled the laughing arguments we had that night about the socially respectable method for moving spaghetti from plate to mouth.

Suddenly I wanted to write about that, about the warmth and good feeling of it, but I wanted to put it down simply for my own joy, not for Mr. Fleagle. It was a moment I wanted to recapture and hold for myself. I wanted to relive the pleasure of an evening at New Street. To write it as I wanted, however, would violate all the rules of formal composition I'd learned in school, and Mr. Fleagle would surely give it a failing grade. Never mind. I would write something else for Mr. Fleagle after I had written this thing for myself.

When I finished it the night was half gone and there was no time left to compose a proper, respectable essay for Mr. Fleagle. There was no choice next morning but to turn in my private reminiscence of Belleville. Two days passed before Mr. Fleagle returned the graded papers, and he returned everyone's but mine. I was bracing myself for a command to report to Mr. Fleagle immediately after school for discipline when I saw him lift my paper from his desk and rap for the class's attention.

"Now, boys," he said, "I want to read you an essay. This is titled 'The Art of Eating Spaghetti.' "

And he started to read. My words! He was reading *my words* out loud to the entire class. What's more, the entire class was listening. Listening attentively. Then somebody laughed, then the entire class was laughing, and not in contempt and ridicule, but with openhearted enjoyment. Even Mr. Fleagle stopped two or three times to repress a small prim smile.

I did my best to avoid showing pleasure, but what I was feeling was pure ecstasy at this startling demonstration that my words had the power to make people laugh. In the eleventh grade, at the eleventh hour as it were, I had discovered a calling. It was the happiest moment of my entire school career. When Mr. Fleagle finished he put the final seal on my happiness by saying, "Now that, boys, is an essay, don't you see. It's—don't you see—it's of the very essence of the essay, don't you see. Congratulations, Mr. Baker."

For the first time, light shone on a possibility. It wasn't a very heartening possibility, to be sure. Writing couldn't lead to a job after high school, and it was hardly honest work, but Mr. Fleagle had opened a door for me. After that I ranked Mr. Fleagle among the finest teachers in the school.

My mother was almost as delighted as I when I showed her Mr. Fleagle's A-Plus and described my triumph. Hadn't she always said I had a talent for writing? "Now if you work hard at it, Buddy, you can make something of yourself."

I didn't see how. As the final year of high school neared its end and it began to seem that even the grocery business was beyond me, my mother was also becoming worried. She'd hoped for years that something would come along to enable me to go to college. All those years she had kept the door open on the possibility that she might turn me into a man of letters. When I was in eighth grade she'd spent precious pennies to subscribe to mail-order bargains in the classics. "World's Greatest Literature," retailing at 39 cents a volume, came in the mail every month, books that stunned me with boredom. *The Last of the Mohicans, Ben Hur, Westward Ho, Vanity Fair, Ivanhoe.* Unread, her attempts to cultivate my literary tastes gathered dust under my bed, but it comforted her to know I had them at my fingertips.

She also subscribed on my behalf to the *Atlantic Monthly* and *Harper's.* "The best magazines in America," she said. "That's where you'll find real writers." The best magazines in America also piled up unread and unreadable in my bedroom. I seemed cut out to serve neither literature nor its bastard offspring, journalism, until my great coup in Mr. Fleagle's English class. Then her hopes revived.

"If only something would come along so you could go to college . . ." became, "For somebody with grades as good as yours, Buddy, there must be some way of getting into college."

Delicately, she spoke to Herb. She could push and haul Herb on matters of household management, but she could scarcely ask him to finance college for me. Grand though his income seemed after her years of poverty, it wasn't big enough to put a boy through college without great sacrifice. There was also a question of taste. I'd done nothing to endear myself to Herb, and she knew it. What's more, with his few years of elementary school education, Herb would have been flabbergasted by the suggestion that a healthy young man should idle away four years in college at vast expense instead of making his own way in the world as he had done.

Still, my mother did speak to Herb, and Herb listened sympathetically. She told me about it next day. "Herb says he thinks he can get you a job as a brakeman on the B&O," she reported.

"Well," I said, "railroad men make good pay."

"Maybe something will come along before school's out," she said.

The idea of becoming a railroad brakeman entertained me for a while that winter. Any job prospect would have interested me then. I was becoming embarrassed about being one of the few boys in the class with no plan for the future. The editors of the high-school yearbook circulated a questionnaire among members of the senior class asking each student to reveal his career ambition. I could hardly put down "To be a writer." That would have made me look silly. Boys of the Depression generation were expected to have their hearts set on moneymaking work. To reply "Ambition: None" was unthinkable. You were supposed to have had your eye on a high goal from the day you left knee pants. Boys who hadn't yet decided on a specific career usually replied that their ambition was "to be a success." That was all right. The Depression had made materialists of us all; almost everybody wanted "to be a success."

I studied the yearbook questionnaire with deepening despair.

I wanted the yearbook to record for posterity that I had once had flaming ambition, but I could think of nothing very exciting. Finally I turned to my friend Bob Eckert in the desk behind me.

"What are you putting down for ambition?" I asked.

"Foreign correspondent," Eckert said.

I loved it. It sounded dashing, thrilling. Unfortunately, it was so different, so exciting an "ambition," that I couldn't copy Eckert without looking like a cheat. And so, turning my mind to journalism, I ticked off other glamorous newspaper jobs and after a moment's reflection wrote down, "To be a newspaper columnist."

In fact I hadn't the least interest in journalism and no ambition whatever to be a newspaper columnist. Though City College published an excellent weekly newspaper, during my four years there I was never interested enough to apply for a job, never knew where its office was located, and never cared enough to find out.

Having solved the problem of finding an "ambition" elegant enough for the yearbook, I returned to reality. Was I really sharp enough to make it in the retail grocery business? Should I become a railroad man?

Matters were at this stage in the spring of 1942 when I discovered my great friend and classmate Charlie Sussman filling out a sheaf of forms between classes one day. Sussman was a prodigious bookworm and lover of education. I admired him greatly for the wide range of his knowledge, which far exceeded mine. He understood the distinction between fascism and communism, subjects on which I was utterly ignorant. He was interested in politics and foreign policy, subjects that bored me. He listened to classical music, to which I was completely deaf. He planned to become a teacher and had the instinct for it. It bothered him that there were such great gaps in my education. Like my mother, Sussman wanted to improve me. He tried to awaken me to the beauties of music. "Start with Tchaikovsky," he pleaded. "Tchaikovsky is easy. Everybody likes Tchaikovsky. Then you'll discover the beauty of Beethoven and Mozart."

Now, finding him bent over a strange batch of papers, I asked, "What're you doing, Suss?"

"Filling out college application forms," he said.

"What college are you going to?"

"Johns Hopkins," he said.

I knew that Johns Hopkins was a hospital and produced doctors.

"I didn't know you wanted to be a doctor. I thought you wanted to teach."

"Hopkins isn't just for doctors," he said.

"No kidding."

"It's a regular college too," he said. "What college are you going to?"

"I'm not going to college."

Sussman was shocked. Dropping his pen, he glared at me in amazement. "Not going to college?" He said it in outrage. He refused to tolerate this offense to education. "You've got to go to college," he said. "Get some admission forms—they've got them downstairs at the office—and we'll go to Hopkins together."

That would be great, I said, but my family couldn't afford it.

"Apply for a scholarship," he commanded.

"What's that?"

Sussman explained. I was astonished. It seemed that this college, of whose existence I had just learned, was willing to accept a limited number of students absolutely free if they could do well on a competitive examination. Sussman himself intended to take the test in hope of reducing the cost to his parents.

"I'll get you a set of application forms," he said, and he did. He was determined that education would not lose me without a struggle.

My mother was as surprised as I'd been. Just when she had begun to lose faith that something would come along, providence had assumed the shape of Charlie Sussman and smiled upon us. The day of the examination she stopped me as I was going out the door and kissed me.

"I've been praying for you every night," she said. "You'll do great."

She'd been doing more than praying. For three weeks she'd worked with me every night on a home refresher course in mathematics, my weakest subject. Night after night she held the math books and conducted quizzes on geometry and algebra, laboriously checking my solutions against those in the back of the books and, when I erred, struggling along with me to discover where I'd gone wrong. Afterwards, when we were both worn out, she went to bed and prayed. She believed in prayer, in the Lord's intercession, but not in the Lord's willingness to do it all. She and I together had to help. The Lord helped those who helped themselves.

The examination was held on a Saturday in May. I hadn't been to Johns Hopkins before, so I gave myself an extra hour against the possibility of getting lost on the streetcar trip to North Baltimore. My mother had written the directions and put them in my pocket, just in case, but the trip went smoothly, and when I reached the campus I was directed to a huge lecture hall reeking of chemicals. I was dismayed to find the hall filled with boys, each of whom probably wanted one of the few available scholarships as desperately as I did.

Unlike my mother, I had no faith in prayer. From early childhood I had thought of God as a cosmic trick player. Though I'd never told this to my mother and went to church regularly to please her, I'd grown up a fatalist with little faith. Now, though, as I counted the boys in the room and realized the odds against me, I decided it was foolish to leave even the remotest possibility untouched. Closing my eyes, I silently uttered the Lord's Prayer in my head and, to leave no base untouched, followed it with the only other prayer I knew, the one my mother had taught me years ago when putting me to bed in Morrisonville. And so, as the examination papers were being distributed, I sat at my desk silently repeating, "Now I lay me down to sleep, I pray the Lord my soul to keep . . ."

At the end I improvised a single line of my own and prayed, "Dear God, help me with this test." It lasted four hours.

My mother was waiting on the porch when I came back down Marydell Road that afternoon. "How'd it go, Buddy?"

"Don't know," I said, which I didn't.

Two weeks crept slowly past and May neared its end. I had only three weeks left of high school when I arrived home one afternoon to find my mother sitting expressionless in the glider on the front porch. "You got a letter from Hopkins today," she said. "It's in on the table."

"Did you open it?"

"I'm not in the habit of opening other people's mail," she said. "You open it and tell me what it says."

We went inside together. The envelope was there on the table. It was a very small envelope. Very small. Hopkins had obviously decided I was not worth wasting much stationery on. Picking it up, I saw that it was also very thin. The message was obviously short and probably not sweet if it could be conveyed in such flimsy form. I ripped the end off the envelope, slid out a piece of note-sized paper, and unfolded it. I saw it was a form letter on which someone had typed a few words in the blank spaces. I read it to myself.

"Well, what does it say?" my mother asked.

I read it aloud to her:

> Sir: I am pleased to inform you that you have been awarded a Hopkins Scholarship for two terms of the academic year 1942-43. This award will entitle you to remission of tuition fees for this period. Please let me know at once if you will accept this award.
>
> Yours very truly,
> Isaiah Bowman
> President

"Let me read it," my mother said. She did, and she smiled, and she read it again; then she said, "Herb is going to be proud of you, Buddy."

"What about you?" I asked.

"Well, I always knew you could do it," she said, heading for the kitchen. "I think I'll make us some iced tea."

She had to do something ordinary, I suppose, or risk fainting with delight. We had helped ourselves, the Lord had helped us in return, and one of her wildest dreams had come true. Something had come along.

Chapter Fourteen

The United States had been at war seven months when I entered Johns Hopkins in the summer of 1942. Through most of my childhood there had always been war. War in Ethiopia. War in Spain. War in China. Dimly, I had been aware through all those years that worlds were burning, but they seemed far away. It wasn't my world that was on fire, nor was it ever likely to be, or so I thought. Sheltered by two great oceans, America seemed impregnable. I was like a person on a summer night seeing heat lightning far out on the horizon and murmuring, "Must be a bad storm way over there someplace." It was not my storm.

I'd just turned fourteen when Hitler and Stalin signed their nonaggression pact which cleared the European stage for World War II to start, but though I delivered the papers that told the story in gigantic headlines, I was baffled when a man bought one from me, glanced at the front page, and said, "So it's war." Wasn't there always war someplace? What was special this time?

For me, World War II began a few days later as nothing more than a mild dispute with my mother. We woke that morning to a radio blaring that the German army had marched into Poland. It was September 1, 1939, and we were still living on Lombard Street. It was one of those rare mornings when Herb was home for breakfast. "We'll be in it before long, mark my words," he said to my mother.

"This is England's war. Let England fight it," she said.

Why another German land grab in the middle of Europe should start a world war wasn't clear to me. I seldom paid attention to news of politics, dictators, and treaties. My interest centered on baseball news, comic strips, murders, and hangings. Herb was better informed.

"We're going to be in it before it's over, you just mark my words," he repeated.

This irritated my mother. She hadn't forgiven the English for denying the great lost family fortune to Papa.

"We went over there once and pulled England's chestnuts out of the fire," she said. "This time let them stew in their own juice."

Still four years shy of eighteen, I quickly calculated that the war would be over before it could take me. If it was a world war, I figured, it would last four years. The First World War had lasted four years, hadn't it? I had the idea that four years was the standard length of world wars. My mother interrupted these calculations to talk business.

"You'll be able to sell all your extras today, Buddy."

I groaned inwardly. "Extras" were the excess newspapers left over after I'd served my regular customers. The *News-Post* always sent more papers than there were customers. It was a sly way of boosting circulation, since they billed me for the extras whether I sold them on street corners or not. Usually I threw them in the trash and took the loss, for when it came to salesmanship I was no less timid than I'd been during my *Saturday Evening Post* career. My mother let me get away with wasting the extras, on grounds that it was more important to spend time on schoolbooks than hawking newspapers. Now, though, she smelled war profits.

"Today you ought to be able to sell every paper they'll send you," she said.

I decided to forget I'd heard her. After delivering the first-edition bundles that afternoon I went home as always to read until the second edition came off the truck. My mother was waiting. "Did you sell all your extras?"

I hadn't sold one, hadn't even tried.

"What kind of newspaperman are you? Take those extras up to the corner where people get off the streetcar and you can make some money."

"Nobody wants to read about this Polish stuff."

"For God's sake, Russell, show a little gumption for once in your life. This is a world war. An idiot could sell newspapers today."

School was to reopen next week after summer recess. "I think I'd better brush up on my schoolwork," I said.

"Are you going to get out there and sell those papers, or do you want me to do it for you?"

She wasn't bluffing. She had once gone out to collect overdue bills from the worst deadbeats on my route after I said it couldn't be done, and she had come back with every penny they owed. I'd felt humiliated by that. Having your mother collect the bill was bound to cost you respect among your customers.

"I'll do it," I said, and went off to badger pedestrians with quiet murmurs of, "Newspaper? Like to buy a newspaper?" In spite of my languid sales pitch I was back home in fifteen minutes with every paper sold and a pocket full of coins.

My ignorance of the world beyond schoolroom, baseball diamond, and family circle was remarkable even for a fourteen-year-old. Except for the previous year's experience at City College I had spent my childhood in the blue-collar world where there was neither money, leisure, nor stimulus to cultivate an intelligent world view. I had never been exposed to art, nor attended a concert, nor listened to a symphony even on records. A phonograph would have been an impossible luxury for my mother. The fierce political passions of the 1930s, the clash of ideas about communism, fascism, socialism, were very remote from the gray depths we inhabited. The debates that engaged the intellectual world filtered down to us in refracted and weakened distortions, like sunlight groping toward the ocean bed.

I knew about Benito Mussolini and Adolf Hitler. They were bad guys. I thought of the world in terms of bad guys and good guys, and I knew Hitler and Mussolini were bad guys , though I didn't know why. Franklin Roosevelt was a good guy of legendary proportions. All Americans were good guys, and America was invincible because it was on the good side of whatever the issue might be. Though Hitler and Mussolini were bad guys, they were also funny comic-opera figures, not only because they looked funny—Hitler with his silly mustache, Mussolini with his strut and bulbous jaw—but also because they acted as if they thought they could whip America. That was silly. Nobody could whip America.

At the movies one afternoon in 1938, my buddy John Heideman and I watched the usual newsreels of nastiness in Europe— Hitler taking the mass salute at Munich, Mussolini strutting like a rooster. In the middle of it, John nudged me and said, "America ought to go over there and clean the whole place out like a rat's nest." I had no doubt America could clean Europe out like a rat's nest if it wanted to. And even if somebody had told me the United States Army consisted of only 227,000 soldiers and had equipment for only 75,000 of those, my confidence wouldn't have fallen. By European standards our army may have looked "like a few nice boys with BB guns," as *Time* magazine put it, but that wouldn't have troubled me. For Americans, I'd have retorted, BB guns were enough to do the job.

What I knew of the world's turmoil came mostly from "War Cards" which, like baseball cards, came packed with penny bubble gum. These depicted Japanese atrocities in China, Italian atrocities in Ethiopia, and slaughters of women and children in the Spanish Civil War. From these I knew that Japan was bad and China good, that Italy was bad and Ethiopia good. The lesson on Spain was confusing. One side murdered nuns and the other bombed helpless villages, but I was uncertain which side was which, and hadn't a guess what the Spanish war was about. The passionate quarrels in intellectual circles about Nazi and Soviet intervention in Spain, and its meaning, and what decent Americans should do about it— only the slightest sense of all this seeped down to the working-class world of southwest Baltimore.

On Lombard Street and in Belleville the great menace of the 1930s was the Depression, not fascism or communism. When I entered City College, where most of my classmates came from more sophisticated families, I was surprised to find boys my own age who worried about Hitler, Stalin, and the future of Europe. Many of my classmates were Jewish, and some talked about relatives in Germany and what was happening to them under Hitler. A few had refugee relatives from Germany living in their homes. One, I was startled to discover, called himself a communist and believed communism was mankind's only hope. When he told me this I decided he was a crackpot, but went on enjoying his friendship. After all, he was a musician. I'd learned on Lombard Street that longhairs were supposed to be a little nutty.

My innocence of modern politics lasted until I went to Hopkins. As a senior in high school I was called for an interview before the Honor Society, a group composed of the school's intellectual elite. Someone had put me up for membership. The interview turned out to be a trial, with the group's president acting as prosecutor. After a few questions about my academic history, he asked, "What's your opinion about the split between Stalin and Trotsky?"

I had no opinion.

"Why not?"

"I haven't heard about it."

My interrogator stared at me. Though he was about my age, he had prematurely thinning hair, a gray complexion, and a gaunt ascetic face, which made him seem much older. He wasn't in my class and we'd never spoken before, but I'd heard of his brainpower. "You must know there was a struggle for power in Russia between the Trotskyists and Stalinists," he said.

Russell, above (right), as a high school senior,
and, at left, at Johns Hopkins.

I confessed I didn't. Eyebrows were raised in the jury box. The prosecutor looked at his colleagues and committed a little shrug, as though to say, "Need we waste more time on this clod?"

A defense attorney stood up, a boy named George Winokur. I scarcely knew him either, but for some reason he'd decided to take my case and somehow had got access to my grades. Like a lawyer leading a witness, he asked, "What was your last mark in Latin?"

It was high, very close to the top of the class. I was strong on the first century A.D.; it was the twentieth I was ignorant about. The prosecutor cut in. "Do you know who Leon Trotsky is?"

I didn't.

"Never heard of Leon Trotsky?"

I hadn't.

Winokur interrupted, trying to limit the damage. "You've also taken three years of French, haven't you?"

I had.

"Would you tell us what your mark was in French last term?"

Since the French teacher marked "on the curve" and I'd scored highest in the class, my grade was 100. Winokur smiled in triumph. He was an admirer of Clarence Darrow and felt as if he'd saved another of society's victims from the gallows.

"Very impressive," sniffed the prosecutor in a tone that conveyed how unimpressed he was. "Now tell us about Stalin. Have you ever heard of Stalin?"

"He's the dictator of communist Russia."

"Well," said the prosecutor, looking at the jury and feigning a smile, "he does know something. He's heard of Stalin." Then turning to me: "You've probably heard of Adolf Hitler, too."

The United States was now at war with Hitler. I understood what I was being told. Though ignorant, I wasn't dumb, and I refused to compound my own disgrace by dignifying his last remark with a reply. They convicted me very quickly, and not without justice, since my ignorance of the modern world hardly qualified me to join the elite.

Lombard Street society would have seemed barbaric to my

prosecutor and probably to most of the boys I admired at City College. To them, 1938 was the year of Munich, when Neville Chamberlain sold Czechoslavakia to Hitler for "peace for our time." In Lombard Street, however, it was the year the dignity of the white race hung in the balance scales of history. While uptown Baltimore debated war and the future of civilization, the men of Lombard Street sat on their stoops in shirt-sleeves, puffed their pipes, and pondered a cruel theological mystery. It could best be stated as a question: to wit, why had God permitted Joe Louis to become the heavyweight champion of the world?

The racial doctrine of our neighborhood was "separate and unequal." Black people were considered unworthy and inconsequential. There was "a place" for black people, and they were tolerable so long as they knew their "place" and stayed in it. Unfortunately, some became "uppity," didn't know their "place," didn't stay in it, wanted to walk right into the fancy downtown stores—Huntzler's and Hochschild, Kohn's—and try on clothes from the rack, clothes that white people might later want to try on. Most stores, of course, didn't put up with that. They didn't refuse to sell to blacks—"niggers," as everybody in my neighborhood called them—but most refused to let them try on garments before buying.

My mother had taught me contempt for bigotry. Though she still had a good bit of old Virginia la-di-dah in her attitude toward blacks, she'd taught me to look down on race baiters as "poor white trash." Blacks were to be judged just like white people, strictly on individual character and merit. On coming to Baltimore, I was shocked by the blatant racism candidly expressed daily in our new neighborhood. After a year or so there I was more shocked to hear my mother tell Uncle Harold one night, "I've got nothing against a Negro as long as he knows his place." Racism seemed to be contagious.

The blacks' place in our neighborhood was Lemmon Street, the back alley between Lombard and Pratt. There they lived in ancient brick dilapidations, tiny row houses two stories high and two windows wide with views overlooking the garbage cans of the whites. There they were tolerated so long as they didn't make an unsightly show of themselves around on Pratt or Lombard where whites presided. This social organization had been in place so long it seemed to have been divinely ordained. The superiority of the white man, the unworthiness of the black—these were assumptions at the very foundation of society. And yet, if this order had been divinely ordained, why, oh why had God permitted Joe Louis to become heavyweight champion of the world?

How could faith in the universal order be justified so long as Joe Louis, a black man, was allowed to pound white men senseless with so little exertion? Joe Louis was a living, breathing mockery of the natural order of things. He had won his title in 1937. Before then and since, he had agreeably stepped into the ring with every white hope willing to have his brains scrambled. Now at the peak of his art, Louis dispatched all comers with such finality that his challengers were called "The Bum-of-the-Month-Club." The ease with which he did the job, often in a round or two without working up a sweat, was gall in the white supremacist's soul.

Louis's exercises were broadcast on the radio and eagerly listened to by the whole community. You heard those awesome words booming out of the speaker from faraway New York: "In this corner—wearing purple trunks—weighing 197 pounds—the Brown Bomber from Detroit—" And then the monstrous roar of that faraway crowd, the gong, the crackling voice of Clem McCarthy: "—Louis measures him—a left to the jaw, a right to the body—" And then it was all over, for Louis was not a man to dawdle at his work.

And then, always, up from dismal Lemmon Street, which lay beneath our open kitchen window, I'd hear shouts, cheering, clapping, a tumult of joyous celebration issuing from the houses where the blacks lived. Out front in Lombard Street, the silence of the tomb. Once again Joe Louis had offended the white neighborhood by giving Lemmon Street a good time.

Lemmon Street people never made much fuss outside their houses. In black districts of Baltimore, celebrators poured out of houses and bars, filling the streets and whooping with pleasure

204

each time Louis finished one of his executions, but there was none of this in white neighborhoods where blacks lived in the alleys. People in Lemmon Street obviously thought too much celebration would be indiscreet. As I discovered in 1938, though, their spirit was not completely lifeless. That summer I witnessed a spectacular development in racial affairs.

For months we had been occupied with the most momentous encounter in the history of sport: Joe Louis had signed to fight Max Schmeling for a second time. Schmeling was the only man who had ever beaten Louis, and he hadn't just beaten him, he had battered him mercilessly, then knocked him out in the twelfth round. This triumph for the white cause had occurred in 1936. Afterwards, Schmeling published a gloating article in the *Saturday Evening Post* explaining how he had found Louis's fatal weakness. Schmeling was a white man. A German, admittedly, and officially approved by Adolf Hitler at a time when Germans were not terribly popular, but, above all, he was a white man. White pulses pounded with anticipation as the second fight approached, and black pulses, for all I know, may have pounded with dread. The white neighborhood awaited the second fight with fevered hopes. Perhaps God had raised Joe Louis so high only to humble him at the fists of the great German white hope.

At last the night of the titanic battle arrived, and I settled by my radio to attend upon the pivotal point of the modern age. What occurred was not the turning of the tide at Gettysburg nor the stand of the Spartans at Thermopylae, but hardly more than a fly-swatting. At the bell Louis left his corner, appraised Schmeling the way a butcher eyes a side of beef—we all saw it over and over again in movie newsreels later—then punched him senseless in two minutes and nine seconds. Paralyzing in its brutal suddenness, it was the ultimate anticlimax for the white race.

From Lemmon Street I heard the customary whooping and cheering rise into the sour Baltimore night. I went to the kitchen window. Doors were being flung open down there. People were streaming out into the alley, pounding each other delightedly on the back, and roaring with exultation. Then I saw someone start to move up the alley, out toward white territory, and the rest of the group, seized by an instinct to defy destiny, falling in behind him and moving en masse.

I watched them march out of the alley and turn the corner, then ran to the front of the apartment to see if they were coming into Lombard Street. They were. They seemed to have been joined by other groups pouring out of other neighborhood alleys, for there was a large throng now coming around into Lombard Street, marching right out in the middle of the street as though it was their street, too. Men in shirt-sleeves, women, boys and girls, mothers carrying babies—they moved down Lombard Street almost silently except for a low murmur of conversation and an occasional laugh. Nervous laughter, most likely.

Joe Louis had given them the courage to assert their right to use a public thoroughfare, and there wasn't a white person down there to dispute it. It was the first civil rights demonstration I ever saw, and it was completely spontaneous, ignited by the finality with which Joe Louis had destroyed the theory of white superiority. The march lasted maybe five minutes, only as long as it took the entire throng to move slowly down the full length of the block. Then they turned the corner and went back into the alleys and, I guess, felt better than most of them had felt for a long time.

On Lombard Street enlightenment was hard to come by. When war began I followed the news as melodrama. Another encounter between the white hats (us) and the black hats (them). I was shocked by the speed with which the Nazis crushed Europe and occupied Paris and planted the swastika at the English Channel. That fall, carrying newspapers with gigantic headlines that told of the blitz on London, I marveled at the destruction of a civilization I'd thought eternal. Like many military thinkers, I guess, I'd expected a rerun of World War I and was surprised to find the script entirely new. Still, it never occurred to me that the Nazis could win. They were the bad guys.

I was flabbergasted when the Japanese attack at Pearl Harbor brought us into the war at the end of 1941. Though by then sixteen, I was still so innocent of the world around me that American involvement had seemed impossible. And Japan! Why in the world had Japan attacked us? I didn't know Japan had anything against us. Sitting by the small radio in the kitchen at Marydell Road that Sunday night, listening to the bulletins from Washington, I thought the Japanese attack was ridiculous. A tiny country like that, nothing more than a few specks on the map, a country whose products were synonymous with junk, a pipsqueak country on the far side of the earth—it was grotesque that such a country should take on mighty America. Settling their hash would be as easy as squashing an ant.

"It'll take about two weeks to finish them off," I told my mother.

She was less confident. "I hope it's over before you're old enough to go," she said.

I laughed. I was still two years shy of military age. In two years we would have forgotten that Japan ever existed.

By the time I entered Hopkins in the summer of 1942 I knew better. Boys I'd known in high school were already in uniform. Others were registering for the draft. Responding to the speeded-up pace of wartime America, Hopkins was operating on a year-round schedule with no summer vacation. I attended classes there the day after graduating from high school. By my seventeenth birthday that August it was obvious the war would not end in the coming year and probably not in the year after that. My mother had been right to worry. Obviously I was going to have to go. I began to look forward to it with pleasurable excitement.

I had been in love with the romance of flying since first hearing as a small boy about Charles A. Lindbergh, the Lone Eagle, Lucky Lindy, who'd flown all the way to France by the seat of his pants. The pinups over my bed had been Captain Eddie Ricken-backer, Wrong-Way Corrigan, Roscoe Turner, Wiley Post, and Amelia Earhart. Enchanted by the glamour of flight, I cut out magazine pictures of the latest warplanes and pinned them up alongside Captain Eddie and Roscoe Turner. In my fantasies I flew over the trenches on the dawn patrol, white scarf streaming behind me in the wind as I adjusted my goggles and maneuvered the Fokker of Baron von Richthofen into my gun sights. Now the war offered a chance to make those dreams come true. The country needed flyers, thousands and thousands of them. While my mother worried about my going to war, I worried too. It wasn't easy to qualify for flight training. I was afraid of being rejected and losing my shot at glory.

There wasn't much glory in college life. I still rode the trolley to school and carried lunch in a brown paper bag. Most of my friends did, too. The people I gravitated to were town boys, different from the tweedy fraternity-house crowd who wore saddle shoes and cared about lacrosse games and campus dances. We were a raffish bunch of overgrown streetwise kids sprawled in the cafeteria, chomping homemade sandwiches, arguing noisily about politics, literature, history, and economics, seething with intellectual contempt for the smooth fraternity crowd and filled with secret envy for the fraternity boys' social polish and devil-may-care ways with women.

Though I'd been an academic whiz in high school, these new companions quickly made me feel like a dolt. They were at ease in organic chemistry and integral calculus, understood the treason of Alcibiades, could argue the merits of logical positivism, debated whether Eugene O'Neill or George Bernard Shaw was the greater playwright, explained why Thomas Wolfe was a romantic sentimentalist who would never rank among the great writers. I struggled comically to catch up to them.

I took physics and calculus, thinking they would improve my chances of getting into flight training. After the first semester the calculus professor offered to erase my "Fail" mark if I dropped the course. Discovering that this was a way out, I dropped physics, too, and concentrated on literature, history, and economics, known on campus as "bullshit courses" because their examinations usually posed essay questions permitting a glib writer to bluff his way through. Sometimes I succeeded, sometimes not. The history professor returned my first test paper with the gentleman's C which Hopkins granted everyone not obviously an idiot and the scrawled, "You find it so easy to be smart that you don't bother to work very hard."

How hard did he want me to work? I was laboring doggedly, yet after six weeks of college I was already six months behind most of my peers. I began looking toward military service as a vacation.

In the spring of 1943, in anticipation of my eighteenth birthday, I applied for enlistment in the Navy Air Corps. It seemed more glamorous than the Army Air Corps. Everybody was enlisting in the Army Air Corps, but the Navy Air Corps was different. It was more dangerous, I thought, therefore more glamorous. Flying off carriers—so hard, so dangerous. Flying over the vast watery desert of the Pacific. So easy to get lost out there, so hard to find a carrier to come back to in that trackless expanse. It took daring, the Navy Air Corps. It took the kind of man who had always wanted to test himself against the great von Richthofen.

I told my mother I was going to enlist. She hid her dread. The training would take fifteen months. She looked for the silver lining. "At least it'll keep you out of the war for fifteen months," she said. "But why don't you try to get into the Army Air Corps if you want to fly?"

"The Navy is better," I said.

"You can't even swim, Buddy."

This was true. I'd spent four years standing in the shallow end of the City College swimming pool without even learning to float. I was mortally afraid of deep water, but in my zeal for adventure I also wanted to challenge that terror. This had been another reason for choosing the Navy.

"Does the Navy take people who can't swim?" my mother asked.

"They guarantee they'll teach you to swim," I said.

The examination was held in Washington and took a full day. I was so fearful of failing the physical that my blood pressure went up. The corpsman who took it said it was too high to suit the Navy. "Have you been eating a lot of potatoes?" he asked.

I ate potatoes every night. Why?

"Sometimes potatoes will drive your blood pressure up," he said.

"I had potatoes for supper last night," I said.

He pondered that. "Tell you what," he said. "Come back here again three days from now and we'll recheck your blood pressure. But lay off the potatoes until then."

Three days later, with potatoes out of my bloodstream, I went back to Washington and was enlisted in the United States Navy under orders to report home and await my eighteenth birthday. My only other physical problem was weight. Stripped bare, I now stood six feet two inches tall and weighed 139 pounds. The Navy doctor noting these figures on the record looked up and said, "You're three pounds overweight."

To weigh three pounds less I would have had to peel off my skin and get down to bare skeleton. But the doctor didn't look like a man making a joke. "I've always thought I was underweight," I said.

He winked. "Young man," he said, "we're going to put thirty-five pounds on you." They did, too, but it took a year.

Orders arrived a few days after my eighteenth birthday. I was to report to Washington with a toothbrush and a razor for transfer to a training base. Most of my friends at Hopkins had already left for war. Charlie Sussman, who'd helped me get there, was being drafted into the Army and was raring to go. "It's going to be a great educational experience," he told me, grinning happily the day we shook hands and said good-bye.

My mother had never been in an airplane—neither had I— and thought of airplanes as infernal machines which none but a fool or a wild man would step into. She knew that training promised to keep me away from enemy gunfire for fifteen months, but felt that flying an airplane was almost as dangerous as being shot at. Throughout my last weeks at home she did her best to keep a cheerful countenance, but I caught her several times looking at me gravely and hungrily, trying to press her memory indelibly with the image of someone she might never see again.

I left the house before dawn on an October morning. Ou

good-byes were said at the door. It was as it almost always was between us in moments of deep emotion. No tears, no clasping in each other's arms, all emotion thoroughly under control, everything correctly repressed to insure against messy outbursts. She looked up at me and with a quick, tight smile said, "Well, you'd better get going if you're going to catch that train," and I leaned down and kissed her briefly on the lips.

"Write me as soon as you get there," she said, and waved me off up Marydell Road to catch the streetcar. I knew she was worried, but didn't realize how badly, and didn't think about it for long. I was too exultant. Boarding the streetcar I had no sense of putting my life at risk. Not a bit. I felt an intoxicating sense of being free for the first time in my life. Adventure. Flight. Freedom. Now at last, all were going to be mine.

By mid-morning I was in Washington and homesick, missing her so much that I telephoned home long-distance, an outrageous use of money in that time. She was so flustered at hearing my voice that she hung up in confusion before we exchanged more than ten words. Late that afternoon I wrote her from the train carrying us south.

"You hung up the telephone so soon I didn't get to tell you anything. The 6:30 train from Penn Station turned out to be a local and I was lucky to get to the Cadet Board on the stroke of 8. They kept us sitting around for two hours, then we ate at the expense of the Navy at a downtown restaurant. After that they whisked us to the Union Station in a truck that looked too much like the Black Maria. I called you from the station and wanted to tell you I'm headed for Pensacola, Fla., but you hung up too soon. . . . Please don't worry. Hold down the fort and keep things running. . . ."

After twelve hours of my adventure in freedom I was yearning for home.

CHAPTER FIFTEEN

FOR the next eighteen months, while old friends and schoolmates were discovering the face of death on battlefields from Bastogne to Okinawa, the Navy sent me on an extended tour of Dixie. After four months at Pensacola came three months at the University of South Carolina. I was in Miami living the good life at Coral Gables when Eisenhower sent the armies ashore on D-Day, and at pre-flight school at the University of Georgia when Patton was racing for the Rhine. I was at Memphis waiting to take off on a flight to Arkansas when a mechanic climbed onto the wing and shouted: "President Roosevelt is dead!" Germany surrendered three weeks later and I was sent back to Pensacola. Because the Navy had overestimated the number of flyers it needed to fight Japan, flight training slowed to a crawl. The Navy had kept one of its promises —it had put thirty-five pounds on me—but its promise of glory remained unfulfilled.

By the summer of 1945 we were flying out of Whiting Field. It was a broiling expanse of cleared land in the north Florida boondocks, one of those ugly, barren, temporary training bases that had been nailed together overnight. The South was strewn with them during World War II. A couple of runways and acres of stark wooden barracks surrounded by a perimeter of back-shadowed piney woods. A water tank on four steel legs. A flag hanging limp in sultry air. Pensacola was an hour away by slow bus. I made the trip to town and back several nights a week on account of Karen, an Indiana girl at the local nursing school. I was in love.

It was a chaste romance. We held hands in the movies and walking the streets. Under a subtropical moon we sat in the grass and Karen confided her dreams, which had to do with owning a horse farm and having a large family, and I talked of mine, which had to do with shooting down Japanese warplanes. We kissed without feeling any fire and went to Walgreen's drugstore for milkshakes, and she went back to the nurses' quarters while I rode the bus back to Whiting Field. I considered our love too fine to be fouled by lust and was offended when my roommate Ozzie, awakening as I returned, leaned down from his upper bunk to ask as he always did, "Did you get deflowered tonight, Bake?"

A big part of my Navy career by then had been spent in the struggle to get rid of my accursed virginity. This had been harder than learning to swim or learning to fly. The swimming had been surprisingly easy, thanks to the Navy's policy of dealing with fear by ignoring it. My fear of deep water left the Navy simply uninterested. On the first day in the pool an instructor with a voice like a bullhorn ordered fifty of us to climb a high board and jump in feet first. The board looked about two hundred feet high, though it may have been only twenty or twenty-five. A line was formed to mount the ladder and jump. I drifted to the end of the line, then stepped out when the splashing started and introduced myself to the instructor.

"I'm a nonswimmer," I said. "You want me to go to the shallow end of the pool?" At City College I'd spent four years in the shallow end of the pool.

"This pool doesn't have a shallow end," the instructor said.

"Well, what am I going to do?"

"Get up on that platform and jump," he said.

The pool depth was marked as fifteen feet at that point.

"I'm not kidding. I can't swim a stroke."

"Up! Up!" he shouted.

"But I'll drown."

"This pool's got the best lifesaving equipment in the Navy," he said. "Don't worry about it."

"Come on."

"I'm giving you an order, mister. Up!"

Quaking in every fiber, I climbed the ladder, edged out onto the board, took one look down, and, unable to faint, stepped back.

"Jump!" the instructor roared.

I stepped to the edge, closed my eyes, and walked into space. The impact of the water was like being smacked on the bottom by a two-by-four, then I was sinking, then—my God!—I was rising irresistibly to the surface. My head broke water. The water was actually supporting me, just as everybody had always said it would. The instructor glared.

"You didn't keep your legs straight," he shouted. "Get back up there and do it again."

Astonishingly, I was able to make a little progress dog-paddling through the water, and, hauling myself out of the pool, I went back up the ladder and did it again. Again I popped to the surface like a cork. Again I was able to move a little through the water. Fifteen feet of water, too. I was swimming. Swimming! A lifetime of fear ended in those few moments. By the end of a year I was able to swim, fully clothed, for hours at a stretch in deep water.

Flying was trickier. My early instructors tried to put me at ease by saying it was a lot like driving a car. I was afraid to tell them I didn't know how to drive a car. Didn't every young man know how to drive by the time he was sixteen? Not knowing how to drive by eighteen seemed shameful. I feared the Navy would wash me out of flight training and send me to scrub decks if they learned about it.

On my first flight the instructor took me to 3,000 feet in a Piper Cub before letting me handle the stick.

"Goddamn it, don't swing it like an axe handle!" he shouted

when I yanked the plane violently up and down. "You wouldn't handle a steering wheel like that, would you?"

This was when we were flying out of a field south of Miami where the instructors were all civilian pilots under Navy contract. Mine was a nervous, middle-aged pilot named Jim, a natty little man with bulging eyeballs usually bloodshot from hangover, a handsome cavalry mustache over his lip, and fear of student flying in his soul. After our seventh flight together, he landed the plane, stepped out, smiled at me, and said, "You take her around."

I was appalled. He was telling me I was ready to "solo." I knew I wasn't. He'd demonstrated the basics during our seven flights and then had me practice while he sat in the front seat. Theoretically I knew how to take off, maintain altitude, bank, recover from a stall and a full spin, and land. Actually I'd never done any of these things. Jim was so nervous about having a beginner at the controls that he'd never yielded either stick or rudder to my command. When I had been supposed to be doing the flying, I'd felt the stick and the rudder pedals doing things that were not my doing. The plane had dual controls, which operated simultaneously in front and rear seats. Jim had been "riding the controls" up front; that is, instead of leaving me free in the back to handle the plane, he'd been actually doing all the flying for me. Several times I had tested him by taking my feet off the rudder pedals, and I'd noticed they kept making the right moves, in and out, as if operated by ghostly feet. Occasionally Jim had even congratulated me on the skill with which he had executed a landing. I'd certainly never made a landing while he'd been in the front seat. Nevertheless when Jim said, "Take her around," I closed the door, pushed the throttle forward, and started to take her around.

The takeoff wasn't too bad, though I nearly skidded off the runway before getting airborne. All I had to do was climb to 800 feet, turn 180 degrees, turn again, put the nose down, and land. It was exhilarating not having Jim riding the controls, but I was surprised, too. The plane seemed to have acquired a mind of its own. It insisted on going all the way to 1,200 feet when I wanted it to level off at 800, then when I tried to get back down it dived

215

all the way to 600 feet before leveling off. It finally consented to circle the field, and I got the nose pointed toward the runway and headed for earth at a civilized speed. When the wheels touched down it looked as if I might survive, and, feeling solid runway underneath, I slammed on the brakes. The plane spun violently through a 180-degree ground loop and wound up fifty yards off the runway in the grass. Since my ground loop hadn't flipped the plane and destroyed a wing, the jury that weighed my case decided to give me a second chance instead of washing me out of the program.

For the longest time, though, I flew and flew without ever being in control of any airplane. It was a constant struggle for power between the plane and me, and the plane usually won. I approached every flight like a tenderfoot sent to tame a wild horse. By the time I arrived at the Naval Air Station at Memphis, where Navy pilots took over the instruction, it was obvious my flying career would be soon ended. We flew open-cockpit biplanes—"Yellow Perils," the Navy called them—which forgave almost any mistake. Instructors sat in the front cockpit, students behind. But here the instructors did not ride the controls. These were courageous men. Many were back from the Pacific, and they put their destinies in my hands high over the Mississippi River and came back shaking their heads in sorrow.

"It's just like driving a car, Baker," a young ensign told me the day I nearly killed him trying to sideslip into a farm field where he wanted to land and take a smoke. "You know how it is when you let in the clutch? Real smooth and easy."

I knew nothing about letting in the clutch, but didn't dare say so. "Right," I said. "Smooth and easy."

I got as far as the acrobatic stage. Rolls, loops, Immelman turns. Clouds spinning zanily beneath me, earth and river whirling above. An earnest young Marine pilot took me aside after a typical day of disaster in the sky. "Baker," he said, "it's just like handling a girl's breast. You've got to be gentle."

I didn't dare tell him I'd never handled a girl's breast, either.

The inevitable catastrophe came on my check flight at the end of the acrobatic stage. It was supposed to last an hour, but after twenty minutes in the sky the check pilot said, "All right, let's go in," and gave me a "down," which meant "unfit to fly." I was doomed. I knew it, my buddies knew it. The Navy would forgive a "down" only if you could fly two successful check flights back-to-back with different check pilots. If you couldn't you were out.

I hadn't a prayer of surviving. On a Saturday, looking at Monday's flight schedule, I saw that I was posted to fly the fatal reexamination with a grizzled pilot named T. L. Smith. It was like reading my own obituary. T. L. Smith was a celebrated perfectionist famous for washing out cadets for the slightest error in the air. His initials, T. L., were said to stand for "Total Loss," which was all anyone who had to fly for him could expect. Friends stopped by my bunk at the barracks to commiserate and tell me it wasn't so bad being kicked out of flying. I'd probably get soft desk duty in some nice Navy town where you could shack up a lot and sleep all day. Two of my best friends, wanting to cheer me up, took me to go into Memphis for a farewell weekend together. Well, it beat sitting on the base all weekend thinking about my Monday rendezvous with Total Loss. Why not a last binge for the condemned?

We took a room at the Peabody Hotel and bought three bottles of bourbon. I'd tasted whiskey only two or three times before and didn't much like it; but now in my gloom it brought a comfort I'd never known. I wanted more of that comfort. My dream was dying. I would plumb the depths of vice in these final hours. The weekend quickly turned into an incoherent jumble of dreamlike episodes. Afterwards I vaguely remembered threatening to punch a fat man in a restaurant, but couldn't remember why. At some point I was among a gang of sailors in a hotel corridor, and I was telling them to stop spraying the hallway with a fire hose. At another I was sitting fully dressed on what seemed to be a piano bench in a hotel room—not at the Peabody—and a strange woman was smiling at me and taking off her brassiere.

This was startling, because no woman had ever taken her

brassiere off in front of me before. But where had she come from? What were we doing in this alien room? "I'll bet I know what you want," she said.

"What?"

"This," she said, and stepped out of her panties and stretched out flat on her back on the bed. She beckoned. I stood up, then thought better of it and settled to the floor like a collapsing column of sand. I awoke hours later on the floor. She'd gone.

With the hangover I took back to the base Sunday night, I would have welcomed instant execution at the hands of Total Loss Smith, but when I awoke Monday morning the physical agony was over. In its place had come an unnatural, disembodied sensation of great calm. The world was moving much more slowly than its normal pace. In this eerie state of relaxation nothing seemed to matter much, not the terrible Total Loss Smith, not even the end of my flying days.

When we met at the flight line, Total Loss looked just as grim as everybody said he would. It was bitterly cold. We both wore heavy leather flight suits lined with wool, and his face looked tougher than the leather. He seemed old enough to be my father. Wrinkles creased around eyes that had never smiled. Lips as thin as a movie killer's. I introduced myself. His greeting was what I'd expected. "Let's get this over with," he said.

We walked down the flight line, parachutes bouncing against our rumps, not a word said. In the plane—Total Loss in the front seat, me in the back—I connected the speaking tube which enabled him to talk to me but didn't allow me to speak back. Still not a word while I taxied out to the mat, ran through the cockpit checks, and finished by testing the magnetos. If he was trying to petrify me before we got started he was wasting his efforts. In this new state of peace I didn't give a damn whether he talked to me or not.

"Take me up to 5,000 feet and show me some slow rolls," he growled as I started the takeoff.

The wheels were hardly off the mat before I experienced another eerie sensation. It was a feeling of power. For the first time

As a seaman recruit (left),
and as a naval air cadet.

since first stepping into an airplane I felt in complete mastery of the thing. I'd noticed it on takeoff. It had been an excellent takeoff. Without thinking about it, I'd automatically corrected a slight swerve just before becoming airborne. Now as we climbed I was flooded with a sense of confidence. The hangover's residue of relaxation had freed me of the tensions that had always defeated me before. Before, the plane had had a will of its own; now the plane seemed to be part of me, an extension of my hands and feet, obedient to my slightest whim. I leveled it at exactly 5,000 feet and started a slow roll. First, a shallow dive to gain velocity, then push the stick slowly, firmly, all the way over against the thigh, simultaneously putting in hard rudder, and there we are, hanging upside down over the earth, and now—keep it rolling, don't let the nose drop—reverse the controls and feel it roll all the way through until—coming back to straight-and-level now—catch it, wings level with the horizon, and touch the throttle to maintain altitude precisely at 5,000 feet.

"Perfect," said Total Loss. "Do me another one."

It hadn't been a fluke. Somewhere between the weekend's bourbon and my arrival at the flight line that morning, I had become a flyer. The second slow roll was as good as the first.

"Show me your snap rolls," Total Loss said.

I showed him snap rolls as fine as any instructor had ever shown me.

"All right, give me a loop and then a split-S and recover your altitude and show me an Immelman."

I looped him through a big graceful arc, leveled out and rolled into the split-S, came out of it climbing, hit the altitude dead on at 5,000 feet, and showed him an Immelman that Eddie Rickenbacker would have envied.

"What the hell did you do wrong on your check last week?" he asked. Since I couldn't answer, I shrugged so he could see me in his rearview mirror.

"Let me see you try a falling leaf," he said.

Even some instructors had trouble doing a falling leaf. The plane had to be brought precisely to its stalling point, then dropped in a series of sickening sideways skids, first to one side, then to the other, like a leaf falling in a breeze, by delicate simultaneous manipulations of stick, rudder pedals, and throttle. I seemed to have done falling leaves all my life.

"All right, this is a waste of my time," Total Loss growled. "Let's go in."

Back at the flight line, when I'd cut the ignition, he climbed out and tramped back toward the ready room while I waited to sign the plane in. When I got there he was standing at a distance talking to my regular instructor. His talk was being illustrated with hand movements, as pilots' conversations always were, hands executing little loops and rolls in the air. After he did the falling-leaf motion with his hands, he pointed a finger at my instructor's chest, said something I couldn't hear, and trudged off. My instructor, who had flown only with the pre-hangover Baker, was slack-jawed when he approached me.

"Smith just said you gave him the best check flight he's ever had in his life," he said. "What the hell did you do to him up there?"

"I guess I just suddenly learned to fly," I said. I didn't mention the hangover. I didn't want him to know that bourbon was a better teacher than he was. After that I saw T. L. Smith coming and going frequently through the ready room and thought him the finest, most manly looking fellow in the entire corps of instructors, as well as the wisest.

Though I'd succeeded in sky and water by the time I was flying out of Whiting, I still had not triumphed with women. In a world where every man boasted of sexual conquest after every trip to town, my innocence was like a private shame. All my efforts to escape it, though, seemed doomed to failure. This wasn't because I lacked a powerful lust. Once the Navy freed me from the sexually stifling atmosphere in which I'd been growing up, the madness of that mania clamped me in a terrible grip. This was inflamed to white heat by the tales told by the Casanovas who infested the barracks.

Listening to this talk, I was paralyzed with envy and desire.

There was scarcely a woman alive, it seemed, who could resist the urge to haul men down onto beds, car seats, kitchen floors, dining-room tables, park grass, parlor sofas, or packing crates, entwine warm thighs around them, and pant in ecstasy. There were many older men among us, Marines who had survived Guadalcanal, Navy petty officers from ships sunk in the Pacific, men who went to town with chests blazing with combat ribbons. I envied those ribbons. They had the power to turn women into groveling slaves subservient to their wearers' vilest desires, or so I judged from the stories that came back on Sunday nights.

Burns, a handsome Marine sergeant of astonishing strength, boasted of having a local debutante so enchanted she would make love dangling from a parlor chandelier. Costello, a chief petty officer, never passed a weekend without having several officers' wives beg him to slake his appetite for flesh in delightfully squalid hotels. Powers, a machinist's mate who'd survived the sinking of the carrier *Wasp*, preferred to have three women bedded simultaneously to perform a variety of sexual services and, he said, seldom had trouble filling the quota.

I discounted a good deal of this talk but believed enough of it to give me pain. If the world was a sexual carnival, I wanted to be admitted, yet all my efforts failed. At first I spent liberty nights standing on street corners in towns packed with sailors, waiting for overheated women to claim my body. All I saw were thousands of other uniformed bodies standing on street corners waiting to be claimed. After midnight, when we all rode buses back to celibate barracks, I lay in my bunk angry and puzzled. If there were so many women out there with smoking armpits and steaming thighs, why did they not search me out? Wasn't I handsome enough, suave enough, desirable enough? Where were all those hot-blooded women anyhow? All I ever saw were 5,000 sailors standing on street corners waiting for something exciting to happen, and nothing ever did. That was Pensacola in 1943.

In Miami there was promise. Lovely Miami, sexy Miami, the hot moon hanging over beautiful Biscayne Bay, the girls so juicy under their light summer dresses, the hot little beads of sweat bedewing their upper lips in that tropical heat. A lush girl picked me up on the street in a Cadillac convertible. A car dealer's daughter, she was game for lippy nuzzling on the front seat but timid about hands fumbling along her thighs, full of "Behave yourself now" and "Be a good boy." I was sick of being a good boy. "It's too public here" was always her final complaint. "Somebody will see us."

I located a very private place south of Coral Gables. We passed it each day en route to the airfield. On a Saturday night I told her to drive that way. She seemed willing enough. We pulled off the highway into marshy ground overhung by great spreading limbs and vines. She switched off the headlights and we embraced in the blackness, hungry for sin. The mosquitoes arrived immediately. Not in squadrons or battalions, not in divisions—the mosquitoes came in flying armies. She was screaming that they were eating her legs. I could feel them tattooing the back of my neck.

She pushed me away, threw on the headlight beams, and crying, "They'll eat us alive!" backed out and roared top-speed back to Miami cursing mosquitoes.

Anticlimax waited to mock me at the end of every encounter. In Atlanta a spare young woman with thick eyeglasses agreed to come to my hotel room after midnight, plopped on the side of the bed, and said, "If you touch me I'll scream for help." I'd heard in the barracks about such women. They wanted to be treated forcefully. I touched her. She screamed. I'd heard of men wrongfully hanged because nervous women cried, "Rape!" I wanted to get her out of the room as quietly as possible, but it wasn't easy. She was determined to stay until I knew her life story. It was long and uneventful.

In Athens, Georgia, a girl spoke to me in a drugstore on Sunday afternoon. "Like to walk?" We walked idly hand in hand. She was young, maybe sixteen or seventeen, and communicated a sense of moist heat. We walked to a ramshackle part of town. "Here's where I live," she said.

It was a small tumbledown frame house, not much more than a shack.

"Like to come in?"

We went into a small parlor. It was separated from an adjoining room only by a sheet hung on a rod. I sat on a sofa with ruined springs. She sat on my lap, closed her eyes, offered her lips, and placed my hand under her skirt. Here was paradise at last. In a moment she was making incoherent noises which I took to be the music of feminine ecstasy. She seemed to be entering a deep swoon. With her body shuddering on my lap, I was near swooning myself when her cries became urgent. "Can't you get out of those pants?" she asked.

I was struggling to loosen my belt buckle when I heard pots and pans clattering on the other side of the sheet.

"There's somebody out there!"

"It's just Mama getting ready to cook dinner," she murmured and gave in to another onset of passion sounds. These had delighted me a moment earlier, but realizing that Mama was not eight feet away, handling pots on the other side of the sheet, took all the music out of them. Now they just sounded like very loud grunts and groans.

"Quiet! Your mother will hear you," I whispered.

"She won't bother us. She never does."

Since I still had Mama's daughter on my lap in a rosy condition, I could only imagine what would happen if Mama didn't run true to form this time but decided to stroll through the sheet. At this point a terribly masculine voice on the other side of the sheet boomed out: "Where'd you put them shoes I left out on the back porch?"

"That's just Pa," the girl said. "He won't bother us."

I hurled her off my lap, stood up, and grabbed my cap. She replied by arranging herself flat on the sofa, opening her mouth wide, and running the tip of her tongue over her lips. She'd seen Lana Turner inflame men that way in the movies, but it didn't work with me. The fire in my blood had turned to ice. Pa had one of those backwoods voices that usually came supported with a shotgun.

"Come on back here," she said, raising her legs to let the skirt fall back to her hips. That did it. I was two blocks away moving at a pace just short of a gallop before I looked back and saw that Pa wasn't on my heels.

Fate seemed to have sentenced me to virginity. There had been the chance to overcome it that weekend in Memphis when the curtain parted briefly on my alcoholic haze and I'd seen the strange woman in a strange hotel room undressing and lying on the bed to initiate me. Where I had met her or where she'd acquired me I couldn't even remember, but bourbon had obviously made me do something right—as it had in aviation—before it turned the tables and left me snoring helplessly on the floor. My sex life was a running joke.

Returning to Pensacola early in 1945 to fly the heavy planes and learn the mechanics of killing, I was resigned to chastity. From my 1943 tour there I knew the odds were hopeless: a thousand Navy men for every female on the streets. Waiting for the bus back to the base with my friends Nick and Carson one night, I was startled when a car pulled to the curb and a handsome woman asked if we wanted a ride. There were two other women in the car. None of the three looked like a casual pickup. Of course we wanted a ride.

The woman driving had a house in the fancier section of town. We ended up there. "For a drink," everybody agreed. But it was soon clear there would be more than a drink. The three women shared the house. They were older women. Women of twenty-five, twenty-six, maybe even twenty-seven, and all married to Navy officers now in the Pacific. They didn't talk much about their husbands. They'd been in the Pacific a long time. We made civilized talk, quiet ladies-and-gentlemen talk. By two A.M. the last bus to the base had left. "Why don't we sleep here tonight?" suggested Nick. Matter-of-factly, the women thought that was the only sensible thing to do. Two of them led Nick and Carson toward the bedrooms and nobody returned. I sat with the woman who'd been driving and had another drink and she finally said, "I'll make up a bed for you on the cot on the sun porch."

When she did I told her good night and she left. I undressed and lay wide awake in the dark for a long time, wondering if she was awake in her own bed expecting me to come to her room. Not likely, I told myself. These were women, real women, good women who missed their husbands and were being kind to three lonely boys who probably reminded them of the men they loved. She came through the sun-porch door and closed it quietly behind her while I was still musing on the nobility of good women.

"Are you still awake?"

She sat on the cot peering down at me in the darkness. I smelled perfume in her nightgown. I was scared. I believed in the distinction between good women and bad women. Good women were to be respected and loved purely. That's what they expected of a man. It was all right to wallow in lust with bad women but not with a good woman, not with a woman who was married to a man, possibly a Navy hero facing death for his country, for his wife, for me, in the faraway Pacific. I didn't want my belief in the good woman shattered. Now, as she sat in her gown on the edge of the cot, saying she couldn't sleep and did I mind if she stayed long enough to smoke a cigarette, I was scared of what she might do. I wanted her only to go away and continue being a good woman.

"Tell me about your husband," I said.

She touched my forehead lightly with her fingertips. "Not right now," she said.

"You must miss him."

Her fingertips brushed my cheek and neck. "It gets lonely sometimes."

"How long were you married before he went overseas?"

"Are you nervous about something?" she replied.

"Why?"

"Do I make you nervous?"

"Not a chance."

"I'm not much older than you are," she said. Her fingertips were now like feathers under my Navy-issue T-shirt.

"How old's your husband?"

"Doesn't matter," she murmured, fingertips still busy.

"Your husband must be quite a guy," I said.

She removed her hand and straightened her back. There was a silence. Finally, "You're really just a kid, aren't you?" she said.

It was very gentle, almost reflective, as though she were talking to herself.

"I guess so," I confessed.

"Don't worry about it," she said, standing up. "You'll grow up soon enough."

"I guess so."

She leaned over and pressed her lips lightly on my forehead. "You're sweet," she said. "I'm glad I brought you home. Sleep well." And she was gone, taking with her my golden opportunity. For weeks afterwards I was torn between feelings of nobility and suspicion that I had acted like a childish idiot.

It was a relief to meet Karen that summer at the nursing school. She was so obviously a good girl. There could be no possibility of anything carnal with her. I happily seized the chance to find peace from the torments of the sexual hunt. Karen was the kind of girl you married and remained faithful to all your life. She was the kind of girl who wanted decent, good things of life—to nurse the ailing, to have many children, to own a horse farm. She was the kind of girl my mother would have approved of. I even wrote my mother about her. "I've met a wonderful girl down here this summer. . . ." I'd met very few girls I dared tell my mother about. "She's the kind of girl I'd like to marry someday."

My mother didn't have too much trouble with the horse farm, but the mention of marriage set off alarms in Baltimore. I'd worked on the campus newspaper at Hopkins before the Navy years, and my mother had persuaded herself this meant I intended to go into journalism after the war. "I hardly see how you could get started in newspaper work if you had a wife to support," she wrote back. "They don't pay that much to beginners, do they?"

It wasn't marriage that occupied my mind that summer, however. It was the forthcoming invasion of the Japanese home islands, said to be scheduled for 1946. I wanted to be in on it. Navy rumor had it that casualties might run as high as a million men if, as seemed likely, the Japanese defended their homeland to the last man. This didn't cool my enthusiasm. I was nineteen and expected to live forever. I wanted glory. Although we would be ready for combat in time for the Japanese invasion, I had begun to worry about missing it.

Germany had surrendered that spring, and what scant news filtered into the backwoods of Florida that summer told of a Japan so devastated that its only effective resistance was the suicide of kamikaze pilots. Movie newsreels of Tokyo burning under B-29 fire-bomb raids depressed me, not because of so much agonizing death but because I suspected Japan might collapse before I could get into the slaughter. Now approaching twenty, I'd lost childhood's common sense and longed desperately to become a death-dealing hero. I wanted the war to go on and on.

On July 16 a group of men whose existence was unknown at Whiting Field tested a new weapon at Los Alamos, New Mexico. It worked. For those of us in Florida awaiting our chance at glory, the age of our childhood ended that morning in the premature dawn exploding over the desert. We didn't know about the test, of course. Doors were closing forever on our past, but we could not hear them slam. Soon the world we had known and the values we had lived by in that world would become so obsolete that we would seem to Americans of the new age as quaint as travelers from an antique land.

The atomic bomb was dropped on Hiroshima on August 6. My mother had written me almost daily since the day I left home. Her letters were mostly homey chitchat. News of a trip to Aunt Sister's, a visit from Audrey, Doris's progress in school, items about the latest trick of my baby sister, Mary Leslie. The letter she wrote the night after Hiroshima was no different. It would have given historians no clue that anything remarkable had happened the day before:

"Dear Buddy, This will have to be a little brief because I took Mary to the park and had a battle to get her to come home. She's in seventh heaven if she can get over there and stand up on the big swings like the older children. She informed me today that she is now a big girl, not a little girl anymore. . . .

"Herbert is now trimming the barberry bushes. There was a big softball game in the park, but I never watch them anymore because the players are all new, and I don't know them. . . ."

And so on.

On August 8, two days after Hiroshima, I wrote her from Whiting Field.

"At this moment I am in a kind of fugitive status. I'm committing the most heinous crime in the Navy and, even now as I write, my hand trembles at the thought of the punishment if I am caught. I am cutting a captain's inspection. They have these things every month or so as a sort of naval religious rite. The inmates all don their best straitjackets and stand at attention in the broiling sun for two hours. During this period, paunchy commanders roam leisurely through the ranks, attempting to catch people who've gotten their shoes dusty while coming through the deserts that surround the inspection field. After everyone's best garments are thoroughly wilted and perspiration-soaked and several persons have fainted, the inspection is formally declared to be over and the daily routine begins. . . ."

And so on.

My mother's letter on August 9, three days after Hiroshima, one day after the Soviet Union declared war on Japan, still ignored the atomic age.

"What's become of my pal? I haven't heard from you since last Friday. Yesterday I sent you a two-pound box of candy for your birthday and tomorrow I'm sending you by mail two books. One is a humorous book and the other, one of the best sellers. I hope you'll enjoy them. . . .

"One of Doris's pals from high school was over and spent the night and we all went to the movies this afternoon. The radio is blaring the news of Russia's victories in her war against Japan. It sure is good news, as I'm sure it will shorten this war. Herb is in an unusually good mood this evening, and he wants me to go for a ride in the car. . . ."

And so on.

On August 9 the second atomic bomb was dropped at Nagasaki. Next night I wrote to my mother.

"Well, today, to all intents and purposes, the war ended. The feeling of extreme elation which I had expected, existed for a bare moment, then life subsided back into its groove and it was just another day. It seems like I'm pulling some monstrous joke on myself when I say the war is over, because I really can't believe it. I didn't expect it to ever end. . . ."

I didn't confess that I hated the war's ending. I knew she had been praying to God to save my skin; I could hardly tell her I was sorry her prayers had been answered. Instead, I composed an essay on peace so fatuous that it might have done credit to a professional editorial writer:

"Tonight, it's almost like a miracle to think that nowhere on the entire earth is there one single, insignificant little war being fought. That is something utterly new in my lifetime, perhaps even in yours. Certainly, this is a strange new era loaded with immense latent possibilities. Let's hope that we can make the most of this opportunity at least."

These pieties were a shade premature, since the war had not quite ended. Still there was no hint in either my mother's correspondence or mine that the arrival of the nuclear age interested us much. My mother, also excited about premature news that the war was over, had less cosmic things on her mind. The night after the Nagasaki bombing she wrote:

"I'm still hoping that you'll go to college when the war is over and study journalism; that is, if you're still interested in that kind of work. Don't lose hope and get married at this stage of the game. Maybe there's still something better in the cards for you. Swell advice from one who's had the noose put on her twice, is it not?"

Eight days after Hiroshima, four days after Nagasaki, Emperor Hirohito, having determined that Japan must "endure the unendurable and suffer the insufferable," ordered the Japanese to cease fighting. It was August 14, my twentieth birthday.

"Dear Buddy," my mother's letter began that night, "On this

happy day I must write to you before retiring. All day we've been hearing the opinions of people on the street in different cities. The story which struck me was that of a newsboy on the street in Chicago. He said he was happy because some man had just bought an 'Extra' and given him a buck for it. This story brought back to my mind the day this war started in Europe. You were serving papers and well do I remember how I exhorted you to put forth your best efforts to capitalize on the big news. Now today as this war finally ends you're a man of twenty years today, and I'll bet it's one birthday you will always remember. . . . I can tell you that your mother's prayers were surely answered, for there's never been a day since you left October 7, 1943, that I have not prayed the war would be over before you had to go overseas, so I feel that I truly should be thankful tonight that at last it's over."

A later generation with hindsight's flawless vision understood very clearly that Hiroshima was a great and terrible moment in human history. The daily log of the war which my mother and I kept showed no such insight.

"I took Mary to the park. . . ."

"I am now cutting a captain's inspection. . . ."

"Herbert is now trimming the barberry bushes. . . ."

"Yesterday I sent you a two-pound box of candy for your birthday. . . ."

A later generation, with hindsight's infallible judgment, found the atomic bombing easy to condemn as a crime in which we had all connived, if only subconsciously. Neither my mother's letters nor mine, however, indicated that we even realized anything very extraordinary had happened.

"I took Mary to the park. . . ."

"I am now cutting a captain's inspection. . . ."

"There was a big softball game. . . ."

"And the daily routine begins. . . ."

"Herbert is now trimming the barberry bushes. . . ."

And so we drifted on, oblivious to history and the future's judgment, lost in the small chaff of humanity's humdrum concerns.

". . . haven't heard from you since last Friday . . ."
". . . people who've gotten their shoes dusty . . ."
". . . box of candy for your birthday . . ."
". . . and the daily routine begins . . ."

CHAPTER SIXTEEN

MIMI did not fit my mother's idea of "a good woman." Because I knew she didn't, it was a long time before I introduced them. Afterwards my mother said, "Mimi wouldn't be a bad-looking girl if she didn't use so much makeup."

I hadn't expected wholehearted approval of Mimi, but I'd thought she would at least be fair and agree with me that Mimi was a stunning beauty. Instead there was only a backhanded compliment—"wouldn't be a bad-looking girl"—slyly poisoned with the remark about "so much makeup." Decoded, it meant, "Not a good woman."

I think my mother realized right away that in Mimi she was meeting her most formidable opponent since the time of Ida Rebecca. Maybe, watching me lead Mimi up to the porch at Marydell Road that Sunday, she caught a glimpse of life repeating itself as an ironic joke and dreaded what was to come. A lifetime ago Ida Rebecca had stood on another front porch and stared at her in disapproval when Benny led her up the steps in Morrisonville. That day she had been the unsuitable young woman threatening the family security of a disapproving matriarch. Now time had

233

played a trick and created a reversal of roles. Now it was my mother's turn to play the disapproving matriarch while a foolish son brought her a dangerously unsuitable young woman.

My mother was more cunning than Ida Rebecca. From her own experience with Benny she knew how willful a son could be in the grip of passion, realized it was dangerous to mount open resistance, and sensed that guile and subversion would be the best weapons for the coming struggle. "Wouldn't be a bad-looking girl" was the first insertion of a very sharp scalpel. "So much makeup" was the twist of the blade. I knew what she was up to, but it was effective. This was in 1946, when I was twenty and shared my mother's belief in the "good woman." Still, my feelings about Mimi were so complex that I was far beyond thinking of her as either good woman or bad. Enchanted by love, I thought of her as a woman so special she could not be catalogued. Now, though, my mother had resurrected the question. It was all very well to keep company with women who applied rouge and lipstick with a free hand, but were such women suitable for presentation to mothers? Could a man who wanted to make something of himself seriously consider marrying such a woman? Vanity fought with love for possession of my soul, and the battle settled into a prolonged stalemate that was to drag on for the next four years.

It was true that Mimi was not promising "good woman" material. Besides using cosmetics, she lived alone, had no family, drank wine and whiskey, entertained men in her apartment, and sometimes touched her hair with bleach. Any one of these defects would have been enough to condemn her before my mother, but beyond these she had no prospect of ever making anything of herself. She had only a tenth-grade education and worked in a department store advising women what rouges, powders, pastes, lipstick, and eyeshadow suited their complexions. Even her name —Mimi—seemed unsuitable. "Good women" were not Mimi or Fifi or Lulu; they were Betty and Mary and Gladys and Lucy and Elizabeth.

She was also much too beautiful not to be suspect. Tall and slender, she had glistening hair the color of dark honey. When she wore it loose, it fell to her waist, a very narrow waist which flared downward into a swelling generosity of curved lines of such subtle complexity that my heart often stopped a moment when I thought of them. She had the carriage of an empress: chin always high and proud, face composed and serene, gracefully sloping shoulders, her long back arched as nobly as if she'd been bred to wear necklaces of pearl.

A friend of mine, meeting her for the first time and seeing us quarrel over something petty and watching her stride off in anger, said, "My God, she's beautiful! If you don't treat her better than that, somebody's going to take her away from you."

I lived in rages of jealous fear that somebody would. Arriving very late one evening at a friend's wedding reception, I went looking for her in the noisy crowd of drunken guests. We'd agreed to meet there, but I couldn't find her. Searching the gallery—it was a hotel ballroom—I looked over the railing and saw her standing directly below. A man I knew casually had her in his arms, and she placed her hands behind his neck, offered her lips, drew his face down to hers, and gave him a wanton kiss. I raced downstairs, hauled her away from him, and took her back to her apartment.

There I accused her of treachery and betrayal. "You couldn't be faithful for twenty minutes if I had to go out to the drugstore," I said.

Since we weren't married, she inquired calmly, why did I feel entitled to abuse her for kissing other men.

"Because there's something fine between us," I said. "Why do you want to destroy it?"

These were shopworn phrases I'd learned in the movies; this jealousy was such a shatteringly new emotion that I had no words of my own to express the pain. She laughed quietly. "Why do *I* want to destroy it? That's good."

"Well, why the hell do you?"

"Why don't *you* want to get married?" she replied.

There were very good reasons why I didn't want to get married to anybody just then, but I hadn't the courage to tell her why I would never get married to her. I wanted her to know, though, that marriage between us would never be possible, so I said, "For you and me, marriage isn't in the cards."

It was another corny old movie line, and she laughed at me for it, but she never forgot it nor let me forget I had said it.

Her full name was Miriam Emily Nash. She was two years younger than I by the calendar but many years older in experience of life. Born in Merchantville, New Jersey, she was the only child of a troubled marriage. Her father was a hard-drinking, perpetually broke ne'er-do-well who did unskilled labor in the Camden shipyard. Her mother was a devout Irish Catholic, awed by the priests, a faithful attendant at Mass, eating the fish every Friday, quick to distinguish evil from good. She hated liquor and what it did to her husband. When he went on a binge she locked the front door against him. Mimi's earliest memories were of her enraged father drunkenly smashing the big glass window out of the locked front door to reach the lock inside. That happened often. On the first Christmas Eve she remembered, her mother spent the day building a toy garden under the Christmas tree and her father stormed in drunk at dusk and kicked it into ruins.

They moved a lot, living in shabby little houses in and around Camden. Mimi was eleven when her mother, who was an epileptic, suffered a severe seizure and was sent to the New Jersey State Village for Epileptics at Skillman. The child was left alone with her father, but not for long. He had often gone away for a week or more—where or why, Mimi never knew. He just "disappeared," and now he "disappeared" again. When he didn't return after several days, Mimi was taken in by a kindly elderly couple who ran the neighborhood grocery. Later she was sent to live with a family who knew her parents.

Her mother came home for a brief period and the family was reunited, and the old uproar with the whiskey resumed, and her mother collapsed and went back to the security of Skillman. The word from Skillman was that her mother would not return home in any foreseeable future. Which left her father with the problem of Mimi. He presented it to the Society for the Prevention of Cruelty to Children, which placed her in the Sheltering Arms, a

236

Mimi as a child of seven (above left) and (above right)
in Baltimore, 1947. Below, during the trip to Charleston.

Camden "home" for orphans, foundlings, and battered or abandoned children.

By the age of fourteen Mimi was wise about the nature of public charities. The police came two or three times a week with bags of stale buns and rolls collected from Camden bakeries. Mimi noticed that the matron and her friends removed the choicest sweets for themselves before setting out the leftovers for the children. The Christmas parties were the worst humiliations. The decent people of Camden were full of Christmas goodwill and eager to do something for misbegotten children, so the inmates of the Sheltering Arms had to be trotted out on Christmas day to stand in local gathering halls and look delighted while each was handed a small gift. Some Christmases there were three or four parties a day at which the orphans were expected to beam with gratitude.

Mimi came to think of Christmas as an occasion when the well-to-do used life's losers to improve their day. Her refuge was books. She had a hungry mind and she read greedily, fairy tales mostly, and books like *Sarah Crewe* in which poor unfortunate children were brought happiness by the hand of beneficent Providence. In high school she enrolled in the college preparatory course. Shocked by such foolish nonsense, the matron ordered the school to transfer her into the business course.

Mimi packed her suitcase and ran away. The police brought her back to the Sheltering Arms next morning. She quarreled with the matron about church. The matron belonged to a fundamentalist Protestant sect presided over by two women preachers who practiced faith healing in services in which hysteria ran high. She insisted that the children of the Sheltering Arms attend these rites. Devoted to the Catholic Church, Mimi was outraged. She wrote to the Catholic bishop of Camden for help. She was being compelled to sin, she told him. She hoped someday to become a nun but now was being torn from her faith. Could the Church intercede for her?

The bishop replied. He wanted her to come see him. She did. Her faith in the Church, she thought, had been well placed. Then she discovered it hadn't. There was nothing he could do to help her, the bishop said. It was her duty to go back to the Sheltering Arms and serve God by being obedient. That shattered her faith in the Catholic Church. She never returned to it.

When she was sixteen and had been four years in the orphanage she ran away again. This time she was cannier. Instead of carrying a suitcase she dressed herself in three layers of clothing and fled to the far side of Camden. She had hoarded just enough money to rent a room. To explain her lack of luggage she told the landlord, "I've just come from out West, and all my suitcases have been lost."

She obtained a Social Security card under the name Judy Grant and took a job in a grocery. A few weeks later she was spotted there by a woman she'd met in the matron's church. Instead of taking her back to the Sheltering Arms, however, the woman offered to take her into her home at Egg Harbor. Mimi moved again, found work in an Egg Harbor clothing factory, and had her first taste of romance—with her benefactress's son. He had just been called into the Army and wanted a girl to remember.

She was seventeen when her father reentered her life. Dropping out of the blue as casually as if he'd "disappeared" only five days before instead of five years, he told her he was living in Maryland, outside Annapolis. Had a house there with a nice couple named Bill and Bertha. He'd like to try to put the family together again. Wouldn't she come and live with him?

Mimi had reason to say yes. She'd become a scandalous figure in Egg Harbor, and it had cost her the love of her Army warrior, who was in Texas. Neighbors had written him that she had been seen driving out evenings with a middle-aged married man of racy reputation. Her first love was infuriated with her and told her and the entire community that all was over between them. Mimi felt herself the object of community scorn. She grasped the opportunity to move to Maryland.

Her father, who was passing through Egg Harbor en route to someplace else, gave her directions. She was to get off the train at Glen Burnie on the appointed day, and he would meet her and take her to their new home. When she arrived at Glen Burnie a week later, he wasn't there yet. She waited. Four hours later he still hadn't appeared. Nor did he appear for four or five days after she'd found her way on her own to Bill and Bertha.

"He's just disappeared for a few days," said Bertha. "He'll come back before long."

He did come back, and he stayed a few days, and then he left again and didn't come back at all. It didn't matter. Mimi was a skilled survivor now. She had befriended people who lived in Severna Park, a middle-aged couple with thirteen children. They invited her to live with them. It was a pleasant house and a pleasant time with pleasant people. One of them had a job in Baltimore at Montgomery Ward's. Soon Mimi had a job there too.

When the mother of the house announced she was expecting her fourteenth child, Mimi decided to move again. A newspaper ad led her to a rooming house on Mount Vernon Place in the center of Baltimore, where, early in 1946, I happened accidentally into her life.

My mother, at this time, had been considering what sort of woman might be qualified to help me make something of myself. Though she never said so, I suspected she thought I might eventually snare an heiress. Mimi's biography, therefore, wasn't one to make her cry out with enthusiasm.

My own interest in Mimi was not high-minded when we first met. In that period I was still struggling to become a sinner. After my unheroic war in Dixie I'd come back to Baltimore feeling much too grown up to go back to college and taken a job in the central post office. It was idiot work—eight hours a day shoving letters into sorting cases—but it was good pay and financed my late nights of searching for lewd women in downtown saloons.

It looked as if my effort to become a seducer would succeed only in bankrupting me. The barflies who guzzled my weekly paycheck came in two varieties: those who lost all motor control before the bars closed and those who at two A.M. suddenly remembered dear old mothers waiting up anxiously for them at home.

The person who saved me from celibacy and cirrhosis was

George Winokur. It was George who in high school several years before had tried to save me from conviction by the Honor Society. We had become good friends afterwards at Hopkins, possibly because we complemented each other so well. George was boisterous where I was sedate, outgoing where I was shy, chunky and square-cut where I was long and angular. He was a scientist, I was a dabbler in the shabbier suburbs of the arts. Where I was sly, George was blunt. George could also make enough noise for both of us.

"You're wasting your time on bar girls," he blared at me in a restaurant one evening in a voice that felt like a load of gravel being dumped on the nerve ends. "The place we've got to crack is the Peabody."

The Peabody Institute of Music was situated on Mount Vernon Place. George, who was now in the University of Maryland Medical School, was well versed in Baltimore's sexual geography. The densest concentration of available women, he said, was Mount Vernon Place, where apartments were packed with sex-crazed musical females. Their desperation, George believed, arose from the fact that most male music students were homosexual. He assured me that musical people, though singularly dumb, were so sexually depraved that we could acquire platoons of budding sopranos for the price of a Coke and a hamburger.

We began prowling this Bohemia after dark. Girls did not pounce upon us. "Let's ring some doorbells," George said, nudging me into a dark vestibule to look for a doorbell with a feminine name beside it. It was hard to resist George. We rang doorbells. Sometimes a girl, sometimes a woman far gone in years would come to the door, and we would introduce ourselves if she looked sex-starved or say we'd rung the wrong bell if she looked too angry or too long in the tooth, and in every case the door was slammed against us.

"We're not getting through to the real Bohemians," George growled one night while we sipped coffee in the Vernon Grill.

"Maybe there aren't any Bohemians."

"They're here. We have to get a foot in the door, that's all."

I was ready to write off Bohemia as a desert when George phoned to say a medical friend of his had opened doors for us. He had arranged blind dates for us with two Peabody girls. The four of us went to the movies. The girls were not overheated. Mine informed me while Bette Davis was speaking that she preferred not to be touched on the knee. We returned them to their rooming house and were invited into the communal parlor for genteel conversation. I had made the genteel conversation and risen and was ready to leave when the parlor door opened and a third girl walked in. It was my date who introduced her. "This is Mimi," she said.

I sat down again. When they put us out an hour later, my life had been irrevocably changed. I didn't realize it, of course. Love is a madness that masquerades under a hundred rational disguises, and at first I mistook it for healthy lust.

Out on the street, the girls back in the rooming house, I found myself unwilling to let go of the evening and urged George into the Vernon Grill to discuss it over coffee. We disposed of our two dates quickly. "Dumb," George said. He'd tried to discuss Dostoyevsky and drawn blank stares while theorizing about Raskolnikov's need to suffer punishment. What could you expect of music students? "The Peabody Institute," he growled. "It would be more accurate to call it the Peabrain Institute."

"What did you think of Mimi?"

"Now that's a very interesting case," he said. "Very interesting. She doesn't have any education, but one thing she isn't is dumb."

"Nice body, too," I said.

George esteemed the female body but had a profound respect for brains. "That Mimi presents a highly interesting possibility," he said. "You and I could probably do with her what Henry Higgins did for Eliza Doolittle."

I knew neither a Higgins nor a Doolittle. "It's Shaw's *Pygmalion*," George explained, and told me the plot: two elegant gentlemen taking an ignorant girl off the streets, filling her with learning, brushing her to a high polish. It was a beguiling idea. ▶

242

liked the notion of playing the elegant gentleman and turning our rough diamond into a glittering jewel.

"Her mind is good and, better yet, almost untouched," George said. "Not quite a tabula rasa, but as close as we're likely to find. We could shape that mind."

I knew we could.

"The first thing she'll have to read is Arthur Koestler's *Darkness at Noon*," said George.

"And *Studs Lonigan* and *The Grapes of Wrath*," I said.

This was the birth of a long campaign the two of us undertook to turn Mimi into a creature who could pass for a princess.

It was not easy to get our project started, though. When I phoned Mimi a few days later she'd forgotten meeting me and, no, she couldn't go out next night, she had something else to do. I phoned her a week later, and again she had something to do. Obviously she didn't like me. I tried to put her out of my mind, but three weeks later an old Navy friend from New York came to town, and I phoned her and suggested we all go to the movies and maybe she could get one of the Peabody girls to come along for my friend. She agreed, not because she wanted to see me, I soon discovered, but because she thought New York men were glamorous. The date was a disaster. Ignoring me, she spent the evening charming New York, and the two of them left the Peabody girl and me alone to exchange icy smiles.

To hell with her, I decided. If she had so little moral character that she could ignore an upright man like me for the tawdry glitter of New York, she wasn't worth thinking about. I kept thinking about her anyhow. After a few weeks I phoned her again. She agreed to go to the movies with me. Alone this time. When I brought her home, she permitted a courtesy kiss at the door. Just one. Its formality angered me. I'd been nothing to her. Nothing. I wouldn't call her again.

Next week I called her again. Again she granted the courtesy kiss and sent me away. "That's it," I told myself. "I'm through with her."

I phoned her a few days later. This time, after the meaningless good-night kiss, she patted me on the shoulder and gave me a smile, as though she remembered having seen me someplace before.

That spring I went back to Hopkins, partly under my mother's badgering—"You'll never amount to anything spending the rest of your life in the post office"—partly because the G.I. Bill would pay the tuition and free me from the tedium of post-office labor. At the same time Mimi moved out of her rooming house and took a small apartment a few doors away with a friend named Jennie, who was serving an apprenticeship as a department-store buyer. Between them they had enough income to swing the rent. It was George who first learned they had an apartment, and he immediately proposed that he and I try to turn it into a center for Bohemian weekend revelry with our male friends and any women Jennie and Mimi chose to admit. To promote this effort I decided to make an all-out effort to ingratiate myself with Mimi. I invited her to make an excursion to Washington. She said she'd like that. She had never seen Washington.

On a sweet day in early May we rode the early train to Washington. A few minutes of languid conversation revealed that she knew absolutely nothing about American politics, government, or history. The urge to play Professor Higgins to her Eliza Doolittle came on me like a fever. I lectured her all the way to Washington about our colonial beginnings, the Puritan tradition, the Mayflower Compact, and the ancient origins of slavery.

We disembarked at Union Station, and I walked her through its spacious grandeur and lectured her on the great age of the railroads and the land swindles of Reconstruction on which they were built. I walked her up Capitol Hill and lectured her on the great Americans whose statues stood in the Capitol Rotunda. I walked her to the House of Representatives, then walked her back to the Senate, where we watched a man addressing an empty room and I lectured her about Daniel Webster, Henry Clay, John C Calhoun, and Thaddeus Stevens, and—in a reprise of my assault on Herb—told her what a bicameral legislature was. I walked her to the Supreme Court and lectured her about James Madison and the separation of powers.

I walked her down the infinite boredom of Constitution Avenue and into the National Gallery and lectured her about Rembrandt and Van Gogh, of whom I knew almost nothing. I walked her across the Mall to the Smithsonian and showed her *The Spirit of St. Louis* and lectured her about the history of flight and the myth of Lindbergh, Lucky Lindy, who'd flown all the way to France by the seat of his pants, and how Lindbergh had become an isolationist before the war began, not neglecting to lecture her on why isolationism was evil.

I walked her down to the White House, and while we stood outside the fence staring at that famous white paint I lectured her about the history of the Presidency, remembering to include Zachary Taylor, Franklin Pierce, and Benjamin Harrison. I walked her to the Lincoln Memorial and lectured her on Abraham Lincoln, the Emancipation Proclamation, Jefferson Davis, Robert E. Lee, Stephen Douglas, Mary Todd, Andrew Johnson, John Wilkes Booth, Dr. Samuel Mudd, Edwin M. Stanton, Salmon P. Chase, Harriet Beecher Stowe, and Simon Legree.

I walked her back toward the Washington Monument and lectured her on the Egyptian obelisk and phallic symbols and classical mythology and ancient Rome and the difference between the Roman Republic and the Roman Empire and the nobility of men like Cincinnatus, emphasizing that he was the man for whom Cincinnati was named, while Troy, New York, was named after a mythical city in Homer, and Cairo, Illinois, after a real city in Egypt. Leading her toward the Washington Monument I said, 'We can take the elevator to the top, but it'll be more fun to walk up."

"Couldn't we sit down a while?"

"You're not tired?"

"You've been talking for the past six hours so you probably haven't noticed that we've walked fifty miles without a rest."

"There's a lot more to cover," I said.

"I can't walk another step," she said, and collapsed on a park bench on the Mall. Well—let her rest a few minutes. Maybe we could skip the top of the Monument. Later we could walk over and look at the Treasury and then we could walk through the Federal Triangle. I sat down and started to explain how Harry Truman had become President.

"Is there anything you don't know?" she moaned.

Was that sarcasm I detected in her voice? Maybe I had overdone it. "I wanted you to have a good time. I didn't mean to bore you."

"You could have fooled me," she said, taking her shoes off to rub her feet.

"Why don't you do the talking for a while?" I suggested.

"What would I talk about? I'm not the expert on the Emancipation Proclamation."

"Tell me about yourself."

"There's nothing to tell."

"Sure there is. I don't even know where you come from."

"Why should you? Nobody could care about that."

"I could. How'd you come to be living on Mount Vernon Place?"

"Well, I come from New Jersey," she began, and bit by bit I began to get the story out of her. I hadn't thought of her as someone who might have had a life before I knew her. What she was telling me now seemed horrible. The Sheltering Arms—did such places really exist? Soon she was talking fluently, pouring out the saga of her miseries and maybe enjoying the tale a bit and making it just a shade more hair-raising to hold my attention. As she talked, love assumed another face, and I felt myself becoming her predestined protector, the strong sheltering male who must never let such dreadful things happen to her again.

When she said, "Isn't there any place to get some food?" I could no longer offer her the hot dog and soda pop I'd budgeted for the trip. "Budget be damned!" I said to myself and feasted her at the Chicken Hut on fried chicken, potatoes, gravy, and cole slaw. I no longer wanted to batter her with education. "If you're tired we can go to a movie and sit down," I suggested.

I paid an awful price for two tickets to a first-run movie and felt not a twinge of pain at the cost. I was prepared to give he everything I had. Nobility soon had its reward. In the darkness she slipped her hand into mine, squeezed it, and left it there.

We were both exhausted when we got back to Baltimore. I was in a mood close to holy exaltation. I despised myself for having once thought of carnal riot with this girl. In that, I had been like all the other beasts who had made her life a misery. Now I would atone by showing her how a gentleman could treat a woman. We climbed the steps to her apartment. She unlocked the door. It was here that she always offered the courtesy kiss and I, lout that I was, had always collected it. This night I determined that I would not.

To my surprise, she didn't offer it. Instead she opened the door wide and said, "Would you like to sit down awhile?"

Absolutely not. Not in my present state of pure love. "I've got to get home," I said, and started down the steps. "Good night."

She followed me to the top of the stairs. "Don't you want to kiss me good night?"

"I'm not that kind of guy," I said, and swaggered out. Love had clothed me in the glory of sainthood.

I let a few days pass before I phoned again. Of course she remembered me. Was I trying to be sarcastic? Why hadn't I phoned sooner? Wouldn't I pick her up that evening? Her roommate Jennie was out of town visiting family for a few nights. It was lonely with no one there.

We took a long walk in the soft spring evening. When I brought her home and she opened the apartment door, I didn't hesitate about stepping in. It was odd how quickly the serenity of beneficence wore off. Closing the door, I put my arms around her and said farewell forever to sainthood. The era of the courtesy kiss had ended.

"When you left the other night I thought you were mad at me," Mimi said later. "I was scared you wouldn't come back."

"Are you crazy? How could I be mad at you? I'll always come back."

And this, it turned out, was God's truth.

CHAPTER SEVENTEEN

THREE months passed before I mustered the courage to introduce Mimi at Marydell Road. Sunday dinner seemed the ideal occasion. Sunday dinner had become a family ritual for my mother, as it had once been with Ida Rebecca, a time when family was expected to gather round and celebrate its unity in food and table talk. It weekly confirmed my mother's pleasure in having given us "a home of our own." It was always a command appearance for me. Doris, now nineteen, helped with the hours of cooking. My mother would preside at one end of the table, and Herb would sit at the other straining to hear the Washington Senators baseball game on the living-room radio while flattering my mother on the crispness of the fried chicken, the texture of the gravy, the excellence of the devil's food cake, the coconut cake, and the apple pie with which the dinner always ended. Their child, Mary Leslie, was big enough now to sit at the table on a pile of books. Uncle Harold and Aunt Sister came frequently, and there were always other guests with blood ties to my mother's family, to Herb's, or to the Bakers.

It seemed the logical occasion for presenting Mimi. Sunday

dinner put my mother in her most gracious mood. With so many people present there would be no chance of matters getting out of hand. I knew Mimi would have instant allies in Doris, who was broad-minded; in Uncle Harold, who liked women; and in Aunt Sister, who liked meeting people.

"I've invited a girl I know to dinner Sunday," I told my mother. "I hope you don't mind."

"Your friends are always welcome here, Buddy. What's her name?"

"Mimi."

"I've never heard you mention a Mimi before."

"You'll like her."

"I'm sure I'll like her if you like her. My boy has good taste."

"She's a lot like you. She's had to make her own way in the world."

"Did you meet her at Hopkins?"

"She's not in school," I said. "She's got a job."

"What does she do?"

"Works in a department store."

"Selling?"

"Sort of."

"Well, I've got nothing against a girl making her own way in this world. Lord knows, I had to do it long enough."

"You'll like her," I said.

"Have you met her family?"

"She doesn't have any family. I guess you could call her an orphan."

"Where does she live if she doesn't have a family?"

"She's got an apartment downtown with another girl."

"Two girls living alone in an apartment?"

"They're both nice girls."

"Have you been there?"

"Once or twice," I lied.

"I see," my mother said, and I suspected she did. She couldn't help but wonder why I had stayed out so many times in recent

249

weeks until four o'clock in the morning. She must have worried about where I might be on those nights, but she hadn't asked. "I look forward to meeting her" was all she said, though.

"You'll like her," I said.

I hadn't told Mimi much about my mother. "You'll like her," I'd said. I suspected neither would like the other, but I was praying.

On Sunday Mimi came out to Marydell Road. I met her, and when she stepped off the streetcar, I felt a pang of uneasiness. Excited about being received into a family, eager to make a fine impression, she had dressed elaborately. She had bought a new dress, a pink clinging fabric that molded itself seductively to her body. She had had her hair done the day before by a hairdresser who, after lightening it with streaks of bleach, had chosen an upsweep suggestive of a Hollywood sex goddess. To present a proper face, she'd spared no expense at the cosmetics counter. Gazing at her, I thought her the most beautiful woman I'd ever seen and knew it was all wrong for Marydell Road.

"Do I look all right?" she asked.

"Terrific," I assured her.

The other guests hadn't arrived, and my mother was waiting alone on the porch when Mimi and I came up the steps. It wasn't until next day that my mother said, "Mimi wouldn't be a bad-looking girl if she didn't use so much makeup," but Mimi understood everything that Sunday night when I took her home on the streetcar. "Your mother didn't like me," she said.

"How can you say that? Of course she liked you."

In fact she had taken pains to be pleasant to Mimi all afternoon. I'd been happily surprised by that.

"She doesn't like me," Mimi said. "She'll never like me."

I was unwilling to believe this even after the next day's "Mimi wouldn't be a bad-looking girl if she didn't use so much makeup." I insisted Mimi come back for another Sunday dinner, and another, and another, and she did. Uncle Harold and Aunt Sister became fond of her. So did Herb. So did Doris. My mother saw only menace. She began clocking my movements.

No matter how quietly I came creeping in at three or four o'clock in the morning, I could count on my mother to be awake. "Is that you, Buddy?" she would whisper from her bedroom.

"Uh-huh."

"What time is it?"

"I don't know. Not too late."

Once in a while: "Where've you been?"

"Out with George," I'd whisper, closing the bedroom door behind me.

One morning, tiptoeing in just before dawn, I found her sitting in the dark in the living room. "Do you know what time it is? I've been waiting up all night for you."

"Is something wrong?"

"There's plenty wrong and you know what it is."

I didn't know how to answer that, so didn't.

"Don't you ever want to amount to anything, Russell?"

I was scheduled to graduate from college in a few months. "I'm not doing too bad," I said. "Let's turn in."

"I've worked and slaved to help you make something of yourself someday," she said. "Now you're throwing everything away because of that girl. She's got you hypnotized."

"That's silly."

"Oh, is it? Where've you been all night?"

"Out with George," I said.

"George doesn't stay out all night. He's in medical school, he's trying to make something of himself. You've been with Mimi, haven't you?"

"Come on, Mom, you're tired. Let's go to bed."

She turned on the light instead. "You never used to lie to me, Russell. Now you lie all the time. Can't you see what she's done to you?"

"What do you want me to do?" In anger at being treated like a child, I was ready to burn bridges.

"I'm only interested in your own good, Buddy. Don't think your mother is interfering."

"That's a fine thing to say. Of course you're interfering. Well, if you want to know—yes, I have been at Mimi's. Does that satisfy you?"

Her face went slack, expressionless. She stared beyond me at something five thousand miles away. "It's in the blood," she said, speaking to herself now.

"What's in the blood?" I asked.

She focused again on me, and, with a look as close to hate as she'd ever given me, she cried, "You're just like your father was. Just like your father."

It was said with loathing. Had she hated him, then? I'd spent most of a lifetime with her and she had rarely told me anything about my father, rarely even mentioned him. It was as if she wanted to erase him from my life. But now, in that hate-filled cry —"Just like your father"—she lit up an entirely different landscape of the heart. There had been some taint in my father's blood. She had reared me in dread that it might reappear in mine. Maybe that had been her reason for taking me out of Morrisonville and away from my father's people before the funeral meats were cold. Maybe she had hoped I could escape the taint of the blood by growing up far away from it among her own people.

I didn't know then nor for many years later that I'd been conceived before she and my father were married. Not knowing that, I couldn't grasp the complex emotions behind her cry: "Just like your father." She must have seen life repeating itself as a macabre dance. It must have seemed that I was reliving with Mimi my father's affair with her, that she was reliving Ida Rebecca's struggle against a foolish son and a wayward girl, and that I was in danger of reliving the disaster that love had made of her own life. She had overcome that and had transformed me from the agent of her disaster into a promise of a triumph for herself. Now the taint had surfaced to threaten everything, and, looking on me for that one terrible moment, she must have seen me as disaster recurring.

"Just like your father!"

After that, Mimi no longer came to Sunday dinner. Lines of battle had been drawn. The time for conciliation had passed.

I had no thought of marrying Mimi and no intention of giving her up. I was only twenty-one, poor, without exciting prospects, and enjoying the indolent sensuous life. Naturally I would marry later, when I was old and stuffy, and when I did I would naturally choose "a good woman," the sort my mother would approve. In the meantime I refused to spoil the joy of youth by parting with Mimi, the only woman with whom I felt happy. Eventually, of course, Mimi would have to be put aside for some drab woman of sound pedigree with all the social graces, but Mimi would surely understand that. She was the most sensible girl imaginable. She would understand the difference between youthful love and the marital requirements of an ambitious man.

In this spirit I let the months go blithely by, and gradually the months turned into years—1946 became 1947 which became 1948 which became 1949—and I was content. Mimi was not entirely content, to be sure. It was annoying when, as she occasionally did, Mimi suggested that she was looking forward to marriage. It was this annoying suggestion that I'd first tried to squelch by telling her, "It's not in the cards." With the passing months, though, she continued to talk rather dreamily about marriage, and, having grown fond of the phrase, I repeated it several times a year.

"Not in the cards," I said. "It's just not in the cards."

After graduating from Johns Hopkins in 1947 I began working for the *Baltimore Sun*. Elliott Coleman had steered me to the job. Elliott had come to Hopkins the previous fall to teach writing. He was a poet, a tall willowy man, prematurely white-haired, with a slightly fey manner and the great writing teacher's gift, which was to identify an ounce of quality in a ton of verbal trash and encourage the student to mine it. When I met him I was enamored of Ernest Hemingway, like almost everyone else in his course, and ground out story after story about sardonic fellows sitting in bars before trudging off to brutal ends. After reading a hundred stories like this, Elliott, who wanted us to discover Marcel Proust, threw up his hands in class one day, cried, "Hemingway's swell, but he's out! out!" and strode from the room.

Even in my embarrassing Hemingway imitations, however, he found something to encourage. "You write dialogue extremely well," he said. It wasn't true, but he'd identified my one skill that might be worth developing. The encouragement kept me from dropping the class. Still, my characters remained hard types who lumbered off to defeat or death with stoic resignation. After laboring through a dozen such tales, Elliott gave me one of the most valuable suggestions I'd ever had about writing.

"Don't you think it would make your tough guys a little more interesting to the reader if once in a while you had one bend down to smell a rose?" he asked.

Learning that I had no job prospects after graduation, Elliott said, "Maybe you should get on at the *Sun*. I'll speak to Dol Emmart."

In my senior year I'd helped edit the campus weekly newspaper, but it had been only a lark. It certainly didn't qualify me to work on Baltimore's great metropolitan daily, the *Sun*. Nor was I much interested in journalism. My passion was to become the new Hemingway, not a newspaperman. The new Hemingway, after all, would be a great artist; what could a newspaperman ever be but a hack?

Elliott spoke to Dol Emmart anyhow. Emmart had had a distinguished career at the *Sun* and was now a highly esteemed editorial writer and a close student of T. S. Eliot, on whose poetry he had spoken in our writing course. Emmart said there was, in fact, an opening for a police reporter at the *Sun*. I must phone Mr. Charles Dorsey, the managing editor, for an appointment. And so in June of 1947, for the first time in my life, I set foot in a newspaper city room.

Mr. Dorsey was precisely what years of movie-going had led me to expect of a managing editor. Encased in a glass-paneled office, looking imperiously out on a confusion of jangling telephones, scurrying copy boys, aged gents in green eyeshades, and marvelously cynical-looking men at typewriters who could only be reporters, he seemed as hospitable as a famished tiger. He was tall, lean, cool-eyed, a man obviously at ease on a telephone to London, placing bets at the $100 window at Pimlico, or firing a reporter for misplacing a fact. Admitted to his glass cage, I wanted to apologize for wasting his time but hadn't the courage to speak.

He ran a hand impatiently through his iron-gray hair, gazed down his patrician nose at me from great height, though he was no taller than I, and snorted loudly at what he saw. A flicker of his solemn gray eyes told me I was a damn nuisance. "Sit down," he commanded.

I sat. "So you think you can be a newsman," he said.

I didn't, but before I could say so the phone interrupted. "I've got to talk to the Washington bureau," he said. "It'll only take a minute."

I sat paralyzed with awe. He was talking to the Washington bureau right there in front of me. To be in a real newspaper office was heady enough. But to sit in the presence of a man who was actually talking to the Washington bureau—"What the hell is Truman up to now?" he was saying.

Somebody at the other end of the line was telling him. It was intoxicating. The rough familiarity with which he spoke of the President of the United States. The Washington bureau at the end of his phone line. A great correspondent of that Washington bureau who could tell him on demand what the hell Truman was up to. Here was glory indeed.

"What's your experience?" Mr. Dorsey was suddenly asking me.

"I've worked on the *Johns Hopkins News-Letter.*"

How ludicrous it sounded. Mr. Dorsey snorted loudly from his altitude, and when I recovered my wits, I realized he was pointing me toward the exit. So much for newspaper work. Still, nobody could take one thing away from me. I had been there when a genuine managing editor talked to the Washington bureau.

A week later the telephone caught me at home at dinnertime. "This is Dorsey," the voice said. "If you still want to work for me, you can start Sunday at thirty dollars a week."

Thirty dollars a week? This was 1947, not 1933. I thought, *Thirty dollars a week is an insult to a college man* and instantly replied, "I'll take it."

Maybe Elliott thought journalism was the obvious way for the new Hemingway to start. I certainly did. The *Sun* thought differently. Two years passed before it let me write a word for publication. I spent those years prowling the slums of Baltimore, studying the psychology of cops, watching people's homes burn, deciphering semiliterate police reports of dented fenders and suicides, and hanging around accident wards listening to people die. I wrote about none of this myself, but phoned the information to rewrite men. They packaged it to fit the space demands of the paper each night. On a slow night a suicide might merit three paragraphs if the deceased had found an interesting way to finish himself off. On a normal night the best he could hope for was a single paragraph, and on a busy night his final deed on earth went unrecorded.

Melodrama among black people, whom the *Sun* carefully identified as "Negro," went at a high discount. When still green on the job, I phoned the city desk in some excitement one night with my first murder story. After saying I had "a good murder," I heard the rewrite man tell the night city editor to listen in as I started to recite the details. After I'd said the dead man had been found in an alley severely beaten over the head with "a blunt object," the night editor interrupted. He knew I was covering a black district.

"Is this guy a jig?" he asked.

"Yes, Negro," I said.

"Hell, don't you know you can't hurt 'em by hitting 'em on the head?" he said, and rang off.

"Give me enough for one paragraph," the rewrite man said. "Maybe we'll need it for filler."

It was all night work. Sometimes I was off at midnight, sometimes not until two A.M. Tedium alternated with Grand Guignol, and Grand Guignol with high comedy. One night, sitting in a West Baltimore police station, patiently hating a skinny little clerk but forcing a smile nevertheless as he described for the hundredth time the pleasure he derived from attending hangings, I saw a cop come in with his ear in one hand and the man who had bitten it off gripped firmly in the other.

I reveled in the raffish upside-down life, passing the nights in a world of gore and vice, getting to bed at four A.M., sleeping till noon. My attachment to Mimi intensified. If I was off at midnight, I dropped by her apartment to drink coffee and talk about the night's grotesque events, like any husband rehashing his day at the office. If I was covering police headquarters, she might pick me up there after midnight and I'd take her to an East Baltimore Street joint to drink a beer, watch strip-teasers bump and grind, and lecture her on the sociology of low life. If I worked until two A.M. and there had been too much horror, I'd telephone her.

"Are you asleep?"

"I went to bed early for a change. Where are you calling from?"

"University Hospital. I've been covering a fire up in the northwest. A whole family on the top floor of one of those rotting slum houses. The father's still dying down here in the accident room."

"Do you want to come by?"

"Not tonight. There were four kids. When they brought them out they were nothing but charred cinders. It was sickening."

"You can come by if you want to."

"I don't think so. Go back to sleep. I just needed to talk to somebody for a few minutes. I'll call you tomorrow."

Friends began to assume that we would inevitably marry. "It's not in the cards," I told George, but I was alarmed by a growing dependence on Mimi and began looking for a way to break it. The chance came when Mimi announced she could no longer afford the apartment. Jennie had moved to New York, and for a while Mimi had hoped to make the rent alone by finding a job that paid better than selling cosmetics. She worked as records clerk for a company that used frogs to make pregnancy tests, then for a few dollars more moved to an electrical wiring company as bookkeeper. She quit after learning she was expected to maintain a double set of books to hoodwink the tax law. The next job—as switchboard operator for a real-estate tycoon—paid less, and the tycoon fired her for not knowing how to work a switchboard.

Why not try show business? she asked herself, and went to the Gayety Theater on East Baltimore Street to ask for a job in the chorus. The Gayety was Baltimore's burlesque house, but not finicky about talent. The manager handed her a set of flimsy transparent garments and told her to put them on right away. She would go on stage in the chorus's next performance. She recoiled upon noting that the G-string was smeared with grape jelly, but she wriggled out with the chorus for one performance. She hadn't told the manager she couldn't dance, but at the Gayety that didn't matter. As soon as the chorus bumped offstage she dressed, left without farewells, and hurried home to take a bath.

Then show business called again. She answered a help-wanted ad for a woman interested in theater. "I've got a dog act," the man told her. "I need a girl to help out on stage and look after the dogs."

They would be traveling constantly of course. He showed her his truck. It contained a double bed and six dogs. "This is where we'll be living," he said. "Cozy, isn't it?"

That was her last stab at show business. She found a job as a drugstore clerk, but couldn't pay the rent on the salary. "So what do you plan to do?" I asked.

"What do you think I should do?" she asked.

"Look," I said, "it's just not in the cards."

Economically it wasn't even possible. My *Sun* salary had just risen, but to a mere $45 a week. There was a terrible quarrel. She said I cared nothing for her, we had no future together. I denied the first and agreed with the second. It was time for her to start a new life, she replied, give up the apartment, find a cheap room somewhere, put me out of her life, start seeing other men. There were bound to be men who would treat her more decently than I ever had. I agreed.

By now we had been together three years. I felt strong enough to make the break. "Give me a chance," she said. "Don't call me again. Don't try to come back into my life."

Mimi in 1948.

"We won't see each other again," I promised.

She rented a room far uptown. I stayed away and tried not to think of her but found I could think of nothing else. Weeks passed. I went to the Saturday-night parties hoping she might make an appearance and went home dejected because she didn't. I asked friends, as indifferently as possible, "Seen anything of Mimi lately?" Sometimes they had.

"I saw her at a party up on Calvert Street last weekend," one of them told me one day.

"Who was she with?"

"Some guy in the advertising business, I think."

"How'd she look?"

"Terrific."

I seethed with hatred for the advertising business and everybody in it. Well, two could play at that game. I tried flirting with a girl named Mary. She was a psychologist. "The ease with which your hand extends backward from the wrist indicates strong latent homosexual tendencies," she said. That ended that.

Then I heard that Mimi had moved again, that she was living in a house in North Baltimore with a friend named Ursula and her widowed mother. The widowed mother was a comfort to me. At least she'd maintain decorum when advertising men came calling.

"What's become of Mimi?" my mother asked.

"I'm not seeing her anymore."

"I thought you've been looking down in the mouth about something lately."

"I haven't thought about Mimi for months," I said.

"I think you've done the wise thing, Buddy," she said. "I always had the feeling Mimi never liked me. I don't know why. I always tried to treat her just like I treated all the other friends you and Doris brought home."

"I know."

"All I've ever wanted, Buddy, is for you to have the chance to make something of yourself, but if you're not happy, all the success in the world doesn't do any good."

"I'm happy," I said.

"Then I'm happy too," she said. "I just wish you'd look a little happier."

At this pass, in fact, I was enjoying a taste of the world's success. The *Sun* had finally brought me in out of the police stations and given me a desk and a typewriter. I was covering general assignments—class reunions, new animal arrivals at the zoo, neighborhood parades, after-dinner speeches. It was tiresome stuff, but I was fast at a typewriter. With a rented Royal and a typing manual I'd taught myself the touch system, and to perfect it, I'd written a 70,000-word novel in one three-month stretch, the summer of 1948. It was about a young newspaper reporter hopelessly in love with an unsuitable girl, and there was a gangster in it so vicious that he never once bent down to smell a rose. I mailed it away to several publishers who mailed it right back. Then I put it in the attic, intending to make some publisher pay a fortune for it after I became famous. Many years later I read Truman Capote's criticism of another novel—"That's not writing; it's typing"—and dug mine out of a trunk and put it in the trash in dead of night. Typing it was, and thanks to the exercise I could make a typewriter rattle like a machine gun. This ability proved far more remunerative than my novel.

The *Sun* was always understaffed. One night its two regular rewrite men were off and I was one of three untested reporters sitting in the back of the city room pecking away at announcements of Hadassah meetings and YMCA elections. Suddenly all hell started breaking loose at the city desk. The editor walked back to my desk. "Which one are you?" he asked.

"Baker."

"Are you the one that can type?"

"A little," I said.

"Come up here and we'll see," he said.

I went up to the city desk and he pointed me to the rewrite desk beside the city editor. "Maulsby's working an eight-alarm fire. You'll have to take it," he said.

It was surprisingly easy. After two years studying what rewrite men did with the facts I phoned them, I knew that journalism was essentially a task of stringing together seamlessly an endless series of clichés. I began feeding takes to the city editor.

"Hold up on the fire story and pick up Carroll Williams. There's an oyster war on the Eastern Shore, and he's got three dead."

Before I was well into that the editor interrupted again. "John Carr's calling from the penitentiary."

I switched to Carr. He was in a fearful state of nerves. He'd been sent to cover the hanging of a famous cop killer. All Maryland had hungered for this hanging for a year, and now, a few moments before he was due on the gallows, the condemned man had slashed his jugular with a razor blade and was bleeding to death in his cell.

"Think you can make it for the first city edition?" asked the editor.

It was simple. By two A.M. I'd written nearly five thousand words, almost the entire content of the local news pages.

Putting on his coat to go home, the editor said, "You ought to be working up here full-time."

Before long I was. Under the *Sun*'s system, a rewrite man held one of the most important jobs in the city room. He worked hand-in-glove with the city editor, made snap judgments about story values, and, because the *Sun* prided itself on its literacy, rewrote a good deal of the copy ground out by the reporters. In recognition of his importance the rewrite man was paid better than most of the staff. My salary soared to $70 a week.

The pleasure of this triumph was oddly disappointing. I had only my mother to share it with. Naturally she was elated, "If you work hard and make something of the job, maybe you'll be able to go to Edwin James and get a job on the *New York Times*," she said.

I had no intention of asking mythical Cousin Edwin to do me a favor. That seemed like cheating. I was cocky enough now to believe I could get ahead without it. My mother's pleasure was gratifying, but there was someone else I needed to share in my triumph, and without her it seemed less than exciting.

One night in the spring of 1949 I abandoned pride and phoned the widowed mother. Yes, Miss Nash was in. Did I wish to speak to her?

"It's me," I said.

"How are you?" she replied.

"Fine. You married yet?"

"It doesn't seem to be in the cards," she said.

I ignored that. "I know I promised not to call you again. Is it all right?"

"I was beginning to think you meant it."

"Have you missed me?"

"I've managed to survive," she said. "How's your mother?"

I ignored that, too. "I've missed you," I confessed, though it hurt me to say it. "I wonder if you'd mind if I came by sometime and paid a visit."

Two nights later I did. The widowed mother met me at the door. We would all sit in the parlor, she said. "Would you care for some tea?"

She brought tea and cookies, and I sat on the sofa beside Mimi, the widowed mother studying me warmly as though I were a gentleman caller on the edge of courtship instead of a fool racked by love. We talked about the climate and newspapers and she told me what a splendid young woman Mimi was. When teapot and conversation were drained, I turned to Mimi in desperation and said, "Would you like to go for a walk?"

It was a balmy night. Strolling along, I poured out the story of my successes at the office, of the mighty $70 a week. "You're just as self-centered as you always were," she said.

"I wanted you to know, that's all."

"Your mother must be very happy."

"Let's forget my mother for once."

"You can't forget her," she said.

"She likes you," I said.

Mimi laughed softly.

"It's true. She asked me not long ago why I never bring you out to the house for dinner anymore. She thinks you're the one who doesn't like her."

"Sure," Mimi said.

"As a matter of fact," I said, "I'd like you to come out for dinner on Sunday."

"Jezebel is to be forgiven?" she asked.

"Don't be sarcastic. Will you come?"

"I'll think it over," Mimi said.

When I walked her home, the widowed mother had surrendered the parlor. Mimi resumed her place on the sofa and didn't object when I switched off the light. When we kissed I realized it was starting all over again. Had it ever stopped? I left a few minutes later whistling in delight and depressed about being a hopeless weakling.

When I told my mother Mimi would be coming for dinner she said, "So you're seeing her again. I'm not surprised." That was all, but I knew what she meant: "Just like your father."

It took courage for Mimi to come, but come she did, and this time she came like a true duchess proudly asserting a claim, a claim on a rightful place at the family table. My mother felt the force and determination of this claim, unspoken though it was. "Mimi's changed since the last time I saw her," she said afterwards.

"What do you mean?"

"She's turned into a woman," she said.

Shortly after this I felt the change too. "How much longer are we going to live like this?" Mimi asked when I took her home one evening and we were standing at the door.

"What are you saying?"

"I'm saying, when are we going to get married, and don't tell me it isn't in the cards."

"It isn't," I said.

"For God's sake, Russ, treat me like a human being. What do I have to look forward to with you?"

"You're talking childish talk. Bad lines out of old Bette Davis movies. Don't be childish."

"You're the child. Twenty-four years old and you're still your mother's favorite baby. Ask Doris. She sees it."

"You're really serious about getting married?" I asked. There

264

was a long silence. "I've been thinking about it," I continued, "and I've done some figuring. I figure I'll be able to afford to support a wife when I'm making eighty dollars a week. On seventy I can't do it. Be a little patient. I'll probably get another raise next year."

"When you're making eighty you'll discover you need ninety, and when you make ninety you'll need a hundred," she said. "Good night." And she slammed the door.

Well, we have evenings like that, I told myself on the way home. Next week she announced she was moving to Washington.

"You're kidding!"

She wasn't. She'd found a job with the Wilmark Agency, a national detective service whose agents spent their lives shopping in client stores to catch employees robbing the cash register. "You can't be a detective," I said. "Everybody will laugh at me for going out with a cop."

"Would you rather get married?"

"Come on."

"Don't say it—it's not in the cards. I'm going to Washington." And she did.

It was maddening having her in Washington. I could see her only once a week and then had to leave early in time to catch the last train back to Baltimore. Still, there was safety in distance, too. It might give her marriage mania time to cool. On my hurried weekend visits she seldom failed to tell me about the parties she'd attended during the week or to report on the sophisticated men she met at them. In glamorous Washington, sophisticated men were so much more commonplace than in Baltimore. She wished she'd moved there years ago. I retorted in outbursts of jealous rage, which always gave her the cue to reply, "Well after all, we're not married, are we? It wasn't in the cards."

In November she announced she was leaving Washington for a six-week southern trip with a crew who would be looking for till robbers in the hotels and retail stores of the Carolinas.

"Six weeks? That means we won't be together at Christmas."

"I'll be thinking of you," she said.

"How many in your crew?"

"Three. One man and another girl."

"You mean you're going to be living in hotels with another man for six weeks?"

"I'll write to you," she said.

She did write. There were six letters in the first two weeks from towns like Rocky Mount, Gastonia, Spartanburg, letters warm with affection that began, "My dearest" or "Darling." This long separation was apparently working to make her appreciate the treasure she had in me. The seventh letter was a poisoned dagger. There was a much, much too casual paragraph referring to the crew boss. What a fun-loving fellow he was, how poised, how manly. He was from Pennsylvania and had been a star running back on his high school football team. But intellectually, of course, not in my class. Awfully nice though. He'd even been teaching her to dance.

A football player! How could a woman I admired take the least interest in a football player? I was in turmoil. After all the years I had labored to improve her mind—a football player. And one, moreover—as she confided in her next letter—who referred to himself as "Kid Muscles."

Oh, there was no doubt she was interested in this football player. I could read her like a book even at a distance of four hundred miles. An entire week passed with no letter from the South, and when one finally came it was not "My dearest" or "Darling" to whom she spoke, but to "Dear Russ." Its tone was guarded, several pages of bread-and-butter ramblings that said nothing. What I read between the lines, however, was betrayal. A football player! It was too much to bear, and unable to bear it, I placed a long-distance call at midnight to the hotel at which she was staying. The operator rang her room. It was the first time we'd spoken since she left Washington.

"Are you alone?" I asked.

"Of course. I just fell off to sleep," she said. "It's nice to hear your voice."

We chatted about work for a few minutes, but I thought her

266

Russell and Mimi, Baltimore, 1949.

conversation unusually restrained. "Is there somebody there with you?" I asked.

"What's wrong? Don't you trust me?"

"You know I do."

"Then quit checking up on me in the middle of the night," she said.

I went to sleep happy and awoke next day tormented. A football player! "Kid Muscles," for God's sake! Well, I'd had enough of trying to raise her to my level of taste and civilized behavior. It was time to give her up and start cultivating ladies. When the great raise to $80 a week came and it was time to marry, I wanted to have a lady—a good woman—ready to accept my proposal.

I knew such a woman. Her name was Beverly. She was a college woman with a degree from Smith. Ancient Yankee blood flowed through her arteries. I'd met her covering a story about a highly social philanthropy with which she was associated. She had explained Jungian psychology to me. An educated woman, a serious woman, a good woman. And—a small bonus here—a woman who was, in George's observation, "built like a brick edifice."

Beverly welcomed my request for a date as though she'd been wondering what had taken me so long to ask her. I proposed the movies. She proposed a tour of the East Baltimore Street strip joints. "I've never had anyone to show me the underside of life," she said.

I took her to the Two O'Clock Club. It was a dimly lit fleshpot where the strippers worked on an elevated platform just behind the bar, so close to the customers you could hear their stomachs growl. I'd spent many a newspapering night at the Two O'Clock Club and become numbed to the erotic vulgarity of the dancers. My pleasure was in watching the owner's skill at simultaneously monitoring three widely spaced cash registers to prevent his barmaids from cheating him. Beverly, though, had eyes only for the strippers. Though she had only one beer she looked drugged when, having stared at a succession of writhing female haunches, navels, and breasts just beyond our reach, she said, "I'm ready to go home."

A good woman, I thought. By bringing her here, I have disgusted her. As soon as I closed the taxi door behind us, she uttered a loud howl, seized my shoulders, flung herself back on the seat, and dragged me down upon her. "Here, here," I said. This would never do. "Think of the cab driver," I muttered, struggling to recover dignity.

She recovered her poise before we reached her apartment. "I'll make us some coffee," she said when we reached the door. I sat in a chair while Beverly went into another room and closed the door behind her. When she came out she was wearing high-heel shoes, stockings suspended with a garter belt, and skin that hadn't a single blemish anywhere between her thighs and her collarbone. What I should have thought at that instant, I suppose, is, "A good woman nowadays is hard to find," but I was too confused just then to think clearly.

For the next week I thought lovingly of Mimi, whose character was so superior to the character of fancy-pedigreed, college-educated women. In Mimi there was true refinement. She had dignity, native intelligence, feminine delicacy of the highest order, and character that royalty might have envied. It was ridiculous to compare her with so-called good women, women like Beverly who played the lady in public and carried the tramp in her soul. Nevertheless, I phoned Beverly again to check my first impressions. It didn't do to jump too quickly to conclusions.

In these excesses of good feeling toward Mimi, I decided to squander another fortune on a long-distance call to wish her a Merry Christmas. I waited until eleven o'clock Christmas night to make sure of reaching her. Her room didn't answer.

I waited until eleven-thirty and placed the call again.

"No answer," said the hotel operator.

This was expensive, since I had to pay for the call to reach the hotel switchboard before learning she was still out. I phoned again at midnight.

269

"Nobody's answering," said the hotel operator.

Not answering on Christmas night? Still out at midnight when she certainly must have known I'd be phoning? Out with that football player, most likely. Why waste a fortune trying to phone a woman who was that insensitive?

I phoned again at twelve-thirty.

"There's no answer," said the operator.

At twelve-forty-five.

"No answer," said the operator.

At one A.M.

"There's still no answer, sir. Wouldn't you like to leave a message?"

"No!"

She wasn't worth a message. A football player! "Kid Muscles," yet!

There was no answer at one-thirty A.M. I hated her, I hated football players. I hated muscles, and I hated myself for a fool who had thrown away every chance to marry her and had now lost her.

But perhaps she was merely out at some great public celebration. . . .

On Christmas night? In Charleston, South Carolina? Who in South Carolina would be entertaining three touring store detectives on Christmas night? In any case, the gala would surely be over by two A.M.

I telephoned at two A.M.

"There's no answer," said the operator.

So love ends.

I went to bed filled with the calm new strength that comes to doomed men once they accept their fate. "She has destroyed everything that existed between us," I told myself. "I never want to see her again."

She was scheduled to return to Washington a few days after New Year's. I'd planned to surprise her by meeting her at the train. It would be an early-morning arrival. I would treat her to breakfast. I scrapped that plan now. I never wanted to see her again. I enjoyed trying to imagine her lonely dawn arrival at Union Station, no one there to surprise her, no one to take her to breakfast. It would be her first opportunity to feel the cold steel wall that separated us and sense the price she would have to pay the rest of her life for discarding my love.

The morning her train arrived at Union Station I was there waiting for her. She didn't look surprised. She looked annoyed, then she looked bored. "Let's have some breakfast," I said.

"I ate on the train."

"A cup of coffee then?"

She shrugged. We sat in the station restaurant. "I tried to phone you in Charleston Christmas night and say Merry Christmas, but you didn't answer."

"I was probably out."

"At two o'clock in the morning?"

"Did you come all the way to Washington at this hour of the morning to give me the third degree?"

"There was something else I meant to tell you that night. I was going to say I've been thinking while you were away."

"I did some thinking too."

"Well, what I was thinking was, maybe it's time I started thinking about getting married."

"Do you have somebody in mind?"

"Are you still interested in getting married?" I asked.

"We've covered all this a hundred times. I'm tired of it."

"Would you like to get married?"

"To who?"

"You know what I mean."

"Well, say it," she said.

"Let's get married."

"After the *Sun* raises you to eighty dollars a week?"

"As soon as you want to. I've been figuring, and I think we can get by on seventy dollars a week, if you promise to quit charging things in department stores."

"Would I have to live with your mother?"

271

"That's a hell of a question."

"I just want to know whether I'm going to have a husband or a mother's boy."

"Do you want to fight or do you want to get married?"

"Is March too soon?" she replied.

I suppose I gasped. March was only eight weeks away. It seemed terrifyingly immediate. "March is fine with me," I said.

Mimi reached across the table and took my hand. "Kiss me," she said.

"Here? With all these people around?"

"It's all right when you're engaged," she said, and we leaned across the table and kissed lightly over the sugar bowl.

Then she leaned back and looked at me as though she suddenly thought me the most improbable creature she'd ever seen. She started to laugh. "What's the matter?" I asked. "Is there lipstick on my chin?"

"Have you forgotten already?"

"What?"

"It's not in the cards," she said.

CHAPTER EIGHTEEN

I N the autumn of 1981 Mimi and I drove down to Virginia to visit
our younger son, his wife, and our three-month-old granddaughter. Afterwards we drove into Baltimore to spend a night with
Doris, who was now widowed after a long marriage, and childless.
Her house was in Catonsville, not far from Marydell Road, and
when Mimi and I were packed next morning for the drive back to
New York I said, "Let's go look at the scene of the crime," and we
drove down there.

The house wasn't changed much since I'd first seen it forty
years ago when Herb had bowed to my mother's insistence that
Lombard Street was no place to raise Mary Leslie and spent a
breathtaking $4,700 for what I considered a palace. Herb had died
there in the bedroom at the corner of the second floor in 1962. Doris
was downstairs that afternoon and heard him cry out and ran
upstairs to find him dead in his bed of cardiac arrest. Now Mary
Leslie was married, with children of college age.

"Remember the first time you came out here for Sunday
dinner?" I asked Mimi.

"What I remember about your mother's house is how clean

and happy it felt, and what a warm feeling there was with all those people there who were related to each other."

"What I remember," I said, "is too much makeup."

Mary and Doris sold the house in 1977 when my mother could no longer keep it up and Doris had brought her to live in Catonsville so she could look after her. It was the only solution to a difficult problem, and it didn't work. To my mother, Marydell Road was the "home of our own" she'd spent her youth struggling to reach. After thirty-five years in it, leaving it was more than she could stand. She'd reared her children there, sent her son off to war from there, cooked a thousand Sunday dinners in its kitchen, painted and repainted its parlor, celebrated the weddings of her three children around its dining-room table, and mourned a husband's death there. She had poured out her strength for thirty-five years in waxing its floors, shining its windows, laundering its curtains, making its beds, tending its stoves, and dusting its shelves. When time came to close it and move to Catonsville, she couldn't understand.

"When are we going back home?" she would ask Doris long after they had made the move to Catonsville.

"This is home, Mother."

"Well, it's all right here, I guess, but I want to go back home now."

Neither Mimi nor I had been back to Marydell Road since its sale, and this day when we drove down to look we stayed outside. The new owners certainly didn't want strangers at the door asking for a house tour.

"You never understood my mother, did you?" I said as we pulled away.

"I understood she was a mean old lady."

"That's not right. She was like a warrior mother fighting to protect her children in a world run by sons-of-bitches."

"And I was one of the sons-of-bitches," Mimi said.

"That's not so," I said. "Don't you remember how good she was about our marriage?"

She had been good about it too. When I braced myself and told

274

her, "I'm going to marry Mimi," she blinked and said, "I always thought you would. When's it going to be?"

I knew she took it as a terrible defeat, but she had suffered defeats before, many defeats, and with so much practice at it, she knew how to accept one with grace. Her first question was in character. "How are you fixed for money?"

Very poorly, was the answer. "Well, don't worry. I think I can help you out."

There was my life insurance policy on which she'd been paying since I was knee high. By cashing it in, she could get me almost $300. That would help with the furniture. She also had "a little money saved up." All her life she had always had "a little money saved up." She could let me have $200. That would help finance a honeymoon. "I don't think we ought to waste money on a honeymoon," I told her.

"You ought to be ashamed of yourself, Russell. How do you think Mimi's going to feel if you don't even give her a honeymoon trip?"

There would have to be a reception, of course. Doris had been married the previous year, and there had been an elegant reception at the Candlelight Lodge. This had depleted the treasury, but never mind, she could manage the reception herself right here at Marydell Road. And oh, come to think of it, she could give us her bed. She was thinking of buying a new bed anyhow. If we took hers it would save us some money on the furniture bill.

"What church are you going to be married in?"

Neither Mimi nor I wanted a church wedding. "That's heathenish, Russell. Don't you want to be married in the eyes of God?"

"Not especially," I said.

"I'll speak to my minister about it," she said.

We were married by her minister in her church. George was the best man. Afterwards he drove us back to Marydell Road for the reception she'd spent days preparing. Turkey, ham, beef, cakes, pies, ice cream. There was a huge crowd. She mingled happily urging everyone to celebrate the great day. So great was it indeed that she dropped the iron bar and, to please my friends, permitted wine and whiskey to be served. When the party was at its peak and Mimi and I were leaving for the railroad station for a three-day New York honeymoon, she led everyone onto the porch and waved me gaily out of her life. It wasn't until we were gone, a friend who stayed behind told me afterwards, that she cried.

Now, thirty-one years later, Mimi was willing to concede that, yes, my mother had had her moments, but not all of them had been so fine. I was driving toward the nursing home to see her before heading back to New York. When I pulled into the parking lot, Mimi opened a book. "Aren't you coming in?" I asked.

"I'll wait in the car."

"Oh, come on. She can't even recognize you now."

"Suppose she does," Mimi said. "She might sit up in bed and start screaming at me."

"She won't know who you are. Don't you want to see her?"

"I'll wait out here," Mimi said.

I went in alone. It had been four years since the fall that broke her last links to the outer world, and her mind no longer whirled in dizzying leaps through time. She was sleeping now. Her thinning hair was as white as the sheets. She weighed only seventy-five pounds. Her wasted body was so tiny it made scarcely a dent in the mattress. I took her hand and felt for a pulse. It was strong and regular, as steady as my own. Assured that she was still alive, I held her hand for several minutes until the warmth of human contact awakened her. She opened her eyes and stared at me in puzzlement.

"Hi there," I said. "Having any good dreams?"

She tried to say something, but it was unintelligible. "Speak a little slower," I said.

She tried again. The words were slurred whispers, senseless, inarticulate mumbles. I leaned over to put my ear against her lips and she tried again, and I was able to decipher it. "How's Herb?" she was asking.

"Let me crank up the bed so you can talk easier," I said. While

I was at it, the nurse came in. "Hello, Lucy," she cried in a loud voice. "You've been getting your beauty sleep?"

My mother attempted a smile. "You know who this man is?" the nurse asked her.

My mother stared at me suspiciously for several seconds. "The preacher," she said with sudden vigor.

"That's not the preacher. That's your son, come all the way from New York to see you. You know what his name is?"

My mother stared at me again as though trying to remember where she'd met me. "Sure I know his name," she said.

"What is it?" the nurse asked.

"Mike?" she asked.

"Russell," I said.

Now she smiled the ghost of an old smile I'd once known. "Hi, Russ," she said. "It's nice to see you, Buddy." She squeezed my hand.

"I've been to see my new granddaughter," I said. "I thought I'd drop by and say hello."

"You've got a granddaughter?"

"You never thought I'd be old enough to be a grandfather, did you?"

"For heaven's sake," she said. "I didn't know that. Did you tell Herb?"

"You're a great-grandmother," I said. "I bet you never thought you'd be a great-grandmother."

"Is it a baby?"

"It's a little baby girl. Next time I come I'm going to bring her in and let you hold her."

"I'd like that." She smiled again. A real smile this time. "I always liked babies."

She closed her eyes and seemed to fall back into sleep.

"Are you tired?"

Her lips moved and there was a sound, but all the strength had faded out of her as suddenly as it had risen, and I couldn't catch her words. "Lucy, don't you go to sleep yet," the nurse said.

Obediently, she tried to open her eyelids and to stare at me. "Who're you?" she whispered.

"Russell," I said.

Her eyelids closed again.

"You remember Russell," I said. "And Mimi. You remember Mimi."

Her mind seemed about to surface again. She got her eyes open. "Who?"

"Russell," I said. "Russell and Mimi."

She glared at me the way I had so often seen her glare at a dolt. "Never heard of them," she said, and fell asleep.